RUFFIAN

BURNING FROM THE START

ALSO BY JANE SCHWARTZ

Caught

RUFFIAN

BURNING FROM THE START

JANE SCHWARTZ

BALLANTINE BOOKS | NEW YORK

Grateful acknowledgment is made to Macmillan Publishing Company for permission to reprint three lines from "In Memory of Major Robert Gregory" from *The Poems of William Butler Yeats* edited by Richard J. Finneran. Copyright 1919 by Macmillan Publishing Company. Copyright renewed 1947 by Bertha Georgie Yeats. Reprinted by permission.

Photo of Ruffian's grave marker courtesy NYRA.
Photos of Ruffian: AP/Wide World Photos.

Library of Congress Cataloging-in-Publication Data
Schwartz, Jane.
   Ruffian: Burning From The Start/Jane Schwartz.—1st ed.
   p. cm.
   ISBN 0-345-36017-6
   1. Ruffian (Race horse)   I. Title.
SF355.R8S39 1991
636.1'2—dc20   90-93532
                                                        CIP

Manufactured in the United States of America
First Edition: August 1991
10 9 8 7 6 5 4 3 2 1

A C K N O W L E D G M E N T S

I was able to write this book, in this way, largely because so many people spent so much time with me, remembering.

My thanks go first and foremost to Ruffian's human family: Frank Y. Whiteley Jr., Jacinto Vasquez, Mike Bell, John "Squeaky" Truesdale, the late Yates Kennedy, Minnor Massey, Vince Bracciale, Jr., and Barclay Tagg. Dan Williams died in 1977, long before I began this project. He was the only person from Ruffian's inner circle whom I was not able to interview.

Many other people contributed to this work. Some of them appear on these pages and some do not, but all deserve my thanks: the late Stuart and Barbara Janney, Jackie Peacock Sanders, Frank Ritz, Eleanor Blades, Jim Prendergast, David Whiteley, Ric Martin, Nick Lotz, John Sosby, Walter Kaufman, Dell Hancock, Buck Jones, Charlie Sullivan, Marshall Cassidy, Dave Johnson, Alex Harthill, William Reed, Manuel Gilman, Pat Lynch, Sam Kanchuger, Lorenzo "Rooster" Carlos, Eddie Drakeford, Hamp Beaufort, Jarboe Talbott, LeRoy Jolley, Braulio Baeza, Frank Calvarese, John Spampinato, Jorge Velasquez, Joanne Norman, Jack Wilson, Tony Alonso, and John Esposito.

Thanks also to all the people who worked in the NYRA Press Office between 1986 and 1990, to the Gulfstream Park Press Office, and to Thoroughbred Racing Communications.

Past issues of *The Blood-Horse* and *The Thoroughbred Record* were invaluable sources of information, and I am deeply indebted to Fred Grossman and the *Daily Racing Form* for giving me access to past issues of that paper which were not available anywhere else, and for granting me permission, in a number of different scenes, to use several lines of dialogue that were lifted directly from its articles.

I read the work of many fine turf writers and am particularly grateful to several who added their personal recollections to my files: Jack Mann, Jack Will, Russ Harris, Bill Finley, Joe Hirsch, Bill Nack, and the late Bill Rudy.

I benefited a great deal from the knowledge and expertise of Steve Haskin, Bob Curran, and John Lee. At various stages of my work, each of them read and commented on all or portions of the manuscript, pointing out my errors and offering many useful suggestions.

Family and friends always encouraged me, and many helped out in unique and specific ways: Charles Schwartz, Susan Bektesh, Gene and Ellie Landesman, Ellen Millman, Joey Gordon, Jack Feher, Marshall Messer, Becky Saletan, Dennis Paoli, Laura Kramer-Carini, Carol Sternhell, Pat Mills, Phyllis Frus, and Billy Mass.

Finally, in addition to Ruffian's "family," there were two people who made it possible for me to do this book the way I wanted:

Ellen Sherman, an extraordinary friend, who has managed over the years—in addition to her own writing, marriage, two children, and a move to another state—to read virtually every word of every draft of everything I have written, and who seemed to understand my vision of Ruffian's book even before I myself could clearly articulate it;

And Bob Wyatt, an extraordinary editor, who has helped me so much as a writer, has always made me feel welcome, and has believed in this book—and in me—from the very beginning.

J.S.
April 1991

... pure-bred horses
And solid men, for all their passion, live
But as the outrageous stars incline ...

—William Butler Yeats
In Memory of Major Robert Gregory

EXTENDED PEDIGREE OF RUFFIAN

RUFFIAN
dk. b. or br. f., 1972

- Reviewer
  - Bold Ruler
    - *Nasrullah
      - Nearco
      - Mumtaz Begum
    - Miss Disco
      - Discovery
      - Outdone
  - Broadway
    - Hasty Road
      - Roman
      - Traffic Court
    - Flitabout
      - Challedon
      - Bird Flower
- Shenanigans
  - Native Dancer
    - Polynesian
      - Unbreakable
      - Black Polly
    - Geisha
      - Discovery
      - Miyako
  - Bold Irish
    - Fighting Fox
      - *Sir Gallahad III
      - Marguerite
    - Erin
      - Transmute
      - Rosie O'Grady

PART ONE

1

Buck Jones yawned and looked at his watch. It was funny how time went late at night. He had started his shift at midnight, relieving Louis Otero, and all he had done since then was pace up and down the shedrow or lean against the wall and sip coffee from his thermos. Yet it was already half past three.

He didn't even have a radio. This was Frank Whiteley's barn, and Whiteley didn't allow radios. Buck could understand that. He'd been a horseman himself for almost twenty years. The boss wasn't paying him to listen to music. Horse watching was a job. Especially in a case like this. The President, the Pope, and the Queen of England all rolled into one couldn't have gotten more attention than this filly had been getting the last few weeks, ever since they had announced the Match.

Buck looked over at her. She was awake now, alert in her stall, ears pricked forward.

"You'll get your breakfast soon enough." Buck smiled and tugged at the belt of his uniform. He was a big man, and he'd put on a few more pounds since becoming a Pinkerton. He could appreciate the filly's appetite.

She wasn't fidgeting or fussing, though. She never did. But there was something about her—Buck had been trying to figure it out all week. He had watched her before, when she raced, but only from the paddock or the stands, like everyone else. Up close, these past few nights, he'd begun to realize what it was: She had the uncanny ability to seem calm and excited at the same time. Perfectly at ease, and yet—eager, intense, wired. He had never seen that in a horse before. Or, for that matter, in a person, either.

The filly stretched out her neck to catch the summer breezes drifting over from the track. Buck thought of the crowds that cheered her every time she ran. If only they could see her now. She was a towering filly, and had always looked magnificent on those bright afternoons when she raced, her near-black coat flashing spears of sunlight as she paraded to the post. But at night, with moonlight filtering down on her, she was even more striking. Silvery, shining, radiant, like something in a dream. Only she wasn't a dream. She was real.

That was hard to believe sometimes, especially if you opened up the paper and studied her form. It wasn't just that she was undefeated: She was perfect. At every point of call, in every race, she had been in front. She didn't always break well, but within a step or two she invariably gained the lead. Five times as a two-year-old, and five times again so far at three. What was even more amazing, she had done it at every distance from a sprint to a mile and a half. Always first. Always on the lead. Perfect.

At the other end of the barn Whiteley's regular night watchman, Hamp Beaufort, was busy getting ready for the four A.M. meal. He muttered softly to himself as he walked through the barn pouring oats into the feed tubs. One by one all the horses poked their heads out of their stalls, nickering and coming to life. Breakfast, they said up and down the line. Morning. Another day. They knew.

Whiteley's assistant, Mike Bell, shifted on his narrow cot and woke up. Although he had an apartment nearby in Elmont, he had long ago formed the habit of sleeping at the barn for several nights before each of the filly's races. When Hamp started back down the row, hooking the tubs inside each stall, Mike squinted up at him, half waved, and turned over, hoping to squeeze in a few more minutes' sleep.

While the horses buried their noses in their oats, snuffling with pleasure, Buck listened to the rumblings in his own stomach. He was looking forward to Red the Baker and his coffee wagon; he needed some of those fresh, homemade rolls to fortify himself. Night was the easy part, watching out for strangers. It was the coming morning that was going to be hard. That's when he'd have to fend off the reporters and photographers and tele-vision crews—people who had flown in from all over the coun-try, from all over the *world*—the same ones who'd been besieging the barn all week. Sure, Mike would be there, and Dan Williams, too—the guy who rubbed her—but they'd be busy with all the horses. It might be the biggest event at Belmont since Secretariat clinched the Triple Crown, but on the backside it was still an-other day at the track: Every single horse had to be fed and exercised and hosed down and cooled out. And though all the horses were treated equally, the filly was the focus of attention. Before long, every person who had managed to beg, borrow, or steal a press pass would be trying to get close to her, crawling all over Buck and the stablehands, asking questions, snapping pictures, trying to push in front.

Buck needn't have worried about handling them alone. Long before it was light, long before the first bleary-eyed reporter even thought about aiming a fist at his alarm clock, Frank Whiteley would show up at the barn. Not that there was a damn thing for him to do at four o'clock in the morning. He just wanted to be with the filly.

Getting up early was nothing new for Frank Whiteley. He'd been getting up early all his life. Everybody got up early on a farm, and he'd been born on one, outside Centreville, Maryland, in 1915, on the strip of the Eastern Shore separated from the rest of the state by the Chesapeake Bay. Frank had always helped out with the milking, the barn chores, and later on, the tilling of the fields. In addition to the cows, his parents grew feed corn and sweet corn and wheat. Nobody had tractors then; they worked the land with mules and horses, so as far back as Frank could remember, horses had been a part of his life. Not the thor-oughbreds, though. The thoroughbreds had come later: first, the broken-down claimers; then the reasonable allowance stock; then, after many years, the champions.

His father gave him his very first horse—a Shetland pony—when Frank was five years old, and he had loved that pony with all his heart. The pony, unfortunately, had not reciprocated the emotion; in fact she hadn't cared for Frank at all. She was cranky and stubborn, and he had to beat on her constantly just to make her move. Once she was actually moving, her primary ambition was getting rid of the irksome boy on her back. The two of them battled it out for a couple of years; eventually, the pony won.

At the age of ten Frank got a real horse. Eighteen dollars! It seemed like a fortune at the time, and when his father handed the money over to a neighboring farmer for the yearling, Frank was thrilled. He broke the horse on his own, figuring out little by little how to introduce the bridle and the saddle and his own weight on the colt's back. He didn't read any books on the subject and he didn't have anybody to teach him. He learned about this horse—as he would insist he learned about each of his future horses—by "fooling around with him" over a period of time. From then on he just kept getting one horse after another, trading or buying up, always learning something new.

Apart from the horses, Frank had only one other passion as a child. That was running. The track and field competitions were the best part of the whole school year to him. Frank was small and quick, and every year from the fifth through the eighth grades he won the 50-yard dash at the county meet. That last victory earned him a trip to Baltimore to attend the state meet, and that meant a ride on the ferry boat and an overnight stay at the YMCA. A trip like that was more traveling than most farm boys had ever done or would ever do for a long time to come. But when he started high school, running got him into trouble.

In the ninth grade, Frank had to compete against upperclassmen. That was okay with him; he was happy to move up from the 50- to the 100-yard dash. He was confident he could beat anyone they threw at him. But the coach wanted one of his graduating seniors in that event, and, fearing that Frank would beat the older boy in the preliminary, qualifying heats, he placed him in the relay instead. "You can do the 110-yard leg, same difference," he told Frank.

Frank frowned at him. It didn't seem fair, but there was nothing he could do about it. At the county meet that spring, he ran the last leg of the relay as hard as he could, but the competing school had opened up a big early lead, and Frank could cut it down only so much. He crossed the finish line bitterly disappointed.

The coach stood there laughing at him. "What happened, Whiteley? I thought you could beat anyone in the county!"

Frank whirled around, eyes stinging with tears, and hurled the baton at the coach's head. "You baldheaded son of a bitch!" he screamed.

The other boys backed away. The coach grabbed Frank and hollered at the officials, "Disqualify this boy! I want this boy disqualified immediately!"

"I don't give a damn if you do disqualify me! I don't care! You just cost me my trip to Baltimore, goddamn you!" Frank wriggled free and ran off, and this time he just kept running—away from the coach, away from the track meet, and away from school forever.

Frank washed his face, ran a comb through his graying hair, pulled on clean khakis, boots, and a short-sleeved cotton shirt. No one else was awake in the house. He sat down at the kitchen table with a cup of coffee and a piece of toast, but gulped them down so quickly he didn't taste a thing. Before he left, he patted his pockets, checking for cigarettes and Gelusil. He lifted his hat off its hook, pulled it down low over his forehead, and shut the door behind him. When he stepped outside, it was still pitch-dark.

His first cigarette was lit before he'd pulled out of the driveway. The streets in his Long Island neighborhood were empty, and Frank pressed down on the accelerator a little harder than usual. Although he stared straight ahead, his blue eyes clear and sharp behind his dark-rimmed glasses, he wasn't concentrating on the road. He was doing what he always did on the way to the barn: thinking about his horses. He worried about every one of them, especially on the days they raced.

That afternoon he had two big horses entered. Honorable Miss was facing a field of colts in the Nassau County Handicap, and Ruffian was facing one single colt in the Match. It was just an odd coincidence, the way that had worked out, the two fillies going against colts in back-to-back races. Odder still that both Honorable Miss and Ruffian were the morning-line favorites.

The guard at the stable gate touched his hat, and Frank nodded at him as he drove past and into the backstretch. He wanted to get Honorable Miss out early; she got so wound up on race days that if she was left inside her stall, she'd start bouncing off the walls and hurt herself. Although she was a five-year-old mare,

she still acted like a kid at the circus. Her excitement was con-
tagious, and the people who worked around her always had a
lot of fun.

The filly was different. Everyone around the filly worried.
They tried not to show it, but it had been that way ever since
her first race. It didn't matter if it was morning or afternoon, if
she was out galloping or in the heat of competition. They could
never watch the filly run without feeling just a little bit afraid.

It had started off as the "Race of Champions," and Ruffian wasn't
even included. The New York Racing Association wanted to pit
the three winners of the individual Triple Crown events against
each other in one special race, tentatively scheduled for the end
of June.

The media protested. What would it prove to throw these
three colts up against each other yet again? They had butted
horns all spring, and on different days, when it counted most,
each had proved himself superior. Foolish Pleasure had captured the Kentucky Derby, the single most prestigious race in
the country; Master Derby had won the Preakness, and Avatar the
Belmont Stakes. But they had never tested themselves against the
undefeated black filly in Frank Whiteley's barn.

"Until these colts are measured against Ruffian, none of
them has much of a claim on the title of 3-year-old champion,"
wrote *The Blood-Horse* in its weekly editorial. "Right now we do
not believe that—even to escape a swarm of Brazil's hybrid Af-
rican honeybees—any of these could catch up with the Stuart
Janneys' big filly."

As a result of the outcry, NYRA officials discussed changing
the race to involve the three classic winners *plus* Ruffian. That
generated much more excitement. Four horses made up an
almost-respectable field, in terms of size, and they were certainly
the best of the three-year-old crop. But just as this idea was heat-
ing up, Avatar's trainer, Tommy Doyle, took his horse back to
California, explaining that the colt was simply not up to such a
race at that time.

While NYRA considered what to try next, Philip Iselin, president of Monmouth Park in New Jersey, made a stunningly simple proposal. He offered a purse of $400,000 for a match race
between Ruffian and Foolish Pleasure. Believing it to be a pro-

moter's dream, he had suggested such a race earlier. Ruffian's enormous appeal was capable of attracting nonracing fans in huge numbers, and the boy vs. girl angle was guaranteed to stir up interest; it was one confrontation that never got old. In fact, it had intensified the last few years, as the media covered the rise of the women's movement. It sold papers, and that was the name of the game.

But it didn't matter how astute Iselin was, or how persuasive his arguments, or even how much money he offered. He didn't have a chance in the world of bringing off such a race in New Jersey. No one said it in so many words, but the reason was simple: Iselin wasn't related to Stuart and Barbara Janney, Ruffian's owners, and Ogden Mills "Dinny" Phipps, vice chairman of the board of trustees of the New York Racing Association, was. His father, Ogden Phipps, was Barbara Janney's brother. If Ruffian was going to be involved in a special race—a race certain to generate nationwide interest and lots of good publicity for the sponsoring track—that race was going to be held in New York.

Confident of this result, NYRA modified its plan and came up with a three-horse "Race of Champions": Foolish Pleasure, Master Derby, and Ruffian. Before another press conference could be called to announce this latest development, LeRoy Jolley, the trainer of Foolish Pleasure, objected. "I just can't bring myself to run in a three-horse race with that great filly," he said. His logic was understandable. In such a race, he would be forced to send Foolish Pleasure after Ruffian right away, to keep a close check on the speedball filly; that could wear them both out, setting it up for the third horse to run away with the race. He was willing to face the filly on her own and see who tired first in a mile and a quarter, but he wouldn't give the race away to someone else.

Mrs. Robert Lehmann, owner of Master Derby, had, over the last few dizzying days, staunchly supported NYRA in all its efforts to create a special event which would depend in part on her participation. The purse for this event had continued to escalate. How could NYRA now tell her, however politely, to get lost?

And yet, they had to. The idea of a true match race—one on one, the filly against the colt—was simply too good to give up.

Especially when there were rumors, soon to be confirmed by an AP news release, that Monmouth was ready to up the ante to an unprecedented half a million dollars to stage what it was convinced would be the sporting event of the year.

On Friday, June 13, Jack Dreyfus, chairman of the board of NYRA, accompanied by Dinny Phipps, made the final announcement. To the assembled crowd in the Belmont press box, he confirmed that he had received commitments from the owners of Foolish Pleasure and Ruffian to allow those two to compete in a mile and a quarter match race to be held at Belmont Park on July 6. The Association had allocated $400,000 in purse money for the race. That was the largest purse ever put up by any racetrack operator for a single event in the history of American thoroughbred racing.

Fifty thousand dollars was immediately skimmed off the top and given to Mrs. Lehmann "as a testimony for her support," which, ironically, she had demonstrated by agreeing to withdraw her horse from the race. That unusual move prompted the snide observation that NYRA could solve much more serious problems, like overpopulation, if it would just extend its offer and pay *everybody* $50,000 for pulling out.

The remaining $350,000 would be divided between the two entrants: $225,000 to the first-place finisher, $125,000 to the horse that came in second. This meant that the winner of the Match would earn $15,000 more than the winner of that year's Kentucky Derby—and, more astonishing, the *loser* of the July 6 race would take home almost $9,000 more than the winner of the Belmont Stakes had received on June 7.

The Match would be held at scale weights: The colt would carry 126 pounds, the filly, 121. It would be run at the classic distance of a mile and a quarter.

Other questions remained to be settled: whether or not there would be betting on the race; whether it would be one of the nine regular daily events or an added tenth race (for which they would need the permission of the New York State Racing and Wagering Board); whether or not there would be national television coverage of the contest; and, finally, at what point on Belmont's mile and a half oval the race would start.

Mile and a quarter races at Belmont were rare. When they were held, they usually started from the chute on the far side of the track, near the parking lot. That was so distant from the stands that many spectators—particularly those less familiar with the sport—might find it difficult to follow the early part of the race. Wanting to accommodate those fans, who would be out in droves for such a special event, Dreyfus said he didn't think it would be too difficult to start the match race on the clubhouse turn, where the action would be more visible.

Frank Whiteley kept his mouth shut. He knew the race was not going to start on the turn. He didn't particularly like the idea of starting it from the chute either, but at least that was a straightaway. There were always risks when you ran a horse, but there were two different kinds: acceptable risks, which you took every time you sent a horse to the gate, and unacceptable risks. One of his jobs as a trainer was drawing the line between them. You didn't start a horse with speed like Ruffian's from the middle of a turn. But this was not the time or place for him to sound off. Let them say whatever they wanted. It was only a press conference.

Frank didn't have to consult with Mr. and Mrs. Janney. He didn't have to get anybody's approval. He didn't have to take into account the fans, the officials, the public relations department, or the position of the television cameras. He had only one thing to consider, and that was his horse. And he knew with absolute certainty that the match race was not going to start on the turn, because if it did, his horse wasn't going to be in it.

One other issue remained to be discussed.

"Mr. Whiteley," a reporter asked, "will Jacinto be riding your filly in the race, or Jolley's colt?"

The room grew quiet.

"You'll have to ask Jacinto that," Whiteley replied. "He's gonna have to make a choice."

2

The Janneys kept most of their horses on their 380-acre Locust Hill Farm in Glyndon, Maryland, where they lived, but seven or eight of their top broodmares remained at Claiborne Farm in Paris, Kentucky, so they could be returned to area stallions each year.

Bold Ruler, the preeminent sire of the sixties, was also kept at Claiborne. He was owned by Barbara Janney's mother, Gladys Phipps, and every year since Bold Ruler had gone to stud, Barbara, or "Bobbie" as she was called, had been given—as her birthday present—one free season to her mother's horse. But in 1970 the situation changed: Bold Ruler was found to have a malignant tumor growing near his brain. In what was, at the time, an extraordinary move, Gladys Phipps, who was eighty-seven years old, sent the stallion to Auburn University to undergo an eight-week series of cobalt treatments. The tumor shrank, Bold Ruler gained weight, and by October he was so much improved that he was returned to Claiborne. One week later, ironically, Mrs. Phipps died.

Bold Ruler made it through the following spring, covering a full book of mares, but then the cancer flared up again and he began to deteriorate. In July, when he showed signs that pain was overtaking him, he was humanely destroyed.

The year that he died, the Janneys had elected to breed their most promising broodmare, Shenanigans, a daughter of Native Dancer, to Reviewer, one of Bold Ruler's sons, who was standing his first year at stud. Stuart and Bobbie Janney were thoroughly schooled in bloodlines and planned each mating carefully. They had been involved in this business all their lives. Still, even with

top quality stock, they knew that breeding racehorses was always
a gamble.

The mating took place early on a warm May morning, in a large
shed with padded yellow mats covering the walls and tanbark
spread out over the floor. It wasn't a spontaneous sex act. It
never was with valuable thoroughbreds. Everyone's first concern
was keeping the two animals from hurting each other or themselves. Kicks, bites, falls—they could do a lot of damage in the
breeding shed. Also, there were only one or two days in a mare's
heat period when she was actually ovulating, and that was when
the cover had to take place.

Shenanigans had delivered a colt one month earlier, and this
was a normal time to breed her again. First a "teaser" was sent
in—a stallion of lesser quality, not good enough to sire future
racehorses—to make sure she was receptive to a male. He would
become aroused, smell and nip and sometimes start to mount
the waiting mare. If the mare showed she was ready, by lowering
her hindquarters and by "winking"—the opening and closing of
her vulva, which revealed the wet pink tissue that was ready for
sex—the teaser was led off and replaced by the stud whose services were being paid for.

Reviewer was relatively new to this procedure, but the men
who surrounded him were not. Since the colt had a reputation
for being difficult, the men who handled him that day were the
most experienced stud men on the farm. They explained what
was in store for him every step of the way, laughing and joking
as they worked, but their attention never wavered from their
job. As soon as the horse smelled the mare, he roared and
dropped his penis, long and erect, out of its sheath. One of the
men was ready with a bucket of soapy water and a cloth, but he
stayed back as the stallion reared up repeatedly, slashing the air.
When Reviewer settled down, the man dashed in and thoroughly
washed the stallion's penis. The last thing anyone wanted at that
stage of the game was to transmit a possible infection or vene-
real disease between the animals. The mare had had her tail tied
up and she, too, had been gently washed with cotton swabs.

Reviewer was brought over. He sniffed and snorted and
danced around. He bared his teeth and tried to savage the man
closest to his head. Finally, trumpeting his dominance—however

illusory it was—he reared up and mounted Shenanigans. He shifted on his hind legs, finding his balance, and settled onto her back; then, with expert guidance from human hands, he thrust himself into the mare.

James Christopher hadn't slept in weeks. He was the head foaling man at Claiborne, and it was spring. Almost every night he was called out of bed for a birth, and every morning he was up early, making the rounds of the still-expectant mares.

It was bright and sunny outside on the morning of April 17, 1972, as James moved from stall to stall, studying each mare, noting their swollen bellies, checking the tubs to see if any of them had gone off their feed. When he came to Shenanigans, he stopped and rubbed her pale nose. It was three days past her due date, but that was nothing to worry about. Vets were no more precise than obstetricians.

"It's your turn, girl," he murmured. "How you feeling today?" She was getting close, he noted. A waxlike substance was forming over her teats; a few drops of milk were leaking down her leg. He ran a hand over her chest, but her coat was still dry.

"Tonight, I bet." He nodded at her. "You'll wait till dark, like most of 'em do. It'll be okay, don't you worry none." He'd been with her a year ago, almost to the day, when she had given birth to a little gray colt named On To Glory. It had been her third foal in three years, each one the product of a different sire—Nearctic, Bold Ruler, and Bold Lad—and each one a straightforward and uncomplicated birth.

"You'll be okay, hear?" James moved on down the line, reassuring the more nervous broodmares with his gentle voice, his hand on their necks.

He didn't return until early that evening. By then Shenanigans had polished off her dinner and seemed to be taking everything in stride, although her gray coat was now splotchy with sweat. She was in one of the specially prepared foaling boxes, a larger version of her stall, with a much deeper cushion of fresh straw. She had started pacing back and forth, not panicked but a little restless, uneasy. From time to time she paused, stopped in her tracks by a wave of cramps.

Quiet as a shadow, James moved up beside her and stroked her buttocks. The muscles had become soft and flaccid, another sign that she was within hours of giving birth. There was round-the-clock surveillance in the barn—she'd be checked every fifteen minutes—but before he left to get a bite to eat and a quick nap, James alerted one of the grooms to Shenanigans's condition.

When he returned that night, the mare's water had broken. She was absorbed in rearranging the straw with her front hoof, then turning and slowly rearranging a different pile. After doing this several times, she lay down and heaved a long, shaky sigh. For a moment she appeared content; then, glancing around wildly, she tried to get to her feet again. When she realized that this was no longer possible, she gave up and rolled over on her side. Her breathing became heavier, rougher. The contractions had begun in earnest.

James talked to her, easing her with his voice. An assistant was nearby, with all the tools of the trade: towels, disinfectant, scissors, antibiotics, thermometer. If anything should go wrong, the farm vet lived on the grounds, only a few hundred yards away.

The contractions continued, more and more rapidly, then suddenly Shenanigans's eyes widened in pain and surprise. Two tiny hoofs pressed through her vagina. She was panting heavily. The foal's muzzle and then its bony nose poked out. James was there, ready to help, but he preferred to stay out of the way as long as things continued to go well. Finally, drenched in sweat but calm and businesslike, Shenanigans shuddered painfully through several major contractions and the worst was over. The head and shoulders were out, nestled in the thick straw.

"One more push," James crooned. "Give me one more good one."

As if on cue, the mare complied. The skinny haunches and back legs slipped through, and a startled foal, sprawled out in the straw, gasping for breath, got her first hazy introduction to the world.

The cord connecting the foal to her dam continued to pulse for several seconds. It usually severed itself when the foal began to move; if not, James would cut it. He knelt down. The stall was full of indescribable baby-scents, the pure, clean smells all newborns carry with them. They mingled with the heavy sweetness of blood. Using a soft towel, he wiped the opalescent membrane off the foal and cleared the mucus out of her nostrils. With the aid of his assistant, he lifted the baby up and carried her nearer to her mother's head.

Shenanigans pulled back at first, but after a minute she began to sniff the foal, then to lick her, long decisive licks to clear away the residue from her nose and eyes. The mare bowed her head over the foal, whose breath was now coming in steady little puffs. The filly looked like an overgrown spider, her dark knot of a body in the center of long, skinny legs. She began struggling almost immediately to get to her feet. Although her legs were nearly three-quarters of their full adult length, they were still weak, and like all foals her bones were so soft that human hands could have kneaded out the slight irregularities that sometimes occurred. In her case, fortunately, there were none.

It took only a few more trials before the foal had pressed herself halfway up. Boom! She collapsed back into the straw. Panting but undeterred, she rested a moment, gathering strength. Shenanigans stretched out her neck and nuzzled the wet little body. The foal's matchstick ribs were outlined against her dark coat. The mare knuckered encouragement. Then, planting her own forelegs firmly in front of her, Shenanigans raised her head and thrust herself up into a standing position, shaking herself to clear away the clinging bits of broken straw. The afterbirth swung heavily between her legs and fell away.

The foal blinked. Her ears pricked up, attentive to the change in her dam's position. With a little grunt she jerked forward, throwing her weight onto two spindly front legs, not quite sure what to do with the hind legs still curled up beneath her. Then, somehow, she managed to unwind her back legs, settle them under her, and begin to push. Once, twice, and there! She was standing—unsteady, breathless, more than a little surprised at herself, but upright. And she remained upright.

James shook his head. Statistically, there was nothing remarkable about this. Most foals were on their feet within twenty to thirty minutes. Evolutionary instinct: Running was the horse's best defense. It was what saved them, and they had to be on their feet to run. Still, the wonder of it all outdistanced logic every time.

The filly butted her nose against the air. James slipped a finger into her mouth and she immediately began to suck. That was all he needed to know. With a smile of satisfaction he backed off, leaving the filly to find the teat on her own. Shenanigans waited as her foal wobbled over, one shaky step at a time, and pushed her little muzzle up against foreleg, then belly, then thigh, until finally her nose slid up against the full warm udder. She cupped her lips around it and began to nurse. Right away she was a good eater: hungry, eager, intent.

James stayed a while longer and noted the filly's markings: a thin white band, higher on the inside, above the left hind foot, with three black dots in it, and an irregular star, high on her forehead, with one ragged point shooting down near the bottom. She'd be registered officially as dark bay or brown. Like all bays, she had some lightness around her muzzle, but she was a dark one—very dark—as good as black to the untrained eye.

Later, one of the grooms would muck up the worst of the bloodied straw and replace it with a clean, fresh pile. When the foal was sleeping, he'd go in and sponge off the mare's hind legs. Then, as long as there was no trouble, he would leave the two of them alone.

James hesitated. There were other horses to check, and paperwork piling up on his desk. Shenanigans was relaxed; the foal was nursing contentedly. He moved quietly out of the stall and latched the gate.

"I've got it," Stuart Janney called to his wife, who had picked up the extension in the other room. He was in his study, going through the morning papers, getting ready for the day's business. Being retired hardly made a dent in his schedule, but that was the way he liked it.

"Yes?" He listened attentively, asked a few questions, then hung up. He turned to see his wife silhouetted in the doorway.

"Well?" They smiled at each other.

"That was Claiborne," he announced.

Bobbie Janney walked over and sat down beside her husband. "Well?" she asked again, waiting.

"Shenanigans dropped her foal at ten minutes to ten last night. Healthy. Up and nursing right away. They're both fine."

Mrs. Janney's china-blue eyes sparkled. *"And?"* she prodded.

Her husband chuckled affectionately as he reached over to touch her hand. "It's a filly," he told her. "A big one. A big black filly with a little star."

3

Shenanigans was led through a gate into a small paddock, and her foal followed, pressing close to her flank. The foal blinked a few times at the glare of sunlight, then her eyes seemed to adjust. She was less than twelve hours old, and outside for the first time. She flared her nostrils, inhaling the deep, sweet, nose-tingling smells. Her tiny hooves made faint impressions in the springy earth, and she picked each one up deliberately, as if testing the ground.

When Shenanigans trotted along the perimeter of the fence, the filly trotted after her. When Shenanigans lowered her head to nibble the sweet grass, the filly stuck her nose down and sniffed. When Shenanigans turned so that her side faced the sun, the filly did likewise, and the brightness melted into warmth against her skin.

Every morning afterwards they repeated the routine, spending longer and longer periods outside, staying close to each other. Even when the foal fell asleep in the thick grass—sleep would overcome her suddenly, many times throughout the day— the mare remained nearby, watching over her.

Like all the new arrivals, the foal and her dam were turned out alone in an individual paddock for the first ten days. This kept the babies safe from the hooves of an unfriendly or nervous stranger. Claiborne had the room to do this. The farm consisted of 3400 acres that the Hancock family owned outright, and another 1600 that they were leasing at the time. But even Claiborne couldn't protect the gangly little foals forever, nor did they want to. They were raising racehorses, not hothouse plants.

They would live in a world with other horses, other dangers, other unknowns. Sooner or later they had to be exposed to it.

So, after the ten days were up, the new foals and their dams were moved to a different barn and divided into groups.

Now, every day, in addition to her ever-present dam, the spindly legged foal had companions her own age—filly foals and colt foals—when she was turned out into the much larger paddock that would be her playground until October. They scampered after each other and jogged along the fences, two and three and four abreast. They kicked up their heels and tumbled in the grass. They shadow-boxed, rearing up on hind legs that grew stronger every day. They jumped and bucked and pogosticked from one end of the field to the other until, exhausted, or spooked by the shadow of a stray leaf, they scattered back to their dams to nurse, nuzzle, rest.

The help at the farm had all been warned: "If you're not in the hospital or being laid out over at the funeral home, you better be here. And be here on time." Everybody understood. It was the first Tuesday in October—weaning day at Claiborne.

They gulped their coffee, pulled on their boots, and arrived at their posts even earlier than usual. Each one knew exactly what his or her role was to be in the upcoming events. The drama they would play out that morning was, collectively, the most wrenching of the entire year; scenes of unrelenting loss and loneliness, separation and fear.

Shenanigans had been through this three times already. She was relatively calm when the man entered the stall and led her foal out by the halter, but the filly planted her hind legs and refused to move when the door to the stall was shut behind her. Her squeals pierced the air. She had been led out of the stall every morning of her life, but never by herself; she had always followed her dam. Ignoring her cries, six men surrounded her, acting swiftly and without hesitation. One man pulled her tail up over her back, the others slipped their arms around and under her and lifted her up into the waiting van. Immediately another foal was loaded in beside her, then another, and another. They parroted each other's frightened screams. The grooms had to watch their own feet as the foals stomped and shifted, trying to rear up or turn around in the confines of the interior box.

"Y'all set in there?"

"Yes, sir!"

The back door to the van was shut and fastened. The six foals pricked their ears at the sound of the engine. They were on their way.

Claiborne had two separate barns for the weanlings. Shenanigans's near-black filly was heading for the one called Raceland, five miles away on the other side of Paris. The van rolled gently over the empty roads. Inside, the foals shuffled about, bleating for their dams.

As soon as the vans were out of sight, the mares were led outside. For the first time since giving birth—except when they had been taken off, briefly, to be mated up again—they were without their foals. Some of them grew frantic, especially the maiden mares who had never gone through this before, and it was always safer to have them buck and run in a fifty-acre field than to leave them caged in a stall. Some of them tore off along the fences, whinnying furiously for their absent foals, but by then the foals were far away.

At Raceland the group of filly foals was unloaded and led into Barn 4. They were weanlings now. No dams waited for them inside their new stalls, and their pitiful cries pitched back and forth in waves under the rafters. The black filly rose up on her hind legs and rolled her eyes. She kicked out at the stall door. She circled the unfamiliar space, smelled the fresh straw, stuck her nose into every corner. There was no trace of Shenanigans. The filly did what the other weanlings did: She whinnied as loud as she could, then froze, ears cocked. Always before, when she had cried out in the field for her dam, there had been an answering cry. Now there was no response.

It was a long, bleak night for the babies, the silence broken only by their own heartrending cries. But by the next morning, most of them cleaned up their feed, and within another day or two they adjusted.

In a few months, if by chance their paths were to cross, dams and foals would not even recognize each other. From then on they would be linked on paper only, through the fact of their shared blood. The near-black weanling in stall number 7 was a daughter of Reviewer out of Shenanigans. She would be known by her dam's name during her eighteen-month stay at Claiborne: "the Shenanigans filly," or just "Shenanigans." If she had a name—if the Janneys had already registered a name for her with the Jockey Club—nobody at Claiborne knew what it was.

4

John Sosby was as close to a "homebred" as any employee on the farm. He had worked at Claiborne full-time since 1957, the year after he graduated from high school, but he had started out cutting weeds when he was only nine years old, and as a teenager he'd built up a few muscles baling hay. He'd been living on the farm since he was three. Sosby's father had worked with the broodmares, and his family had lived in one of the houses on the grounds. Now Sosby and his wife—high school sweethearts—and their four children were doing the same thing.

In 1967 Sosby had become yearling manager. That year Buckpasser, a Claiborne foal of 1964, was battling with Damascus and Dr. Fager for Horse of the Year honors. Now both Damascus and Buckpasser were standing at stud at the farm, another turn of the wheel completed. Damascus was owned by the Bancroft family, and had been trained by Frank Whiteley; Buckpasser was owned by Ogden Phipps, Mrs. Janney's brother.

Ogden Phipps also owned Reviewer, and the Janneys had bred Shenanigans back to him shortly after she gave birth to the near-black filly in 1972. This time the mare had been barren, so there had been no foal for her the following spring. About that time, however, John Sosby started noticing her yearling filly. She had caught his eye even earlier, as a weanling, but that was only because of her size; she was hard to miss. But around the time that she was chronologically a year old, in April, he began to see a distinct personality emerge. She was a tomboy, pure and simple. More like a colt than a filly. She was tough. Not vicious-tough, not violent, but aggressive, independent, and very self-possessed. Sosby was curious to see how these qualities would

23

survive the next stage of her training, when they put a rider on her back and a bit in her mouth.

Those next hundred days—the "breaking" of the horse, as almost everyone still called it—were pivotal in the development of the thoroughbred. They marked the transition from carefree youngster to budding professional. From now on there would be a gradual winding down of the hours the horses spent outside running free. They would still have their playtime, but a bigger and bigger chunk of every day would be devoted to school.

The fillies would continue to be turned out in their groups of ten or eleven, but the colts would never again be allowed to romp all together in the fields. Now it was too risky. They were becoming too rough. Most were separated into pairs, and all were restricted to smaller paddocks than before.

"I think you'll fit her pretty good." John Sosby smiled as he informed Nick Lotz that he would be breaking the Shenanigans filly. Nick grinned back. The matchup was obvious. Although he weighed only 125 pounds, Nick was five feet, ten and a half inches tall, about six inches taller than the average exercise rider, and the Shenanigans filly was by far the biggest of the bunch at Barn 4; she was the biggest yearling filly on the entire farm at that time, and, in fact, she was bigger than many of the colts. Size wasn't the only factor to be considered in matching up horses and riders; experience came first, but Nick had that, too. And he was smart. The height was a bonus.

Although Nick had never handled the filly before, he was familiar with the family. He had broken her half brother, Icecapade, Shenanigans's first foal. Icecapade had been a trial. When Nick first took him outside, he had bucked and jumped every day for three weeks, channeling his formidable energies into a constant battle with his rider. He was always testing, always challenging. He had not been a sneaky horse, he never tried to duck out from under Nick, but he had fought openly and honestly every step of the way. Then one day he had simply settled down.

Nick had also followed Reviewer's career enough to be interested in the foals from his first crop. Many people considered Reviewer to be the second fastest son Bold Ruler had ever sired. The fastest, of course, was Secretariat, the phenomenal red colt who only the month before had become the first Triple Crown winner in twenty-five years. Secretariat had set a record in the Kentucky Derby of 1:59⅖—the first horse to run that mile and a quarter race in under two minutes; he had established what virtually everyone accepted as a record in the Preakness—1:53⅖ for the mile and three-sixteenths as caught by Gene "Frenchy" Schwartz, the chief of clockers for the *Daily Racing Form*, and others—although a malfunction of the electronic teletimer would rob him of the mark in the official record books; and in the Belmont, he had destroyed the rest of the field, winning by an astonishing 31 lengths and setting not just a stakes and track record, but a world record as well. His 2:24 for the mile and a half was a watershed in thoroughbred racing, not unlike Roger Bannister's breaking of the four-minute mile. No one was going to come close to that performance for a long time.

Reviewer, who had been so promising, had fractured the cannon bone of his right hind leg three years in a row. Twice he had come back—at three and then again at four—his blazing speed still intact. He even set a Belmont track record for nine furlongs that year, in the Nassau County Handicap, but after a third fracture, he was retired to stud.

In 1960, when he was ten years old, Nick Lotz persuaded his father to take him on vacation to several of the great Kentucky horse farms. Nick had ridden a horse for the first time the year before, and the die was cast: He knew what he wanted to do for the rest of his life. On that visit to Claiborne, he had been taken in hand by the venerable Ed "Snow" Fields, a middle-aged black man who started as a groom at the farm in the 1930s and would work there for fifty years before he finally retired.

Snow introduced the boy to many of the famous stallions standing at stud there, among them Princequillo—who would sire the dam of Secretariat—and Bold Ruler himself. Princequillo's most famous son, Round Table, had been foaled the very same night, in the very same barn, as Bold Ruler—April 6, 1954—and, in a script even Hollywood couldn't have conceived, he had gone on to become Bold Ruler's archrival at the track. Round Table raced until he was five, and had only recently joined the stallion band at Claiborne. When Nick got to Round Table's stall, he innocently reached out to pet the champion, and the stallion lunged towards him, screaming, ready to break down the stall door. Snow threw his hand up to ward off the charge, and reminded Nick never to reach for a stallion without first getting permission.

"They bites!" Snow informed the child. "Sometimes lots of 'em bites me." He held up his hand as proof, and Nick stared at it, wide-eyed: Snow had four fingers, but no thumb.

Nick never forgot that visit. The summer he was sixteen, he went down to Claiborne and asked for a job. First he worked as a groom with the yearlings. Gradually, over the next five years, he got a chance to start riding them. By 1970 he had become a full-fledged exercise rider.

By then he was also halfway through his undergraduate studies in animal sciences at the University of Kentucky. This created a minor conflict. The school year ran from September through May. The process of breaking the yearlings ran from late July until the middle of November. Nick had to make a decision.

The choice was easy. Nick hoped eventually to have his own farm, to breed and race his own thoroughbreds. Horses were going to be his life, and the horses could teach him more about themselves than any school. Anyway, the university was still available in the spring, when the yearlings weren't. So Nick went to school for one semester every year, and devoted the summer and autumn to working with horses on the farm.

When Nick arrived at Raceland on the last Wednesday in July, he looked a little different from most of the other riders and stablehands. In college he had grown a mustache, and his dark hair was several inches longer than it had been in high school. He got a few sideways looks, and he was greeted with "Hey, hippie!" every now and then. Most of the teasing was friendly, because he was good with the horses. That was what counted when you went to work.

He spotted his assigned filly right away. She was a hand taller than any other yearling in the barn. A hand was a full four inches, measured at the withers, and that was a big difference in a horse at any age. Even standing in her stall, she made an impression.

For this phase of training, a groom was assigned to each rider to serve as his or her tack man. They operated as a team, going from set to set, from barn to barn, working together with nine or ten yearlings a day. Nick was working with a young man named Donnie Bussell. To get ready on that first day, Donnie had removed the feed and water buckets from the filly's stall even before Nick arrived. That left nothing inside for her to get tangled up with if she got wild and flipped over or started bouncing off the walls.

Donnie's next job was to slip a Chiffney bit into the filly's mouth, fasten it to the halter, and let her get used to it for a little while. He'd held the steel bit under his arm to warm it up before introducing it to the filly. She played with it, tongued it, and when she appeared to have accepted that new item, Donnie attached the leather shank to her halter. He glanced over the stall door. "You ready, Nick?"

"Yeah, I am." Nick slipped inside. He was carrying a saddle-cloth, a saddle pad, and a surcingle. "Hey, you be a good girl now, hear? Just be a good girl now. That's right." He had begun rubbing the filly on the back and side, easing towards her belly. She stiffened and pointed one ear back. "I'm just gonna put this little saddlecloth on you. There. You see, that's not too bad now, is it?" He was already smoothing the thin piece of cotton. "Now this is the next part. This is just a pad, see? It won't hurt." Nick laid the pad, made out of pressed felt, on top of the cloth, and folded the front end of the cloth back over the pad. "Okay, that's a good baby, good baby. Now this is the part you won't like, I bet. Just let me get this around you, you got a big old belly, you know that? You're kind of fat for a little baby, aren't you?" He pulled the surcingle over the pad and around her girth and fastened it. It was not tight, but the filly had never had anything strapped around her before, and she let out a loud squeal. When the strap stayed on, she stamped her feet and tried to back away from the groom. Donnie kept a firm hold on the shank, but left just enough play in it so she wouldn't feel trapped. When she shook her head and hollered a second time, he gave it a few sharp jerks. "That's enough now! I mean it, young lady! Behave yourself!"

The filly stood still, eyes wide. Nick stepped up to her and tightened the surcingle by one notch. Like many horses, the filly had instinctively swelled up against the binding when it was first attached. They waited a minute. After she had relaxed again,

Nick tightened the surcingle a final time and backed away. The filly bared her teeth, and Donnie jerked on her shank. "Come on now, that ain't too tight. Come on now. Let's take a little walk. Come on. See if you'll be a good girl." He turned her around one time inside the stall and she followed perfectly. He turned her one more time.

"Hey! She's doing good, ain't she, Nick? You wanna belly this horse now?"

Nick nodded. He double-checked the stall door to make sure it was closed tight—horses had been known to bolt the first time they felt a rider on their back—then he stepped over to the filly's side. Without letting go of the shank, Donnie leaned forward, grabbed Nick's left leg, and boosted him up so that he was lying across the filly's back, his stomach against her spine.

For an instant she stood absolutely still, as if stunned. Then she put her head down and bucked once, not too hard, took a few hops sideways, and quieted down. The groom turned the filly twice, with Nick still lying across her back. When she made no further objections, Donnie grabbed hold of Nick's left foot, allowing the rider to slip his right leg over the filly and straddle her. Upright, Nick relaxed into her back, his long legs dangling loosely on either side. While he stroked her neck and praised her for being such a good horse, he made sure to keep watching her ears for any sign that she might try to dump him. Nick could feel her muscles tighten, but she did not act up. Instead, she stood there at full attention, waiting to see what was coming next.

Similar scenes were being enacted in all the stalls in the barn. Most of the fillies were much more nervous than Nick's; their screams echoed under the roof. Because horses so often imitated what they heard and saw, they could work each other up into a frenzy. Nick was pleased that his filly seemed to ignore the others.

Donnie led his duo around inside the stall for several minutes. Then Nick slid off and patted the filly but did not untack her. They waited; after a brief pause, Donnie lifted Nick back on. The groom turned them for a while, and again all went smoothly. Nick dismounted. This time he undid the surcingle and rubbed on the filly's back and neck, telling her what a good job she'd done.

They spent ten days like this, inside the stall. On the third or fourth day, they added the bridle and saddle, minus stirrups. Once the rider was aboard, Donnie left him alone in the stall to turn his horse in slow figure eights, letting her feel the pull of the bit on both sides of her mouth. The groom waited just outside the door in case of trouble. Nick's filly got in a few good bucks, then quickly picked up on what was expected. On the fifth day they added the stirrups. On the sixth day they added the martingale, or yoke, a leather strap that attached to the girth, ran up between the front legs and split to attach to the reins, allowing the rider more control of the horse's head. That was all the equipment the yearlings would get at Claiborne. Anything extra would come later, from their individual trainers: blinkers, run-in bits, shadow rolls. Now they were being schooled in the basics, and if they had no problems, they could go the rest of their lives without needing any additional tack. After they had been introduced to their equipment, they spent several days getting used to it. They repeated the same simple exercises in the familiar confines of their stall. Then, on the eleventh day, they were moved.

Their new barn was on a nearby farm called Xalapa, which Claiborne was leasing at the time. It had a mile track and it served as the training center for the yearlings. On their first day, they stayed inside and skipped their lessons. The following morning they returned to school.

Nick and the other riders watched as the grooms led the fully-tacked yearlings out into the shedrow and walked them around in a well-spaced line. They were like any bunch of kids entering a brand-new classroom: Some were curious, some cautious, some reticent, some bold. They put their heads down, they sniffed the rail, they shied from unexpected shadows, they investigated every post and water tub. Nobody hurried them. There was no point in starting the day's work until the class was ready to respond. Usually, one slow trip around the shedrow was enough. That also gave the grooms a chance to make any final adjustments with their tack, to check if a girth was pinching or a saddle had started to slip.

John Sosby studied the line as they filed past. It was his job to notice everything, but at that moment he was particularly interested in whether there was one horse who remained calm and did everything right. If so, he might be able to use her as a leader. Monkey see, monkey do. That equine instinct could be made to work in a positive way in this setting. A few years later Claiborne would start taking the yearlings to the track with a lead pony—a mature, well-behaved horse who could often settle down a bunch of nervous youngsters—but in 1973 that was not yet part of the program.

"Okay, now. Stand 'em up." Sosby checked everyone as they came to a halt. The riders approached and the grooms gave them a leg up. "Walk 'em around one more time, then unshank 'em and let the riders do the work!"

Nick thought briefly of Icecapade. "You be good, now, hear?" His voice softened as he took the reins. "Be nice, young lady. Don't go crazy when I get up there." He eased into the saddle. The filly took a few sideways steps, then collected herself. Nick and Donnie nodded at each other. They were on their way.

There was nothing glamorous about training a racehorse, even the best racehorse. It was a process that consisted of countless small steps, patiently applied, with lots of repetition. There were no shortcuts and no holidays. Exercise was not called off because of heat, or heavy rain, or mud, or snow. Only for lightning or extreme iciness did the horses forgo their morning constitutional. They were a 365-day-a-year responsibility, and try as everyone might to school them properly and keep them fit and healthy, only a small percentage ever made it to the racetrack.

Sosby monitored the slow, steady progress of the yearlings as they were ridden under the shedrow. The first day the grooms walked the horses counterclockwise—the direction they would run on all North American tracks. The second day, after three or four turns in this direction, they halted the horses, turned them, and walked them clockwise for a while.

At this stage the grooms were especially patient when they were tacking up. They made a point of playing with the horses' ears, getting them thoroughly accustomed to having that part of them touched. They checked and double-checked that the bridle wasn't pinching their skin or pulling their hair. The bridle was the single most important piece of equipment that they wore. These horses could conceivably be ridden without a saddle, but not without a bridle. And no one wanted to receive yearlings who constantly shook their heads or shied away every time you went to tack them up.

The Shenanigans filly would sometimes squeal when she was being tacked up. Sosby had noticed that about her from the beginning. She was a quick study when anything new was introduced, and for the most part she was a willing worker, but she had a need to assert herself from time to time, to keep a certain boundary between herself and her handlers.

Sosby wasn't worried about her behavior. She was from "that line," he would tell the riders. Reviewer. Bold Ruler. Each of them had been a little tough to handle, and by the time you went back one more step to Nasrullah, Bold Ruler's sire, you came up against an animal that was as close to a wild horse as a stallion could be while still remaining domesticated. He proved himself well worth the trouble, though, siring 99 stakes winners, a record for the time. But he had passed a certain temperament on to many of his offspring, and they, in turn, had done the same. "Truth is," Sosby confided, "given her background, I'd be more worried about her if she didn't make any fuss at all!" A squeal, a few bucks—that was all within reason for a healthy horse. Nick agreed. Compared to the hell he'd gone through breaking Icecapade, this filly was a piece of cake.

Another ritual that started during this time was the daily bath, and the filly didn't like it very much. Ever since they first put the tack on her, Donnie had sponged her off a little bit each time they untacked, preparing her for the full-scale bath that would follow every morning of her life after her exercise. She didn't mind the first spongeful of water on her face, dripping over her forehead, between her eyes and down her long muzzle; she didn't mind the splashes down her neck and back; but she most decidedly resented the intrusion under her tail and between her hind legs. In that respect, she was like many other fillies, but because she was noticeably bigger and stronger than most fillies, she could do more damage when she acted up. Once or twice Sosby had to send over another man to help out; he didn't like to have to put a twitch on a horse, but it was important that she learn that water and a sponge weren't going to hurt, even back inside her legs. The brief pain of the twitch on her upper lip distracted her enough so that she couldn't go wild and hurt either her handlers or herself. After a time or two she settled down. She might toss her head or occasionally kick out, but her protests were in vain: Donnie had a job to do, as would all her future grooms. He was as delicate as possible, he worked as quickly as possible, and he tried to keep out of her way. The filly learned to tolerate it.

By the tenth day under the shed the yearlings were covering about a mile. Mostly they would walk and jog. They had become accustomed to working in a line, to stopping and starting, to turning around. Now they were ready to go all the way outside into a paddock. That was always a gamble.

John had decided to try Nick's filly on the lead. "Just walk her over there," he'd said. "That Shenanigans seems pretty confident, don't you think? She may try something, but I want a steady horse up there, and she's a good one. She's not flighty."

Nick smiled. No, she certainly was not flighty. She might put a hump in her back the second they got out under the open sky, but she was not going to skitter around and surprise him. If she didn't like something, she would be direct.

It was a hazy August morning, the prologue to a long, hot day. Nick had been working since seven, and by nine o'clock, when the set with the Shenanigans filly went out, the air still had a trace of coolness to it, though the humidity was beginning to seep through. Horses as well as riders could work up a sweat on a day like that.

There were ten fillies in their set, and the riders lined them up each morning according to John Sosby's orders. Sosby might have them walk single file around the paddock, then switch and do some figure eights, then jog a bit, or do an easy gallop. There were plenty of bucks and jumps and squeals, but after ten days of being outside with the riders up, the fillies were ready to head over to the track.

From then on they did something different all the time. They might pair off, or run three or four abreast. Sosby tried to mix up the order so that each horse experienced what it was like at the front, at the back, and in the middle of the pack. They took turns along the rail and on the outside. They learned how to behave in each situation. After they had all been shuffled up a few times, Sosby and the riders knew a lot more about their horses than they had before. The nervous fillies who shied from every shadow were kept off the lead and away from the inside rail. The more confident individuals were allowed to remain in front, on the theory that they would set a good example and stay out of trouble.

At this stage of the game, the riders had very limited goals. They wanted to teach the horses good manners, which meant responding to instructions and behaving under all circumstances. They wanted the horses to learn to maintain whatever gait and position they were in and not bolt off. Everyone at the farm was working towards a single end result: to lay a foundation for well-trained, responsive thoroughbreds who could be handled as easily as possible in every aspect of their daily lives.

By mid-September the yearlings had been using the one-mile training track for several weeks. They followed a basic routine: They would walk off, jog an eighth- to a quarter-mile, then start cantering.

No one was asking the horses for speed. The riders weren't trying to discover if they had the next Secretariat under them. That was not their job and this was not the time. They were simply trying to teach the youngsters to cooperate. To do this, they depended on the basic "aids" to communicate with the horses: their legs, seat, and hands. And their voice. The words didn't matter; it was the reassuring tone that often helped to calm a green horse, especially in the new situations they were facing every day. It was not unusual to hear riders singing to their mounts, soothing and distracting them, as they worked their way around the track. Conversely, the sharp tone of a reprimand would ring out from time to time, and that, too, could be effective.

The yearlings were never tested. Their soft bones and tender shins could not take the pressure of short, fast works. Even galloping, a number of them bucked shins and had to lay off training for months. Every precaution in the world could be taken with these horses, at every stage of their careers, but they could never be completely safe. They were racehorses. For them, running would always be a double-edged sword.

Nick was pleased with the progress of the Shenanigans filly.

Sometimes he'd have to get after her, but she usually behaved. She learned quickly, too; she was smart. And as they started doing some easy gallops, he noticed one major difference between the Shenanigans filly and the rest of the set: She had excellent wind. When Nick pulled her up after their mile, she'd blow once and recover; the others went off huffing and puffing.

One Sunday, John Russell flew down to Claiborne to have a look at the yearlings who would soon be shipped to him up at Belmont. He was the trainer for Wheatley Stables, which had been started by the late Mrs. Phipps. He stood at the rail with John Sosby, watching the set, and when he saw the filly Nick was on, he could hardly believe his eyes.

"My gosh, look at the size of her!" he exclaimed. "I've got to take a picture of this one to take back to New York and show people! They're not gonna believe how big she is!" When the set was finished and the horses were walking back to the barn, Russell was shaking his head.

Nick was amused. The filly was big, and impressive, but he had gotten used to her. Russell was the first outsider to take special note of her, and Nick was proud that she had received that recognition. In a few weeks the Janneys themselves would stop by for a day as they always did, spring and fall, to look over their stock. Nick hoped that they, too, would have the same response.

The rest of the fall was spent putting a bottom on the horses, building up their stamina by continuing to exercise them a mile a day. In October, as the days grew cool and the nights started to leave a trace of frost, the schedule for turning out the horses was reversed: Now they were put up in their stalls in mid-afternoon and kept inside through the night. In the mornings they ate breakfast, went over to the track, and exercised. They came back and were bathed and hotwalked. Only then were they turned out in the open field for a few hours of play. Their free time was gradually being cut back; the time spent inside their stalls was being increased. Everything was leading up to a future at the racetrack, where most of them would not be out of their stalls for more than an hour or two every day.

At this point in their training the yearlings were also walked through the starting gate. The doors weren't closed on them, but the horses were led through or halted inside for a moment, to give them a brief exposure to another element they would soon encounter. At first the Shenanigans filly bolted right through the gate. It was only forty inches wide, and horses were wary of being so rigidly confined. Nick settled the filly down and brought her back around to try again. Horses were creatures of habit; simple repetition was the best way to ingrain a lesson in their minds. Since nothing could be explained to them in words, they had to be shown there was nothing to fear. It was when horses felt helpless and afraid that they became dangerous and destructive.

Sosby relied on a few basic principles of training. He tried to make the lessons interesting; he relied on persuasion rather than force, unless force became absolutely necessary; he was consistent; and he remained flexible and responsive to individual needs. These were the qualities that made a good teacher in any field. It was no different with horses.

What the filly learned early in life would always be a part of her. That mattered a lot to Nick. He would never be the one who jumped off the horse in the winner's circle; he would never be the object of the crowd's cheers; he would never get written up in the newspapers. But he'd be a little tiny part of every horse he ever worked with. No one could teach a horse to be fast, and no one could teach it to have courage. The only thing that people could do, all the people who came in contact with a racehorse, was to help create the conditions under which the horse could flourish; to help it develop into whatever it was destined to become.

November twelfth was a big day at Claiborne Farm that year. Secretariat was arriving from Belmont Park to begin his new career at stud. A film crew, journalists, photographers, and special visitors were on hand to witness the event. After all, this was the horse who had already appeared on the covers of *Time, Newsweek,* and *Sports Illustrated* during his Triple Crown triumph. This was the horse who now had his own personal representative from the William Morris Agency in New York.

The powerful red colt was led into the stall formerly occupied by his own great sire, the late Bold Ruler. Snow Fields, who had been Bold Ruler's groom, let it be known that the colt would have some mighty big shoes to fill in the breeding shed, and that was a fact that nobody could dispute. His success at stud would have economic repercussions for the syndicate that now owned him, and it certainly had the potential to influence future generations of racehorses. But to the people who admired and loved him, the people who had seen him race, it didn't really matter what he did from now on. His performances at the track had been more than enough. He was one of the immortals.

Four days later, while everyone's attention was still focused on Secretariat, the Shenanigans filly that Nick Lotz had been riding for the past three and a half months was walked up a ramp without any fanfare whatsoever and loaded into a horse trailer. Her days at Claiborne were over. Nick would never see her again.

5

"**H**ey, Miserable, you gonna stick around today?"

Jackie Peacock turned to face Frank Whiteley. She was a young woman with dark blond hair pulled back in a ponytail; nice-looking, friendly, secretly pleased whenever Frank called her something slightly derogatory. That was a sign of affection with him, a sign that you belonged.

"I don't know. Why? What's today?"

"I just asked, are you gonna stick around?"

"Well—yeah. I guess so. I can." She continued scrubbing the saddle she had balanced over the rail. After a minute she remembered. "Is that when the shipment's coming in from Claiborne?"

"Maybe."

Jackie grinned. If Frank had any idea how transparent he was, he would die of embarrassment. He was trying to act like it was no big deal, like he wasn't excited about a new bunch of yearlings. Not that he showed it, exactly. But Jackie had been galloping horses for him for three years; she could tell. In fact, he had driven over to Kentucky only a few weeks earlier to have a firsthand look at these babies in advance.

Jackie concentrated on rubbing sponge over leather in small, deliberate circles. She'd grown up around horses, in Virginia, and she was meticulous. When she was finally satisfied, she hauled up saddle and bridle and headed for the tackroom. "You expecting something special?"

Frank was watching the line of horses being hosed down in front of the shedrow. "Never know till they run," he said. "Never know till they run."

"Oh, Frank!" Jackie shook her head. "That's gonna be your epitaph, you know that? They're gonna write on your grave, 'He never knew till they ran.' "

Frank snorted. Well, it was true. Nothing could make a liar out of you faster than a racehorse. He'd been around the track since the thirties, and he'd learned long ago that the only thing you could count on in this game was unpredictability.

Frank was living in a room in the Mona Lisa Motel near the center of Camden, South Carolina. Before, during his marriage, he and his wife Lillian had rented a house every winter when they came down with the horses, but in the years since his divorce Frank couldn't be bothered. All he needed was a place to sleep at night and take a quick nap in the afternoon. Or, occasionally, to put his feet up and read through the copies of the *Racing Form* that piled up in his post office box every few days.

He woke up at four-thirty every morning and headed over to Mrs. Thomas's, a typical eggs and grits diner on Broad Street. It was one of the few places open in Camden at that hour. Frank would have a cup of coffee and a piece of toast, or maybe a doughnut. Then he'd drive through the gates of the Training Center and be ready to start the morning workouts around five.

That morning, in addition to the twenty-five or so older horses he already had, he was to receive six yearlings that had been born and raised at Claiborne, colts and fillies whose names he wouldn't even want to know until they began to race. They would be referred to by their bloodlines, or coloring, or size. Like "that big, black Shenanigans filly." Mr. and Mrs. Janney's filly, Frank thought, smiling. He'd noticed her right away when he was out there. She stood out over everything, big and beautiful. He had never seen anything like her, a yearling that size, that commanding, with all the ease of a much older horse.

Of course, he reminded himself, you didn't really know anything about them till they raced, and that was months away—if everything went smoothly. She had good breeding, though. The Janneys had bred her themselves, out of their own mare Shenanigans, who had already produced the stakes winner Icecapade, a gray colt by Nearctic. Frank had trained him, too. This filly coming in was from the first crop by Reviewer, who had raced for three years and won nine of his thirteen starts. But each year

he had fractured the cannon bone in his right hind leg. Speed
could do that to a horse. The good ones always got hurt, sooner
or later. The bad ones didn't run hard enough to do themselves
any harm.

The maroon and cream-colored Mills van slowly turned the corner and rumbled past the entrance gate. The driver was very
careful as he made his way along the dirt roads inside the Training Center, wending his way over to Barns 8 and 9, near the top
of a gentle rise, close to the edge of the forest. He had six yearlings in the back, attended to by stablehands, and he'd had no
trouble the entire trip. When the horses stepped down off the
ramp, they would be Frank Whiteley's responsibility.

Frank was ready. "Rooster!" He pointed to one groom. "Grab
ahold of that little chestnut. You, Minnor!" he ordered another
man. "You take that black filly." One by one the yearlings were
paired up with their grooms. The ten-hour trip from Kentucky
to South Carolina was the longest they'd ever been cooped up
in a van. They had to be watched closely when they got off.
Often they'd have a temperature, or trouble with their bowels.

Several of the exercise riders had waited to have a look at
the new shipment. They stood around drinking coffee or cleaning their tack. Jackie slipped off her extra sweatshirt. These November mornings could fool you. Only a few hours ago it had
been freezing; now, with the sun up and no wind, it was almost
warm.

"That's a nice-looking bay," she commented. "Oooh, look at
that filly, you guys! Do you believe how fat she is?"

Squeaky Truesdale—the best, most experienced rider Frank
had—was standing nearby. "She big, all right," he answered
softly.

"Big!" Jackie cried. "She's huge!"

The other riders nodded. They couldn't help noticing her.
She was by far the biggest yearling in the bunch, the biggest
many of them could remember, a freak.

"Squeaky, what do you think she weighs?" Jackie asked.

"Oh, 'bout nine hundred pounds, I bet. Maybe a little more."

"You think so? That's awful big for a yearling, isn't it?"

Squeaky shrugged. "She pretty, though."

"Aw, Squeaky, you always think they're pretty!"

Squeaky dipped his head and smiled. It was true. To him, they were all pretty.

"Well, I got to get home." Jackie jumped down from the rail. As she passed Minnor, she called out to his horse, "You old baby, you are the fattest thing I've ever seen! Mr. Whiteley's gonna work that blubber off you, I can promise you that!" She playfully smacked the filly's side. The filly snorted and bared her teeth.

"Hey, hey," Minnor crooned, tightening his grip on the shank. "Behave yourself now. You be good."

"Sorry!" Jackie said. "Aren't we touchy? Here, let me try again." She reached over and stroked the filly; long, firm strokes. This time the horse appeared indifferent. "Okay, fatty, now I know better. You're one of those dignified types that doesn't like to be slapped. I'll remember that."

A minute later a chestnut colt walked by and Jackie gave him a few swats on the shoulder. He whinnied with pleasure. Jackie laughed out loud, picked up her helmet, and headed for the car.

6

Sunlight splintered through the wall of pines and dappled the deep green grass. Frank climbed aboard Sled Dog, his stable pony, and followed the first set out for morning exercise.

Since the mid-sixties, Frank had been wintering in South Carolina, and had come to like it better than Florida as a place to freshen his horses. It might get frosty, but it seldom snowed. If it rained for a few days, plenty of sunshine followed. Best of all, from November to April the horses could experience three distinct seasons. The change was good for them. Frank was convinced they liked variety in their climate as well as their routines.

The Marion du Pont Scott Training Center—that was its formal name, which no one ever used—was in the heart of Camden. It could accommodate 450 horses, in wooden barns painted the traditional white with green trim, and it offered plenty of choices for morning exercise. There was a one-mile dirt track known as Wrenfield; a huge, grassy polo field; and on the other side of the polo field, a second training track, this one a half-mile. The woods themselves were tall, shimmering, long-needled pines, cut with trails on which Frank often sent his sets back and forth to the track. That took a lot more time, but Frank wasn't in any hurry. Some days he let the riders hack their mounts through the woods for an hour or so and skipped the track completely. That was the whole point in going away for the winter: to give the horses a break, a change of pace. If the horses were happy and interested in their work, they would be less likely to go stale when they were returned to the more severe limitations of the racetrack.

Minnor Massey, a tall, thin groom with a round face and a slight goatee, had worked with horses all his life except for one four-year stint in a funeral home. He was a sharp dresser and a fun-loving, cheerful man who had come to Frank in 1970 after working for several locally based trainers. Minnor had been assigned to the Shenanigans filly, and, like all the other yearlings, she was walked under the shedrow without a rider for the first few days after she arrived. Minnor encountered no problems with her. She did not shy away when he rubbed her or cleaned out her feet with a hoof pick; she was a good "doer," finishing all her oats; and she shifted quietly around the stall, staying out of his way, as he moved from one spot to another forking out the soiled straw.

When it was time to get the babies fully tacked up, Frank stood outside the row of stalls and watched. Everything was going smoothly with Minnor and his filly until he leaned down to tighten the girth. Suddenly there was a flash of teeth and wide pink gums as she snapped at Minnor's skinny arm.

"Damn!" Minnor jerked back just in time.

"Fooled ya, huh?" Frank chortled.

"Did you see that? Damn! She's quick, ain't she?"

"She's gonna get a piece of you one of these days if you don't watch out."

"Don't you worry, I'm gonna tie her up from now on! What's the matter with you, girl? I'm not hurtin' you, am I? Come on now, behave yourself."

Minnor led her out. The flare-up lasted just that moment, the tightening of her girth. Then she was once again perfectly calm.

New Year's came and went. All thoroughbreds in North America automatically became one year older on January first, regardless of when they had actually been foaled. From now on Frank would gradually start asking more from his brand-new two-year-olds. He'd gallop them farther, school them in the gate, and by late February, early March, he'd start breezing them—giving them shorter, faster workouts to develop their speed. When that phase started, he'd add lunch—a third meal—to the babies' schedule. The harder they worked, the more fuel they needed to do the job. They'd be ready for it.

By late January everybody had been on the filly at least a couple of times, and they had begun calling her "Sofie," as in "Sofie the Sofa," because she was big and soft and easy to sit on. She was mild-mannered enough to have served as a beginner's horse in a riding school, but the babies still hadn't done any real running at this stage. They spent a lot of time at the polo field, walking and trotting, trotting and jogging, and doing endless figure eights as they learned to change leads. When horses ran, they always reached out first with one front leg, called the lead, which took an additional stress. Although horses naturally changed leads on their own when covering a distance, it was important that they also learn to switch at a signal from their rider.

When those lessons were pretty far along, they moved over to the main track. One of the last times Jackie Peacock rode the filly was at Wrenfield. Frank had asked the riders to gallop out in sets of four, and Jackie could not get her horse to pick up the pace.

"Make her run!" Frank hollered from the rail.

"I'm trying!" Jackie hollered back. She was urging with her hands, kicking with her heels, but the filly just lollygagged around, enjoying the scenery. "Hey!" Jackie shouted in the filly's ear. "Come on, you! Let's go now!" She kicked again. There was no response.

Jackie made a laborious trip around the track, working herself up into a sweat without producing any noticeable increase in the filly's speed. When they finished and got back to the barn, Jackie turned to Frank. "She just wouldn't run, Frank! She wouldn't go!"

"You got to make her go! That's your job!"

"I tried! She's just fat and lazy! I don't think she even likes to run!"

"Is that a fact?" Frank watched the horses being led out for their baths. He didn't seem the least upset; if anything, he was amused by Jackie's report. Nobody could know yet whether this filly or any of the other babies liked to run, because they hadn't ever really done it. Running—competitive running—would come later on. Maybe some of them would pick up on it down at the Training Center; others not till they were in a real race. Some horses had a taste for it and some didn't. Some could be taught and some couldn't. Frank had a feeling the filly just needed a little more experience, a little more guidance, before she caught on. And he knew just the person who could give it to her.

"Squeaky!" he called out.

"Yessuh, Mr. Whiteley?"

"Squeaky, I want you to get on that big filly tomorrow, hear? Old Miserable here tells me she don't like to run."

John "Squeaky" Truesdale was only twelve years old when he received his nickname. He was a small, quiet child, and he had not yet developed the muscles that would later give him the appearance of a middleweight boxer in his prime. All his life he had been in love with horses. The horses, however, existed in another world. The only way a boy from a black family in Camden could get close to them was to hang out over at the polo field, by the Training Center, and offer to muck out stalls. Sometimes, as payment, he would be allowed to hop on one of the thoroughbreds. This reward was by no means guaranteed, but John was willing to do almost anything for a chance to ride.

He had spent most of one afternoon shaking out stalls, hauling manure over to the pit, and raking the shedrow when two owners, who had been hanging around drinking, started making fun of him and giving him a hard time. John had long ago learned to ignore them, even when—or, perhaps, especially when—their teasing took on an ugly tone.

Suddenly, for no reason other than simple meanness, they grabbed the boy, carried him over to the tackroom, and hung him up by his shirt on one of the highest hooks on the wall. It was a long way to the floor, and the floor was made of cement. John looked down from his precarious perch and started to cry. There was nothing else he could do; if he struggled, he might choke himself or fall loose and smash onto the hard floor. The two drunken adults sprawled in lawn chairs and made jokes while John, terrified, cried and cried so hard he lost his voice.

They left him there for an hour and a half. Then, two other men who had driven by to check on their horses noticed what was going on and put an end to the torture. John tried to say something, but all that came out was a peeping sound, a thin whine. "You sound like a little squeak-mouse, you know that?" one of them said, not unkindly, and sent him on his way.

The next afternoon, after school, he was back at the barns. His voice had returned to normal, but by then everyone had heard the story. "Little squeak-mouse" they called him, and, over time, "Squeak-mouse" turned into "Squeaky." The name stuck. For over twenty-three years everyone had been calling him by this name.

Squeaky had come to work for Whiteley through a groom named Dan Williams, a family friend of the Truesdales who had been like a father to him. Dan had arranged his first real job for him with a local trainer when Squeaky was only sixteen, and had looked after the boy as they traveled the Eastern circuit of race-tracks, teaching him how to shop and cook and handle his finances. At that time they were paid twice a month, and on the first and the fifteenth Squeaky always stopped at the post office to mail home a money order to his mother.

Given the chance, Squeaky quickly developed into an excellent exercise rider, earning a reputation first for schooling jumpers and later for his ability over the flat. Although he and Dan frequently had to hire on with different outfits, they managed to work together off and on over the years. In the early seventies they both found themselves back at Frank Whiteley's barn. Their timing couldn't have been better.

7

The Shenanigans filly was coming into her own. She was galloping easily and coming back fresh. Squeaky jumped off one morning and told Minnor he thought she had the makings of something good; while the other horses were wanting to pull up, this filly was ready to take off all over again. Before he left the barn that morning, Squeaky even tried to get Frank to bet him one paycheck, double or nothing, that this horse was a future stakes winner. Frank just laughed.

Towards the end of February, when it was time to see if she had any speed, Frank began putting a rider named Ric Martin on the filly most of the time. Ric was forty pounds lighter than Squeaky, who weighed about 160, and any trainer had to be concerned with weight once the youngsters started running. Two-year-olds had notoriously tender shins and soft bones. Like many of the babies, the big filly had already popped a couple of splints during this early training phase. Splints appeared as a swelling on the bone, usually just below the knee. They were technically an inflammation of the connective tissue between the cannon bone and the fourth metacarpal, resulting from physical stress, and were almost as likely to occur while a horse was running free in a paddock as they were while the animal was exercising on a track. Ice and cold-water hosing usually solved the problem. Since Whiteley was in the habit of icing and hosing anyway, as preventive measures, outsiders could never tell for sure if one of his horses had a problem or whether it was simply business as usual around his barn. If a splint was severe, the horse might be taken out of training and rested for a while. Splints could become dangerous if they went for weeks or months unattended, but if they were caught early, they produced little damage and had no lasting effects.

"Goddamn it! I told you to stay with those damn horses! What the hell's the matter with you?"

Whiteley shouted at Ric as he struggled to pull the big filly up. The rider was still catching his breath, but the flame in his cheeks came from anger rather than exertion. What the hell was the matter with Whiteley? Ric had tried his best to do exactly what the old man asked: gallop out head to head with the other two horses in the set. It wasn't his damn fault that the bitch he was on was twice as big as every other horse out there, with a stride three times as long. In order for her to stay comfortable and relaxed, she just naturally went faster than anyone else.

After he had untacked her, Ric tried to explain. "Mr. Whiteley, that filly's all business nowadays! You can't hold her back with them other horses! She's rarin' to go! You can't expect a powerhouse like her to lope along with them other babies!"

"I don't need you to tell me what to expect from a horse, goddamn it! When I say stay together in the set, I mean it! You want to train horses, go get your goddamn license!"

Ric kicked at the dirt and started to stomp off.

"Where the hell you think you're going? Hold that filly for Minnor and then you hotwalk her."

"I got to get up on that colt in the next set! Can't you let someone else walk the damn horse?"

"No! You walk the damn horse!"

Damn that damn horse! Ric got so mad he couldn't even think straight sometimes. Whiteley was just doing this to punish him. He was sure of it, treating him like a little kid. He was almost twenty, and there was no reason on earth he should have to hotwalk horses anymore. He was a professional jockey now; he'd won some races for Whiteley the past year, up at Delaware and Maryland, and he'd come down to Camden for the winter to recover from a spill and take it easy for a while. But Whiteley, Ric thought, was living in the dark ages, the time when a jock was a slave to the trainer who held his contract. Ric had done that for almost two years now and he was sick of it; he had one year left on his contract, and he didn't think he should have to do all this other stuff anymore. Whiteley thought otherwise.

There was nothing personal in Whiteley's attitude. Everybody who worked for him was treated the same way. In New York he occasionally made Jacinto Vasquez, one of the leading jockeys in the country, pony sets out in the morning. Even his assistant, Barclay Tagg—who already had his own trainer's license and could have worked elsewhere, giving all the orders— was sometimes called on to scald feed tubs or shovel shit or unbale the hay. Whiteley didn't pay much attention to job titles or to rank. Each person was expected to do whatever needed to be done. The highest praise Whiteley could give someone— though he never said it to their face—was that the day wasn't too long for them. Hard work was his life. If you didn't want to make it yours, you had no business being in his barn.

It wasn't the filly's fractions that impressed Ric—he had no idea how fast she was moving when they started breezing two and three furlongs that spring—but rather her frame of mind when she hit the track. She was beginning to catch on. Some ancient instinct was being aroused in her; she wanted to beat those other horses. That's why it was increasingly difficult to hold her back, in spite of Whiteley's tirades. It was so unfair, Ric thought. Why should he have to put up with this constant verbal abuse over something that was beyond his control?

He didn't understand that it wouldn't have made any difference who rode that particular horse, or how good they were, or even how perfectly they followed orders: As long as Whiteley had that filly in his barn, he was always going to be yelling at someone.

8

Frank had given the first set instructions to go out the lower gap when they were done and head straight back to the barn. He wanted the track completely cleared so there would be no distractions when he broke a couple of two-year-old fillies from the gate. It was late March, and some of these babies might be racing within a month.

One of the riders in that first set was John Bruno, a man in his mid-thirties. He was on a three-year-old filly named Yankee Law, and he caught up to Squeaky as they finished galloping their mile and a half.

"Who's coming out of the gate, do you know?" Bruno asked.

Squeaky shrugged.

"I bet he's breaking that Shenanigans filly," Bruno said. "He's been schooling her in the gate a lot."

"Maybe. You never know what Mr. Whiteley gonna do."

"You and Ric been riding her the most. You think she's any good, Squeaky?"

"She gonna be a stakes filly, I think. They still just babies, though. You can't never tell."

"I'd like to see how she goes, you know? If she's got any speed."

Squeaky smiled. "She got some speed all right." He guided his horse over to the gap. Bruno decided not to follow him out. He wheeled his horse around and proceeded up the track in the opposite direction, heading for the outside rail, to watch the black filly run.

Back at the gate, the two babies were all business. Jackie was up on the little one, a daughter of Damascus named Lady Portia. Ric was aboard the Janneys' horse.

When the bell rang, both fillies sprang out together and started pounding up the track. Lady Portia was on the outside, running faster than Jackie had expected. Ric's filly was moving, too, strong and smooth. Both displayed the exhilaration of a real break, the awareness of competition. Frank had wanted them to stay together, two abreast. For the first furlong they were. It was an excellent start, and Frank leaned quietly against the rail, drinking it all in.

Then, at almost the same instant, everybody realized they were in trouble. Straight ahead, looming like a rock, stood Yankee Law. She had panicked and started backing up across the track; then, suddenly unnerved, she had frozen directly in the path of the oncoming fillies. Bruno was frantically kicking and whipping and shouting, but Yankee Law refused to budge. Whether it was from stubbornness or stupidity or sheer terror didn't matter. Two horses were bearing down on her at better than 35 miles an hour, and it was too late to stop them.

"Noooooooooooooooo!" A single scream pierced the air, followed by the sickening thud of horses colliding at high speed.

Frank's heart stopped. The thought flashed through his mind that they were all going to be killed. He was in his car and over at the spot so fast he didn't even remember driving there.

The scene that confronted him was not reassuring. Lady Portia lay unmoving on her side, bleeding from her nose. Jackie had been hurled a hundred feet through the air, and she, too, was still. Yankee Law, knocked to her knees, was slowly righting herself. Bruno was sitting up in the dirt, stunned. And off in the distance—Frank was almost afraid to look, he didn't want to see her staggering down the track—but no! The black filly was still flying! She had somehow managed to swerve, had never broken stride, and was now racing around the turn untouched, running for all she was worth!

Frank absorbed all this in a split second as he rushed to Jackie's side. Her eyes were open. "I'm okay, Frank," she gasped. She'd had the wind knocked out of her, but was now trying to get to her feet.

"Don't move!" Frank hollered.

When she saw how pale he was, she tried to smile. "I'm okay,

Frank. Nothing's broken. Really. I'm okay." Then she saw her filly. "Oh, God," she whispered.

Frank started back towards the fallen horse. They were all thinking the worst when suddenly Lady Portia flicked her ears, shook her head a few times, and scrambled to her feet. Frank grabbed the reins. Her breathing was labored and she seemed dazed, but she was standing squarely on all four legs. She seemed to be okay. Miraculously, everyone seemed to be okay.

By then Ric had managed to pull up his filly and was heading back to the scene of the accident. "You goddamned son of a bitch, Bruno! You almost got us all killed out there! Goddamn idiot! Did you see that, Frank? Did you see what he did?"

Frank didn't answer. He would take care of Bruno later. Now all he was interested in was making sure everyone was all right. He studied the black filly. She was dancing in place, pleased with herself, with her extended run. If she was aware that she had narrowly escaped disaster, she gave no indication.

They all waited under the shedrow for the vet's report. When he emerged from Lady Portia's stall, he was cautiously optimistic. She had had a concussion and would need to be watched closely for the next twenty-four hours, but he believed she would make a full recovery. She'd have a stiff neck for a couple of weeks, and she'd be plenty sore—there was no avoiding that—but it looked like she was going to be just fine.

Frank went through the rest of the morning as he always did, checking his horses' legs, supervising their baths and bandages, mixing their afternoon feed. He altered his routine just long enough to give John Bruno a chewing out the likes of which no one had ever heard around that barn before—and they had heard plenty under those eaves. But to everyone's surprise, Whiteley stopped short of firing him. Why bother? Frank knew Bruno would never again dare to disobey an order.

That night, alone in his room, Frank stretched out in bed. He was exhausted, but for once sleep did not come easily. It was hard not to think about the accident. It had been such a close call. He could have lost three horses and three riders. They could have all been badly hurt. Ruined. It had been a matter of inches; fractions of a second.

He could have lost the Janneys' filly. It was that simple. Before she'd ever had her chance. It wouldn't have been the first
time a promising horse had vanished before it ever ran a race.
Horses disappeared like that all the time, before anyone had
even heard their names.

Frank flicked off the light. And yet, for all that, she had
survived. She had survived untouched. So, in addition to everything else she had shown him over the past four months—speed
and strength, an easygoing disposition, intelligence, beauty,
nerves of steel—the filly had had one more thing going for her,
on this one day at least, and it was the most elusive quality of
them all: luck.

PART TWO

1

As soon as the match race was announced, the New York Racing Association offered both trainers the additional protection of round-the-clock Pinkertons at their barns. Under normal circumstances, the guard patrolled the entire backstretch area, covering all the barns in the course of their rounds. The upcoming match was an extraordinary event, so the increased security was welcomed.

With one proviso. Frank marched into the Pinkerton office and asked to see the man in charge. Their conversation was short.

"I want Buck Jones over at my barn at night," Whiteley said.

"Well, we're gonna have to check the schedules, Mr. Whiteley, and see if he's free. He's usually working days now."

"You tell him I asked for him over at my barn. Nobody else is coming over there at night, understand?"

"Yessir, we'll see what we can do."

"Ain't nothing to see. Just get Buck."

Although the Match was still two weeks away, word had already reached the backstretch that there was some real money being wagered on the race. Frank didn't like that at all. "Real" money meant the big-time—organized elements outside the track, people who were capable of influencing the outcome of a race. There had been a recent wave of that. The story hadn't broken publicly yet, but it was a hot topic on the rumor circuit; not just in New York, either, but all over the Northeast. During the past year there had been more than the usual grumblings about fixed

races, horses being held, suspicious bets—especially trifectas—
being cashed.

These charges were very hard to prove. Riders had to make
split-second decisions all the time, and half-ton horses running
at high speeds didn't always cooperate. Just because a jockey
timed his move wrong or got himself caught in a traffic jam
didn't mean he was deliberately trying to throw a race. Still, a
study of the mutuel betting patterns and payoffs in certain races
would have revealed some disturbing results. Several years would
pass before reports of the scandal erupted in the press; meanwhile, those trainers who had established solid personal rela-
tionships with one or two key jockeys were holding on to them
as if they were gold.

Frank Whiteley thanked his stars for Jacinto. He knew that
Jacinto's name, along with those of Angel Cordero, Jorge Velasquez, Braulio Baeza, Eddie Belmonte—many of the top riders in
New York—had been whispered in connection with the race-
fixing rumors, but that was one score on which Whiteley personally had no doubts. Jacinto had always been a hundred
percent with him. There were very few people in all of racing
that Frank Whiteley trusted. Jacinto Vasquez was one of them.

It hadn't always been that way. Frank Whiteley and Jacinto Vasquez had met for the first time six years earlier, during the
summer meeting at Delaware Park.

"I don't ride no Por-ta Ricans." That's how Whiteley pronounced the word. "You know that. What are you wasting my
time for?" He was talking to a man called Fats, and it was the
middle of the afternoon. That was not the time of day when
jockey agents usually did their business, but Harold "Fats" Wisc-
man was not a run-of-the-mill jockey agent. He was over six feet
tall, weighed almost 300 pounds, and was plagued with a variety
of ailments, the most serious of which was diabetes. He had
handled some of the best jockeys in recent years, including Walter Blum, but he and Frank knew each other from the lean old
days in Maryland, where Fats had started off as a boy selling the
Racing Form from the steps of Pimlico while Frank was still gyp-
ping from one half-mile track to another. Playful, bullying, affectionate, and corrosive by turns, Fats was proud of his

reputation as a teller of tall tales. But there were some people he didn't fool around with. Frank tried many times to trap him, but he had never caught Fats in a lie; he was the only agent who was always welcome in Whiteley's barn.

"First off, you know good and well he ain't no Puerto Rican," Fats answered. "He's from Panama. That other boy from down there won the Derby in 'sixty-three. This boy can ride a horse."

"Can't trust no son of a bugger I can't talk to."

"Talk to me! What the hell am I here for? Anyway, the boy speaks okay English, what's the matter with you? He's a good rider. Would I take him if he wasn't good?"

"Huh." Frank looked around.

"Give him a chance, Frank. Put him on something in the morning. I'm telling you, he can ride. And he knows horses. He's smart, not like these other pinheads around here. He can think. Pain in the ass sometimes, I won't lie, but he's good. And he's an honest little hell-raiser. He won't screw you around."

"Don't waste your time, Fats. I told you, I ain't riding no Porta Ricans."

The next morning Fats made the introductions. Frank looked down at Jacinto and repeated his position.

Jacinto shrugged.

"For cryin' out loud, put him on a horse!" Fats bellowed. "He's the best rider around!"

"Who says so?"

"I say so! Have you looked at the standings? The boy's winning races here every day!"

"Then he don't need to get on my horses, if he's so damn busy!"

"Come on, Frank, don't be so fucking stubborn! I'm gonna have a heart attack arguing with you all day!"

"Aw, hell! I'll do anything to get you off my back, Fats." Whiteley turned to the jockey. "You know how to ride a thoroughbred?"

"Yessir. I ride anything you got."

"Take that chestnut bitch over there and gallop her a mile and a half with this next set. Rooster!" Whiteley hollered.

"Yessuh?" The groom poked his head out from the stall.

"Give this goddamn Por-ta Rican a leg up on that filly when she's ready, will you? See if he can stay on." Whiteley turned back to Fats. "Goddamn it, now are you satisfied?"

Fats winked at Jacinto. Jacinto pulled on his helmet. It was exactly like Fats had said it would be. Exactly. Fats had sat him down the night before and told him that Whiteley would make a lot of noise and insult him and call him names—and then he would give him a chance.

That was all Jacinto wanted. Just a chance.

The first time Jacinto climbed over the fence onto the backstretch of Remon Racetrack, in Panama City, the guards chased him away. The second time he made it. He scurried off unnoticed and found a trainer who allowed him the privilege of rubbing seven horses a day for no pay. That was fine with Jacinto. He was twelve years old and had run away from home, in the town of Las Tablas, leaving his father and nine brothers and sisters—his mother had died when he was five—because he wanted to become a jockey.

He lived with a family on the backstretch and, during the next few years, while he dreamed of fame and glory, he watched in awe as a young jockey named Braulio Baeza—only four years older than himself—went out and smashed every riding record ever set in Panama. Baeza became the idol of a generation, but his success only increased the frustration that Jacinto was beginning to feel: The trainer he worked for had forbidden him to so much as sit on any of his thoroughbreds. How was he going to become a racerider if he couldn't get on the horses?

But nobody was around at three o'clock in the morning. Jacinto decided that would be the ideal hour to go for a ride. One night he simply crept into the barn, saddled one of the horses, and, in the darkness, rode over to the track. There, for the first time, he galloped a thoroughbred. It was nothing like riding the workhorses on his father's farm. This was a wild surge of speed and power, a magical rhythm of muscle and bone.

Night after night he repeated the experiment, riding one or two or sometimes even three horses. Afterwards, he cooled them out and left them quietly in their stalls. In the morning he watched those same horses being led out again for their daily exercise. They never showed any signs of wear and tear; Jacinto was convinced that they actually benefited from their extra run, that they were the fittest horses on the track. The trainer didn't agree. When he discovered what was going on, he kicked Jacinto out of the barn and told him never to come back.

When he first came to the United States, in 1960, the railbirds dubbed him "Baby." Panamanian newspapers picked up the nickname and featured stories about Jacinto Vasquez, "El Bebé," another local jockey seeking his fortune in the greener pastures up North.

It was easy to see where the name came from: Jacinto looked much younger than his sixteen years, with his smooth round face and earnest, wide-spaced brown eyes. He could eat three big meals a day then—if he had the money—and still tip the scales at a scant 103. And it didn't matter if his English was just beginning to take root; when he spotted a pretty girl in the crowd, all he had to do was raise his eyebrows and grin.

He was as wild on the track as he was off. During his first few months in the United States he got set down for rough riding so often that he spent as many days on the sidelines as he did in the saddle. Then his luck changed—for the worse. On January 4, 1961, his seventeenth birthday, he broke his leg in a spill and was out for six months.

Jacinto's first experience in New York was a disaster. Between suspensions, general cockiness, and a lack of good mounts, he did not make a favorable impression. He returned to the lesser tracks of Arizona, New Mexico, Nebraska, Louisiana, and gradually established a solid reputation. By the late sixties he was riding regularly in Kentucky, Delaware, and New Jersey. Then he hooked up with Fats.

At the urging of his agent, Jacinto shifted his tack to New York in 1970. This time he made it big. He led all riders there in the number of races won for the year. Having achieved both recognition and some financial security, he had married a woman named Patricia Vurgason, whom he'd met three years earlier in New Jersey. They moved first to an apartment in Forest Hills, and then, a couple of years later, to a house in Garden City, Long Island, where Jacinto was happily surrounded by females—his wife, mother-in-law, and two young daughters.

He had come a long way from the farm in Las Tablas. In fact, by sheer coincidence, he was now living directly across the street from the man who had been his hero in those early days, the man who was now his competitor and friend: Braulio Baeza.

Whiteley took one additional security measure. He got hold of some old wooden sawhorses and set them up so that they blocked the path leading to his barn. They could not really stop anyone, but they might discourage casual onlookers and deter some of the less familiar, less aggressive reporters as well. Frank instructed everyone at the barn to double-check the special credentials issued to the media for this one race, and then, on top of that, to get his permission before they let any stranger, even with the credentials, into the barn.

Whiteley was not paranoid. He wanted to protect his filly not only from possible threats—the likelihood of anyone actually harming her was quite small—but also from the stress of constant interruptions: the hassles, noises, and demands that would inevitably distract her and interrupt her rest.

Whiteley felt the weight of a tremendous responsibility. The Racing Association couldn't come right out and say so, but it was obvious which horse was the centerpiece of this race. As good a colt as Foolish Pleasure was, it was not his presence that had generated the intense media coverage of this event, which was now going to be televised by CBS to a projected audience of almost twenty million people. It was not Foolish Pleasure's participation that had lent the Match its timely social overtones. And it was not Foolish Pleasure whose importance—whose *symbolic* importance—had transcended the world of racing and even sports in general. It was the larger-than-life filly with the perfect record; the coal-black daughter of Reviewer and Shenanigans; the speedball, the beauty, the female, the freak.

2

In April, Whiteley sent his assistant, Barclay Tagg, ahead to Belmont Park with a dozen horses who were ready to run. Whiteley had been stabling in New York only the past two years, but he had a national reputation in the sport, for he had trained Chieftain and Tom Rolfe and Damascus. Those were the kind of horses people liked to be involved with, so as soon as the word went out that Tagg needed an exercise rider, Yates Kennedy presented himself for the job.

Everybody on the backside knew Yates. Although he had ridden his last race in 1951—the horse was named Woc, and Yates liked to tell people that its class could be determined by spelling its name backwards—he had remained jockey-size, a scant five-feet, two inches, lean and wiry, with a narrow leathery face and sharp blue eyes. His taste in clothes ran to Western-style shirts, jeans or khaki pants—always clean and pressed—and a cowboy hat. He was as well-known at Esposito's Tavern as he was on the track, and, at fifty-nine years of age, he could still pass for a hard-living forty.

"You understand it's only temporary, though," Barclay explained as they agreed on terms. "When the boss comes up, he'll want to hire his own riders."

"No problem," Yates replied. "Only I got to be finished by eight-thirty or nine, though, 'cause I drive the van all day for Ralph Smith."

"That's okay. See you at six."

After Yates had been going to the barn for three or four weeks, Barclay stopped him one day and handed him a check.

"Boss's coming up tomorrow, so I don't think I'll be needing you anymore."

"Okay," Yates said. That was how it worked. There were no hard feelings.

"But come around anyway and see Mr. Whiteley in the morning. Maybe he'll hire you back."

Next morning, before he'd taken three steps under the shedrow, Yates was accosted by a man his own age who stepped out from one of the stalls.

"Who're you?" The man scowled at Yates from behind dark-rimmed glasses.

This had to be Whiteley, Yates figured. "I'm the guy that's been getting on your horses."

"Oh. You're the guy only wants to work half a day."

"No, no," Yates replied calmly. "You got that wrong. I work a day and a *half*. I get on horses in the morning and I work the rest of the day driving the van."

"Well, I can't use anybody like that."

"Okay, no problem. See you later." Yates checked his watch. He had almost half an hour before he had to get on a colt for another trainer, so he headed over to the track kitchen for a cup of coffee.

Twenty minutes had passed when Barclay appeared in the doorway, spotted Yates, and walked over to his table.

"How're you doing?" He hesitated. "The boss wants to see you."

"Can't." Yates stood up. "I got to go get on some horses."

"Oh." Barclay hadn't considered this possibility. "Okay." After a moment he turned and left the room.

When Yates had finished riding for the day, he checked in with his dispatcher and was told he wouldn't be needed till the third race. He ambled back over to the kitchen and pulled up a chair with some other riders who were trading real estate stories. "Real estate" referred to land they "owned" on the track itself: the spots where they got dumped most often. Distances at the track were marked off by poles and calculated backwards from the finish line. The quarter pole was one-quarter mile *before* the wire; the three-eighths pole a furlong before that, and so on. Yates claimed he had a bigger piece of property than anyone else over by the five-eighths pole. He couldn't explain why, but almost every horse that had ever tossed him had done so at that same exact spot. As he elaborated on some of his more memorable spills, everyone got to laughing so hard they didn't even notice Barclay enter the room for the second time that day. He walked straight over to Yates, and this time he skipped the preliminaries.

"Boss says for you to be there six o'clock in the morning."

Yates glanced up. For a split second it was impossible to tell what he was thinking. Then the grin returned. That Frank Whiteley was one goddamned son of a bitch! Yates was starting to like him already. "No problem," he said. "I'll be there."

Whiteley's full shipment of twenty additional horses arrived the next morning from Camden. They were unloaded and led immediately to their stalls in Barn 34. Frank was busy supervising everything and hadn't said half a dozen words to Yates, but he'd been watching him out of the corner of his eye. When the rider was getting ready to leave, Frank called him over.

"I got a big black filly I'm gonna put you on." He nodded in the direction of the stall nearest the tackroom. "It's the fastest horse you've ever been on!"

"I ain't too sure about that, Frank."

Whiteley turned and looked him directly in the eye. "It'll be," he said.

Yates walked off shaking his head. What the hell did Whiteley know about the horses he'd ridden? *Fastest horse he'd ever been on?* Shit. They'd see about that.

Two days later Yates got on the filly for the first time and decided Whiteley must have been joking. He must have meant the "fattest," not the fastest. She was the biggest two-year-old Yates had ever seen, that was all: a big, soft baby. But he knew better than to say anything. He rode her under the shedrow, as Whiteley had told him to, letting her get used to everything. She was a very tall filly, mild-mannered, and she seemed completely at ease in her new surroundings.

On Friday, Yates took her to the track. Frank rode beside them on Sled Dog. The black filly was in a playful mood. She seemed to like Frank's cranky old pony and bumped up against him as they walked.

They entered the track at the gap near trainer Allen Jerkens's barn. Yates jogged her halfway around the oval the wrong way to warm up, then turned and galloped her for a mile. She was sweet and responsive and well-behaved, but Yates couldn't see anything extraordinary about her.

Later, talking to Squeaky, Yates mentioned the filly and asked him if he knew her name.

"Me and Minnor and Dan call her Soul Sister, you know, 'cause she black." He spoke in his sleepy South Carolina drawl. Big and strong as he was, everything about Squeaky conveyed a kind of gentleness; it was one reason he got along so well with the horses that he rode. "Nobody know her real name. Not till Mr. Whiteley run her. But she be a stakes filly, all right. I sure wish I didn't have to leave."

"Where you going, Squeaky?"

"I got to go down Delaware. You know, freelance. I go there in the summertime 'cause I make a lot more money freelancing than I can here. I got a lotta customers there. Then I go back home to Camden for the winter, work for Mr. Whiteley again. But I sure wish I could stay this year, watch this filly run."

"Maybe he'll run her once before you leave. You think so?"

"No telling with Mr. Whiteley, you know. But I sure hope so."

One morning after he hopped off the filly, Yates asked Frank directly when he was planning to give her a real work.

"You training the bitch or am I?" Whiteley replied, and that was the end of that conversation.

A couple of days later Frank stopped Yates as he was leaving the barn. "Can you get here a little early tomorrow?" Something in Frank's voice told Yates it was important, and he agreed to be there.

It was still dark when Yates entered the barn at twenty minutes past five. Minnor was tacking up the filly by the light of the naked overhead bulb in her stall. Other grooms were cursing or humming as they rubbed their horses and picked out their feet in preparation for the first set. Yates joined Whiteley and they sipped coffee from paper cups. Frank hadn't said anything, but

Yates was certain he was getting ready to work the filly. Usually she went out with the second set, but today she was heading out first. That meant Frank was trying to hide her from the clockers. He was finally going to let her run.

As they headed towards the track, Frank kept close by on Sled Dog. Just before they reached the gap, he took a long draw on his cigarette and flicked it away.

"Take her out there and go a slow three-eighths. *Slow.*"

Yates nodded. Just as he suspected. Not a fast work, not all-out, just a little breeze. A slow three-eighths meant three furlongs in about 37, 38 seconds. You'd want faster in a race, of course, but this was just to get some idea of the filly's speed without taking too much out of her.

He steered her onto the track, warmed her up, and then, taking a big hold of her—by now, he'd learned that she liked to run; he wasn't about to let her get away from him—he asked her for some speed.

One of the things Yates prided himself on was his sense of pace. Many a trainer had valued him as an exercise rider because of the clock inside his head. Yates didn't have to think about time too much; he felt it. He concentrated on the way a horse was moving, and the time took care of itself. The filly had a very long stride, even longer than what might be expected from such a tall horse. Yates would be ready for her to touch down *now*, but she'd keep hanging in the air for an extra fraction of a second. It took a little getting used to, but it was a wonderful feeling, as if she put up a sail between strides and let the wind catch hold of it.

Almost before he knew it, they had completed the three-eighths. Yates pulled the filly up, rising high in his stirrups, and for the first time he had to summon all his strength to rein her in. The outrider was heading over to help, but Yates waved him away.

Frank and Sled Dog were waiting up ahead, and the filly began to slow herself down when she spotted the pony on the track. Frank was glaring at Yates, but he didn't say a word. As they headed over towards the barn, Whiteley asked Yates if he had any idea how fast he'd gone.

"Oh, 'bout 37, 37 and one." Yates thought about it for a minute. The filly had been going so easy, he hadn't worried too

much about the time. It couldn't have been too fast or he would
have felt some exertion on her part. And he'd kept such a tight
hold of her. Of course, on the other hand, she did have that
beautiful long stride. "Maybe a little faster," he conceded.

"Damn fool! Went too goddamn fast!" Whiteley clucked at
Sled Dog, who condescended to move a half step in front. Then
Frank looked around, making sure no one was nearby. "Went
35 and change!" he hollered. "Thirty-five and change, goddamn
it! You call that *slow?*"

Yates didn't let himself get upset. He had been riding horses
for fifty years. He knew the difference between a 37- and a 35-
second work.

"I think your clock is wrong, Frank," he answered mildly,
with all the sweetness of a man who knows he is right, who can
indulge a misunderstanding on someone else's part. After all,
Yates had been on the filly's back. He was the one whose shoulders would be stiff the next morning, aching from the effort of
holding her back. But what was the sense of arguing? You
couldn't win an argument with Frank Whiteley.

Back at the barn, Yates caught Barclay alone for a minute.
"What's the name of that filly I worked today?"

Barclay looked away. "I don't know," he mumbled.

Yates shrugged. Fine. If nobody wanted to tell him her damn
name, he had other ways of finding out. One of the clockers
would know. They had photographs and records of each horse
on the grounds, and in spite of the trainer's efforts, they had
probably identified her and caught her workout. They would
tell him her name, and tomorrow he'd check her time in the
Racing Form. Then he'd show Whiteley who was right.

3

Mike Bell was lying in bed in his furnished room, staring at the cracks in the ceiling and trying to make up his mind: Should he stick it out in New York or return to Kentucky? He had gotten as far as throwing some dirty clothes into an open suitcase, but then doubt had overcome him.

Part of him wanted to go home. He missed his friends and family. He missed his dog, Rebel, a black Lab who went everywhere with him. Although Mike was only twenty-six, he had been out on his own as a full-fledged trainer for several years in the Midwest, winning races at Latonia and River Downs. If he went back, he could easily pick up where he'd left off.

But he didn't want to be a quitter. He knew that certain people back home might have been shocked to see him living like this, for he came from a prominent Kentucky family. His grandfather, the late Hal Price Headley, had been a successful owner and breeder of thoroughbreds and a founder of Keeneland racetrack in Lexington. His mother, Alice Headley Chandler, divorced his father when Mike was two and later went on to develop her Mill Ridge Farm into a highly respected breeding operation. She had bred the great Sir Ivor there, and he had won the English Derby in 1968.

Mike possessed the same love of thoroughbreds that had driven both his mother and his grandfather, and he didn't care what anyone else thought. He was determined to carve out a career on his own terms. Maybe he was naive, but that's why he had come North: to work for one of the top trainers, someone he could learn from. For years a litany of names had run through his head: Jerkens, Miller, Stephens, Ward, Whiteley. These were the trainers he kept reading about in Charlie Hatton's column in the *Form*. That's what he thought all the New York trainers would be like.

He'd had a rude awakening. To a lot of people he'd met in New York, racing was just another business. They didn't seem to notice if the stalls weren't as clean as they should be; they were too busy playing golf to supervise their grooms in the afternoon. Why learn about splints or quarter cracks? They paid vets and farriers to take care of those problems. And who had time to graze their horses in this day and age? Horses got used to spending the whole day inside their stalls. Some of these trainers were good salesmen, though. Owners always seemed willing to put horses into their hands. Mike had been at Belmont eight months now, and he was confident he could always find work on the backstretch. But that wasn't enough anymore.

Before he fell asleep that night, Mike decided on a plan of action. He would screw up his courage and go around to each of the trainers he really admired. If none of them wanted him, then he would return to Kentucky. That wouldn't be quitting, because he would have done his best. But he wasn't going to waste his time visiting any second-rate outfits. What they had to teach him, he didn't want to learn.

His first stop would be Frank Whiteley. He knew Frank's son David a little. David also trained in New York, and sometimes Mike ran into him at Esposito's. He decided to go the very next day.

In the morning, Mike pulled on his jeans and fished out a wrinkled shirt from the pile on the floor. He was an even six feet tall, with a lean, athletic build and a prematurely receding hairline that didn't quite fit his young, open face. He had played football all his life, and though he was generally easy to get along with, he was not afraid to settle a serious difference of opinion with his fists. But the nearer he got to Frank Whiteley's barn, the more he felt like a little kid on the first day of school. He rubbed his palms against his jeans. At least it'd be over pretty quick. Whiteley was known as a man of few words. Mike figured a simple yes or no would decide his immediate future. He paused, then headed down the shedrow.

Whiteley didn't look up. He was sitting there fiddling with

something, and as Mike drew closer he could see that the trainer was using a rubber band to repair one of his bridles.

"Hello, Mr. Whiteley, I'm Mike Bell. I been working for Jim Conway and I'd like to know if you could use some help."

"Pull that chair over here and sit down."

Surprised, Mike did as he was told.

Whiteley finished with the bridle and set it aside. "What can you do?"

Mike briefly recounted his experiences, mentioned his family background, and explained what he'd been doing in New York.

"Tell me something, Bell," Whiteley broke in. "Do you drink?"

Oh, shit, thought Mike. Shit, shit, *shit*. He was thrown completely off guard. Well, of course I drink. Hell! What am I supposed to say?

"Yes, sir," he answered politely.

"You ever go to Esposito's?"

Mike started to squirm. Aw, please! Just tell me yes or no and let's get this thing over with. I didn't think I was gonna have to have a whole damn personal interview!

"Yes, sir," he said again.

"You ever see David over at Esposito's?"

Mike started to get up. He wasn't gonna get this job, no way. There was no use lying. Whiteley must have known that David went to Esposito's or he wouldn't have asked. Mike sighed.

"Yes, sir, I have."

"You ever see *me* at Esposito's?" Frank snapped.

"No, sir!" Mike fell back into his chair.

"And you never will, either!"

There was a brief pause. Whiteley asked him a couple more questions, which he managed to answer. He didn't wear a watch, so he didn't know how long he'd been there, but it felt close to forever when Whiteley abruptly stood up and said, "Okay. Be here in the morning."

For a moment Mike was too surprised to reply. Then he found his voice. "Yes, sir. Thank you, sir." He stumbled out of there as fast as he could, not even noticing where he was until he emerged onto Plainfield Avenue. When he looked up, he realized that Whiteley hadn't told him what he'd be doing or how much he'd be paid. And Mike hadn't even asked. What's more, he discovered, he didn't even care! *He didn't care.* He would gladly have paid Mr. Whiteley for this chance. Slowly, slowly, it was beginning to sink in. He had just gotten exactly what he wanted. The very thing he had dreamed about back in Kentucky. And he had come so close to leaving! Yesterday, he had almost given up.

Suddenly he felt so relieved, so excited, so nervous—so damn *happy!*—he was practically overwhelmed. There was only one thing for him to do. He crossed the street to Esposito's and got drunk.

4

Every two weeks the condition book came out. It listed the upcoming races and the "conditions" under which each would be run: the distance, the age and sex restrictions, whether it was on grass or dirt, whether it was a claiming race, allowance race, handicap, or stakes race. Frank flipped through it in the Racing Secretary's office, then stuck it in his pocket to study at home in the evening.

There was no doubt the filly was ready for a race. Frank just had to find the right spot for her. When he did, he gave Stuart Janney a call.

"How's she doing, Frank?"

"Looks good, Mr. Janney. Still having fun with her. Thinking of putting her in a race next Wednesday."

"All right, Frank. How far are you going to run her?"

"Five and a half furlongs. Maiden special. Hundred and sixteen pounds."

"Sounds good. We'll be there."

"Well, that's fine. See you then."

Frank dialed another number. "Hey, Patty! How you doin'? Let me speak to that no-good husband of yours."

Jacinto got on the line. "Hello?"

"Hey, Por-ta Rican! Think you can get your ass over to the barn by six o'clock tomorrow?"

"What's up?"

"Can you be there or not?"

"Okay, I be there."

Frank was in the stall early, helping Minnor tack up the filly. He had already made a point of double-checking her feet. Frank was one of the few trainers who refused to shoe his horses till they started racing. If he had his way, he would never shoe them. Let them run natural, he thought, and their feet would stay a whole lot healthier, a lot more sound. But shoes gave them an edge. They helped horses grab the track a little better, which improved their time. Once they started racing, Frank wouldn't deny them that advantage, but he could and did put it off as long as possible. On this morning, less than a week before the filly's first race, she was still completely barefoot behind, although she had finally gotten steels—flat shoes, without the toe grabs—put on up front.

Yates poked his head in. "Morning. Who'm I getting on first?"

"Y'ain't getting on her today. Just stick around."

Honorable Miss peered over from the next stall and whinnied for attention. Yates stepped over and rubbed her nose.

"Aw, hush, you old thing. Nobody forgot you. You're going out next." He scratched her enormous ears, which had earned her the affectionate barn name of Ugly, and she settled down.

Jacinto arrived, carrying his helmet and stick. "Hey, cuz," he greeted Yates. "How you doin'?"

"Hey, yourself, cousin! What're you doing getting up with the chickens?"

"How the hell I know?" Jacinto laughed. "Mr. Whiteley say be here, so I here. What he want me for anyway?"

Frank stepped out of the stall and Minnor started walking the filly around the shedrow. "If the two of you'd shut up for a minute I'd tell you. First, get rid of that." Frank pointed to the whip. "You won't be needing that. Think you can do what I tell you for a change, Por-ta Rican?"

"I always do!"

"Huh. Like hell you do. I want you to take the filly to the gate, understand? She's got to be approved out of the gate."

"Oh, yeah? When she gonna race?"

"What do you want to know for?"

"Oh, I just like to know when she gonna start. Maybe I be busy that day."

"Who says you're riding her to begin with? Fats tell you he had the mount?"

"Hell, no!" Jacinto grinned. "My agent don't tell me nothing! He just try to get me kill, that's all, putting me on eight, nine horses every day!"

"Well, don't come crying to me about it. Now listen." Whiteley's voice became serious. "Here's what I want you to do. Just break her out of the gate and pull her up. Nice and easy. I don't want you working her, understand me? Slow and easy. Quarter-mile or so. Don't try anything! Pull her up soon's you can."

"Okay."

"Come on, then." Whiteley gave Jacinto a leg up. It was the first time he had ever been on the filly.

"She a big horse," Jacinto said admiringly.

"You scared, Por-ta Rican?"

"Sure I scared," Jacinto joked. "She a lot bigger than me."

"She's a hell of a lot stronger, too, cousin," Yates warned. "You watch it out there."

The starting gate was set up on the backstretch, near the seven-furlong pole. As Jacinto approached it, he recognized a couple of LeRoy Jolley's horses who were getting ready to load into the gate. Good horses, too; Jacinto was riding a lot for Jolley, and he knew these two horses by sight. There was one of David Whiteley's, too, a colt called John Bryn. Fast little colt; Jacinto had worked him already, and he'd be riding him when he started to race. As a matter of fact, half the youngsters entering the gate that morning were going to be his mounts. Jacinto was at the peak of his form, and everybody wanted him. Fats had no trouble lining up business.

Frank and Yates had positioned themselves over by the rail.

"Slow!" Frank called out. "Remember—I said *slow!*"

Jacinto nodded.

Frank turned to Yates. "He's gonna go *fast*. Ain't nothing you can do about it. She's gonna run."

"You got that right, Frank."

"Just hope he can pull her up okay."

"Well, she's something else. I don't have to tell you."

"I know it. That's why I let him take her to the gate. Let him

get the feel of her one time before a race. I don't want no surprises. I want him to be ready for her."

Yates nodded. He didn't like to admit it, but Whiteley had
been right the week before: The filly had worked the three furlongs in 35⅖ seconds, just like the trainer said. The clockers had
verified her time. Thirty-five and change wasn't anything extraordinary in itself—it was a good time, a very good time for a
two-year-old—but nothing noteworthy. What stunned Yates was
the fact that he had been a full two seconds off in his estimation.
That had never happened to him before, and he began to believe that Whiteley's prediction might come true. This big, fat
baby might turn into something special.

The gateman motioned for Jacinto to come closer. "Horse's
name?" he asked.

"What?"

"What's the horse's name?"

"How the hell I know?"

"Jacinto, cut it out! How many years you been riding up
here? You know I can't sign the gate permission for you unless
I have the name!"

"What I suppose to do? Mr. Whiteley don't give me no
name."

"Well, that's the rules. You want to go ahead and break her
out of here this morning, that's fine with me, but you're not
getting a slip till you bring me her name."

"Okay, I bring you tomorrow."

Jacinto circled around and chirped at the filly to move into
the gate. Even though they had to wait for a while for the outside
horses to settle down, she remained calm. Then the bell rang
and the gates sprang open. The filly did not break well. She
didn't do anything wrong, exactly, but there was a split second
when she didn't move, when she seemed to be gathering herself,
and in that instant everyone except John Bryn got off ahead of
her. Then she started to run.

In two jumps she had settled into a stride that could only be
described as dreamlike. It was too long for a real horse, even a
big, tall horse like she was; too even, too easy, too smooth. She
floated, then came back to earth and did it again, stride after
stride, with such a steady, easygoing rhythm that Jacinto almost

forgot she was running at all. It was like taking a stroll in the park. She had hardly started to roll—they had gone less than a furlong—when Jacinto was surprised to see a wall of horses directly in front of him. They had all got the jump on his filly, but already they were coming back to her. If he didn't do something pretty quick, she was going to start climbing right over them. He tried to check her, but she was stronger than he thought, and she was intent on overtaking the other horses. He needed all his strength to pull her up and take her way around to the outside, over to the middle of the track where she could have some room. Then he just nursed her along for a half-mile. The easiest half-mile you could imagine.

Only afterwards, back at the barn, did Jacinto find out she'd gone that half-mile in 47 seconds. After a slow break. And being taken back. And way outside. And no shoes on behind. He didn't even try to hide his excitement. "Who's the hell is this horse anyway?" he sputtered at Mr. Whiteley.

"You do the riding and I'll do the training. When I put her in a race you'll find out who she is."

"But I got to give the gateman her name!"

"Don't worry about it. That's my problem. You just ride the horse."

Whiteley grabbed Jacinto the next morning and told him to get on Sled Dog and take the set over to the track. Like everyone else, Jacinto hated riding Sled Dog, but he did as he was told. When he was in the saddle, Whiteley handed him a piece of paper. "Give this to the gateman when you get over there."

Jacinto stared at the word in the center of the paper:

RUFFIAN

Ruffian? he said to himself. It was just like the Spanish, *rufian*. A bully. A mean guy. A fighter.

"This a joke?" Jacinto looked at Whiteley. "What the hell kind of name is this?"

"You wanted to know her damn name, that's her name. Now get out of here."

It just didn't fit. Not that names meant anything. Often,

names were registered when the horse was foaled, or even reserved by the owners in advance, when they didn't have anything
to go on but the bloodlines. Jacinto knew that as well as anyone.
Still, he thought, she was such a dignified horse, such a lady.

Jacinto gave the paper to the gateman and after a moment
got back a signed permission slip. It meant that the filly—that
Ruffian—could now start in a race on any track in New York.
He studied the paper. Ruffian. *Rufian.* Well, if you thought about
it, the day before she *had* beat up on the competition. In her
own way—with her sheer speed, her desire to get in front, her
will to win. *Rufian.* Ruffian. What the hell. It didn't matter what
her name was. He'd got himself a racehorse.

5

Frank had been around the racetrack too long to have any illusions. The help on the backstretch wasn't going to be perfect. They worked seven days a week for low wages, and grooms in particular labored long hours in which they were called on to do just about everything except jump on the horse's back. Frank hired the best people he could, but they were human. Sometimes they showed up late. Occasionally they got into fights. A few of them fooled around with drugs. And, frequently, they drank. An awful lot of people, at all levels of the game—from owners on down—drank too much. The problem was so widespread in racing that many people simply accepted it as part of the territory. Frank couldn't fire his employees every time they took a drink. He'd have no help left, and the horses would be the ones to suffer. He needed hands and bodies to run a barn, and he needed them every single day of the year. But there were other problems he could control.

One morning, in front of everyone, Frank turned to Barclay. "I'm taking this next set out," he said.

Frank always took the sets out, unless he had a sick or injured horse at the barn who needed his attention. There was no reason for him to announce his plans. Barclay shrugged and went about his business.

Frank gave the riders in the set their instructions and accompanied them as far as the gap; then, instead of settling into his spot along the rail, he wheeled Sled Dog around and headed back to the barn. He had been gone less than ten minutes.

He glanced around the shedrow, jumped off the pony, and handed the reins to Mike Bell. "You seen Minnor?" he asked.

"No, sir," Mike answered.

"You?" he asked Barclay.

Barclay nodded towards the bunkhouse. This was just what Whiteley had suspected. In spite of strict rules against cooking in the rooms, Minnor had developed a well-known habit of filling a big pot with chicken wings and spices every morning and setting it to simmer on a hotplate. This required tending several times a day, which meant he had to leave his post at the barn. He was never gone very long—the bunkhouse was just across the way—but it didn't take very long for something to go wrong, and this year Minnor had the filly. Frank was taking no chances. He surprised Minnor coming back around the corner.

Mike turned away, embarrassed to witness what he thought would be an ugly scene. He expected a shouting match, a tirade of some sort, and then the inevitable sack for the groom. Instead, Whiteley's voice was calm and steady. "Sit down here, Minnor." He pointed at the footlocker in front of the tackroom.

"Minnor," Frank said, "goddamn it now, don't blow it, you hear? You're rubbing the fastest filly in the country. Do you understand that? The fastest filly in the country!"

That was all he said, but Minnor understood. "Yes, sir."

Frank stood there a minute, shaking his head. Then he walked away.

On Tuesday afternoon, May 21, as soon as the overnights came out—the list of all the horses entered in each of the next day's events—word flashed through the barn that the filly would be starting in the third race. This caused a ripple of excitement among the stablehands, who'd been waiting for her to make her debut. Most of them learned her name for the first time when they saw it printed in the entries. That was okay with them. The longer Whiteley managed to keep a low profile on this horse, the more chance they had of getting a decent price on her when she ran.

Mike Bell didn't quite know what to make of all the fuss. He was the new kid on the block, having joined the barn only ten days earlier, but he had worked around thoroughbreds all his life. This filly, as nicely put together as she was, still seemed much too round and roly-poly to him. She did not fit his image of a finely tuned racehorse. And yet he had heard Mr. Whiteley, whose judgment he respected, tell Minnor Massey that he was rubbing the fastest filly in the country. Not just in the barn, or even in all of Belmont Park, but in the *whole country.*

In the end, though, Mike had to rely on his own instincts. In spite of what everyone else in the barn was doing, he decided not to bet on Ruffian in her maiden race. Why throw away good money? he reasoned. The filly was just too fat.

6

Jacinto laid out the cards for another round of solitaire. He barely glanced up at the TV monitor for the first race, a low-priced claimer which was distinguished only by the appearance of one of the worst-named horses in the history of the sport: a colt called Grundgy Twerp. As usual, Jacinto seemed relaxed, lounging in his terry-cloth robe and flip-flops, occasionally trading bad jokes with the valets and the other riders, but for the most part keeping to himself. When the second race flashed on, he looked up long enough to watch Vince "Jimbo" Bracciale trail in next to last on the 2 horse, more than thirty lengths behind the leader.

In a few minutes Bracciale returned to the jockeys' room with the other riders.

"That horse was a piece of shit," he muttered, tossing his number onto the table. He stomped back to his locker.

"Aw, forget about him." Jacinto was slipping off his robe. His valet, Harold Timmons—"Timmy" to everyone around the track—was holding out the silks he needed for the third race. Without looking, Jacinto slid his arms into the sleeves and stuffed the billowing tail into his riding pants and inside his underwear, to hold it down flat. White silks, cherry hoop, cherry sleeves. Of course, they didn't use real silks anymore; almost everyone's colors were nylon. "You watch this race." He traded his flip-flops for riding boots. "It's that horse Mr. Whiteley's I told you about."

"Oh, yeah?" Bracciale's face brightened. He'd been waiting to see this filly run.

"Yeah. If she run like I think she can, she gonna be a race-horse." Jacinto fastened the snaps at his waist and stepped over to the scale to weigh out, carrying his saddle and saddle pad. The needle pointed to 116 pounds, of which 112 was the man himself, stripped. He stepped down and handed the tack to Timmy, who went immediately out to the paddock. Jacinto walked back over to his locker and unwrapped a piece of gum. He always chewed gum during a race; it helped him think better, helped him concentrate. He still had time before he had to go up—Jack O'Hara, the Clerk of Scales, wouldn't even give the jocks their first call for another five minutes—but Jacinto was a little restless. He wasn't worried exactly, and if he was more excited than usual he didn't show it. But he was eager to ride this filly. He'd only been on her once, that morning last week when he'd worked her out of the gate, but in fifteen years of raceriding he had never felt anything move beneath him the way that filly did.

He checked himself in the mirror, smoothed his hair, and pulled on his helmet.

The basement halls were empty as Jacinto climbed the two flights of worn stairs that led him out of the bowels of Belmont into the open air tunnel that connected the paddock to the track. Eyes straight ahead, avoiding the fans scattered along both rails, he tapped his whip against the side of his boot as he sauntered into the emerald circle. Every jock had his own walk. If you watched them long enough, their strides became as familiar as their faces.

Nine times a day, six days a week, the riders took this route as they filed into the paddock, singly or in pairs, talking to each other—if at all—not about their waiting mounts, but about their golf swings or their Cadillacs or the heavyweight title defense or the new blond ponygirl with the big ass who had a thing for Spanish jocks. These were the professionals, the top of the line, riding on the toughest circuit in the country; if they were nervous, they kept it to themselves. Even the tight, drawn lines on their faces were misleading: It wasn't tension, but the hours in the hotbox making weight, that left them looking taut, exhausted.

Across the paddock, Minnor was walking the filly back and forth in front of the stalls. Mr. and Mrs. Janney, who had flown in from Maryland, and Frank Whiteley were watching in silence. As Jacinto headed over in their direction, he noticed that the trainer Woody Stephens was also staring at their filly. He had the favorite in the race, a bay named Suzest, so far going off at 1-to-2.

"You better look now," Jacinto boasted to Stephens as he passed by. "Take a *good* look," he added, " 'cause all you gonna see in the race is my filly's black ass!"

The Janneys shook hands with him, and while they all stood around, waiting, Jacinto stole a glance at the tote board. They had his filly at 9-to-2. Good. He was gonna make some money on this race. Earlier that morning, at the barn, Fats had grilled him one last time. "You really think that filly's gonna win? You sure?" Jacinto answered him the same way he'd been answering him all week: "I think that filly gonna be a racehorse." Fats would be watching now, over in the office with Racing Secretary Kenny Noe and his assistant, Charlie Sullivan, and a bunch of other jockey agents. And he, too, would have put down a little something on the race.

Ruffian looked good. The crowd noticed her immediately, and many pointed and stared. She stood out like a full-grown mare in a field of yearlings. It wasn't just her size, though she was already sixteen hands; or her girth, which, at 75½ inches, was bigger than Secretariat's had been at that age. It was more the way she held herself, a certain presence, that made people turn and take a second look. A lot of fillies, especially the two-year-olds, acted "silly." It was a stage they went through, like nervous adolescents, jumping at the slightest touch, skittering away from imaginary shadows, overly sensitive to every change in the tone of your voice. Not Ruffian. Ruffian never had a silly day in her life. Playful, yes. Nipping and nudging Minnor in her stall; bumping old Sled Dog as they headed for the track in the morning; snipping at leaves on the low-hanging branches. But never silly.

She seemed to know instinctively what was called for in every situation; to understand, her first time in the paddock before a race, that she was on display. Head high, ears alert, and not—as Whiteley had worried—in the least bit nervous in the face of the crowds and the noise. Not a drop of sweat marred her shiny black coat. She remained poised even as Minnor brought her into the enclosure to be saddled. She stood calmly until Whiteley tightened her girth. Then, as usual, she made one quick swipe to the side, but Minnor was prepared; he had shortened his hold on the shank so she couldn't reach very far. The filly immediately relaxed again, docile as ever. Still, Whiteley had directed Minnor to skip the tour of the walking ring once Jacinto was aboard. Just take her right out to the track, he'd told him. Maybe he was being overprotective, but he couldn't see taking a chance. A horse that powerful, that full of herself—you just never knew what could happen the first time out. But for once his worries were unfounded.

"Riders up!" cried the patrol judge.

The ten horses were spread out around the paddock, and near each one was a little cluster of people, shaking hands, smiling, conferring. Trainers were giving last minute instructions to their jocks, some of whom were getting on their mounts for the first time. The jocks were nodding seriously, some paying strict attention, others inwardly formulating their own strategies. Since Jacinto rode regularly for Whiteley, worked horses for him in the morning, and was well aware of this particular filly, he knew in advance exactly what was expected. Still, for the fun of it, to tease him, get him to relax, Jacinto looked up earnestly at the trainer.

"You got any orders for me, boss?" He tried not to smile.

"Yeah," Whiteley growled.

A flicker of surprise crossed Jacinto's face.

Whiteley took a final drag on his cigarette and crushed it beneath his boot. "Don't screw up."

Ruffian warmed up beautifully, relaxing as Jacinto steered her past the clubhouse turn and onto the backstretch where the starting gate had been set up, 5½ furlongs from the finish line. The horses filed into the gate from the rail out, Ruffian in post position number 9. She went in smoothly, and as soon as the doors closed behind her, Jacinto grabbed a fistful of her mane and twisted it around his hand, bracing himself for the start. His face was buried in her neck, eyes front, knees pressed against her shoulders. When the last horse was in place, when there was an instant of relative stability among the excited entrants, George Cassidy pressed the tongs of the starter's gun together and the gates sprang open.

The first four horses broke in post position order. Ruffian was one big jump behind them, but it was a good clean start. Then, before you could look down to check your program, Ruffian had moved out in front, cutting across the field as Jacinto guided her to the rail. After the first quarter-mile, she had three lengths on the closest horse. Her time flashed on the tote: 22⅕ seconds.

"Goddamn! Goddamn!" Fats was on his feet in the Racing Secretary's office, his mismatched plaids and checks a blur of activity. He grabbed Charlie Sullivan, was pounding on his arm. "I knew she was a good one! I knew it! I told you sonsabitches I had something!" His face was beet-red and he was grinning from ear to ear. "Goddamn it! I bet three thousand dollars on this filly!"

Nobody said the obvious—that there was still a half-mile left in the race, and a lot could happen in a half-mile—because the way the filly was moving, nobody thought it would make any difference.

Behind Ruffian the next three horses were heads apart. Suzest began to draw away from Precious Elaine and Great Grandma Rose, whose first quarter had already wasted them. But it was no longer a horserace. Jacinto had Ruffian under tight control, but she poured out over the track like water, like a river overflowing its banks. Five lengths after the first half-mile, and Jacinto could feel her aching to run. Eight lengths at the top of the stretch, still under a big hold. Jacinto glanced over his shoulder. They were alone now, she was flying down the stretch, she owned the track, with her long flowing stride, and he hadn't even asked her for anything yet, he was holding her back, his hands low on her neck; she could just coast on in, she had destroyed the field.

And then Jacinto heard a noise from the crowd, a wave of sound rising off to his right. Maybe something was coming, he thought, though he knew this was not so. Maybe he ought to— just once, just in case—he knew he shouldn't, Mr. Whiteley would kill him, but he couldn't resist, like a child sneaking cookies, just once, one test—*there!*—so quick, with the whip in his right hand, just once, on her belly, and later the films were mangled, there was no complete record of this race, and the announcer never saw it and the trackman missed it and none of the reporters noticed—so unnecessary!—they'll all swear he never touched her—and yet, just once, he had to find out, just once, just hard enough to ask the question—and *yes!*—she accelerated instantaneously—Jacinto had his answer—effortlessly, not with anger or indignation or fear, but with the pure joy of someone who has been waiting to be asked, who has been waiting a lifetime for just this moment. She simply kicked into another gear and pulled even farther ahead, and you blinked your eyes and she was in front by ten and then by twelve and you didn't understand how it was possible—she was going so easy, there was no sign of effort on her part—and then thirteen and you were shouting, and then fourteen and you felt a shiver up your spine, and then fifteen as she crossed the finish line! Fifteen lengths in front! Ruffian had broken her maiden first time out, and that was the correct time on the tote board: 1:03 flat! She had tied the track record! A two-year-old, a filly, in her first race, *under restraint*, had tied the track record for 5½ furlongs! The crowd was on its feet, and even the losers were cheering for Ruffian.

In the jockeys' quarters, those riders not in the race had been crowded around the TV in the rec room. Now they started talking excitedly, half of them screaming for their agents, plans to submarine Jacinto dancing in their heads. This was a horse with a future, they thought. They wanted that mount for themselves.

Bracciale didn't join in the chatter. Not just because he was friends with Jacinto, or because he knew that Whiteley never listened to the agents anyway—half the time he didn't even let them in the barn. That was not why Bracciale was so quiet. Bracciale had been around horses all his life, since he was in diapers—raised in a trailer while his dad was riding at Charles Town, West Virginia. Respect for horses was in his blood, and he knew that he had just witnessed one of the great ones. He felt proud, privileged almost, to have seen something as beautiful as that filly's first race. And there were other riders in the room who felt the same way. Bracciale didn't say anything because there was nothing to be said. He ran his hands over his well-muscled arms. His arms were covered with goose bumps.

Jacinto jogged Ruffian back to the winner's circle. She was not even breathing heavily, and there was still no sweat on her huge frame. She looked around, curious, her ears flicking at the noises from the crowd, as if to say, Let's do it again; I had a good time.

Minnor met them in front of the gap. He slipped on the shank, and Stuart Janney led her into the enclosure, where the obligatory photo was taken. Jacinto jumped off, undid her girth, and grabbed the saddle to weigh in.

Looking slightly stunned, Minnor led the filly off. He wasn't surprised that she had won, but the way she'd done it—the power of it, her assurance—had been overwhelming. She tossed her head and fanned her nostrils, still pumped up, excited from the race. Now she'd had a taste of the real thing, and it was clear to Minnor that she liked it. She had won. Not only won, but dominated the field. And she understood exactly what had happened. Some horses had to learn, over time, what a race was all about, but Ruffian knew right away. Minnor would be extra careful with the filly for the next day or so; she might need a little time to wind down completely from this trip.

Whiteley and Jacinto followed them back through the tunnel, studying the filly's legs. She seemed fine. Her motion was the same as always: She lifted and placed each small hoof gracefully, as if there were only one precise spot where each belonged, not a half-inch to the left or right, but *here* and *here* and *here* and *here*. No sign of her favoring one leg, no sign of any soreness. Whiteley was relieved.

Then he gave Jacinto a look, and the jockey knew he was going to catch hell. Not now, but later, in private. Now they walked in silence, lost in thought, for unspoken between them had come a dream: the once-in-a-lifetime horse, the horse who changes everything.

"Hey, Mr. Whiteley!" a reporter called out, interrupting the moment. "You got anything else like that back at your barn?"

"I hope not," the trainer replied. "It'd scare the hell out of me if I had another one."

At the stairway, Jacinto stopped.

"Well?" Whiteley said.

Jacinto looked away. "She a racehorse all the way," he answered.

"I can see that, goddamn it! That's not what I'm asking you!"

"What?" Jacinto put on a schoolboy's expression, wide-eyed and slightly wounded.

Whiteley was not fooled. "You goddamn little sonofabitch! I oughta kick your ass! You know damn well what I mean!" He glared down at him. "What the hell did you hit her for?"

"Oh, that." Jacinto hesitated, then he told the truth: "I just wanted to see what she would do."

"Hey, Vasquez, where'd that horse come from?" someone called out as he entered the jocks' room. "She was really something!"

Jacinto snapped the rubber bands at his wrists, seemingly absorbed in the act of taking off his shirt. "She not bad," he shrugged. But when Bracciale caught his eye, he grinned. "What I tell you?" Jacinto said, and you could hear the strut in his voice.

He was not riding in the fourth race, so he grabbed his robe and went off to sit by himself for a while. His thoughts crowded together, but he was a thinker who did not always want to think. Ruffian had stirred up some of his deepest feelings, his most private dreams. Many of these feelings would never be shared with anyone, for that was the way he was. Some, perhaps, would remain hidden even from himself.

He needed something to distract him till his next race. He reached for the deck of cards. Slowly, deliberately, he began to reshuffle.

7

The Fashion Stakes was named in honor of the famous mare who had defeated her male rival, Boston, in a match race out on Long Island in 1842. It was the first stakes race of the year for two-year-old fillies in New York, but because it came so early in the season it rarely attracted much notice. Horsemen usually waited until late summer, early fall, to pay attention to the youngsters, especially the young fillies, but this year they were buzzing in June.

One reason was a bay filly named Copernica. She had been born blind in her left eye, and there was some doubt whether she would ever race, but she was from the first crop of foals sired by the prominent European champion Nijinsky II, so her owners wanted to give her every chance. They sent her to trainer Mack Miller.

Miller was a tall, patrician-looking Southerner who was known for his unflagging graciousness, jaunty straw hats, and unlimited patience in bringing along two-year-old thoroughbreds. He took his time with Copernica, and it was not until May 15 that he decided she was ready for a race. She rewarded him by romping home fourteen lengths in front of her nearest opponent, covering the 5½ furlongs at Belmont Park in 1:04⅕. That was the best time of the year so far for any two-year-old—colt or filly—in New York, and she was hailed as a "comer," a live horse, one to watch. The crowd loved her.

True to form, Miller remained guarded about his filly. Yes, he admitted, she had looked good wiring the field in her debut. But what would happen when she got dirt kicked in her face? What if her partial vision made her skittish when she got boxed

in in the middle of a field? There was even the possibility—
Miller didn't think this was the case, but it was conceivable—
that she ran so fast in the first race simply because she was
scared.

On June 3, when she ran back, all those questions were answered. She won again, decisively, by more than five lengths,
repeating her time of 1:04⅕. This time she prevailed in spite of
sand in her eyes and a generally better field. Miller was somewhat relieved. So were the fans who backed her, though once
the race was over they acted as if she had been a lock.

Copernica had everything going for her: good breeding, two
fine performances, an outstanding trainer, and the emotional
backing of a lot of fans. Under normal circumstances she would
have gone off the heavy favorite in her next race, the Fashion
Stakes, on June 12.

But "normal" didn't apply that year. Between Copernica's
first and second outings, Ruffian had been to the track, and that
changed everything. Though both fillies won their maiden races
by similar margins—Copernica by 14 lengths, Ruffian by 15—
their times reflected the difference. Copernica had been clocked
in 1:04⅕; Ruffian covered the same distance in 1:03 flat, equaling the all-time track record for horses at any age.

As if that weren't enough, you had only to look at the two
of them—Copernica was a nice-looking, fit, average filly; Ruffian
was a knockout.

The day before they were to meet, Ruffian had a workout
that left chief clocker Frenchy Schwartz in awe. He had seen a
lot of great fillies work, but he insisted he had never seen a move
to match this one: Ruffian had gone a quarter in :21⅗, three-
eighths in :33, and was eased up to finish a half-mile in 45⅗
seconds. A lot of top horses on the grounds—older horses, stakes
horses—couldn't come close to those figures.

Mack Miller joked that he had expended less energy training
his filly than he had trying to get Frank Whiteley to run Ruffian
in the Colleen over at Monmouth rather than in the Fashion.
Unfortunately, he conceded, his efforts had failed.

And this time Whiteley let Ruffian parade around the paddock like everyone else. She behaved beautifully, as if she were
incapable of making a false move.

In addition to Ruffian and Copernica, there were four other

fillies in the race. Jan Verzal had been unbeaten in two starts, including a stakes at River Downs. Witchy Woman had finished second in that race. Sun and Snow had won her single previous start, and Precious Elaine had already met up with Ruffian, on May 22, although it wasn't exactly a close acquaintance, since she had crossed the finish line a full seven seconds after Ruffian, which meant that she was roughly 35 lengths behind.

On June twelfth it didn't matter that Copernica had only one eye. One eye was more than enough to take the measure of that afternoon's overwhelming favorite. Ruffian radiated confidence. She had won one race and now she owned the track. This was her place. As she moved out of the shade, her huge hindquarters rippling with muscles, a murmur passed through the crowd.

Copernica went calmly into the gate in post position number 2. Ruffian moved in beside her, into the third slot. That was the last time they were ever really close.

There was a moment at the head of the stretch, when the rest of the field had fallen away and only the two best fillies remained, when Copernica made a move on Ruffian. Ruffian had led all the way, under wraps, by a length and a half. Now Copernica showed what a game filly she was. She dug in and stuck out her nose and went hard after the leader. But Jacinto had been holding Ruffian back, and as soon as he let out a notch in the reins, his filly surged ahead. Two, then three, then four lengths. Copernica fought back, she kept on coming even as Ruffian opened up another 2¾ lengths before she crossed the wire, again tying the track record at 1:03; again, without even trying. Copernica, a solidly beaten second, was thirteen lengths in front of the next finisher.

Mack Miller's filly had clearly outclassed the rest of the field. Even as she was being trounced, this half-blind daughter of Nijinsky II had refused to collapse; she struggled on, giving everything she had. It just hadn't been enough.

After that race, what did it matter that Copernica was better than "everyone else"? What good did it do to stand out among losers, to outdistance everyone who didn't win? The game was horseracing; the point was to get home first. The best horses knew that, and they understood it when they failed.

The defeat didn't end Copernica's career. She went on all summer, running up a string of second-place finishes, but she never regained the form she had shown before her meeting with Ruffian. On the backside, people attributed this to a simple phenomenon. Copernica, they said, had "got her heart broke." It wasn't something that could be explained scientifically, but it was something people saw if they stayed around the track long enough: a good horse destroyed in a race by a better horse. Some horses didn't seem to mind. They came back with all their lights flashing to try again. Others reacted like fighters who had taken one too many blows to the head. They came away dazed, unnerved.

After only two races Ruffian had earned herself a formidable reputation. She was more than just another winner, more even than just another record-setter. Now she was the toughest of all horses to beat: a heartbreaker.

Over in the winner's circle, Mr. and Mrs. Janney were beaming, and for once even the same old questions didn't irritate Frank. The reporters, sensing this, closed in.

"How's it feel?" they asked.

"Feels great!" Frank answered. "I'm 'specially pleased with the second win because sometimes they go the other way—the first win's their best."

"How does Ruffian compare to other fillies you've had?"

"Well, I have to say I've never had a filly as impressive as this one is now."

The Janneys nodded their agreement. They had enjoyed many successes as breeders and owners and, some years before, as amateur steeplechasers. Stuart Janney had won the Maryland Hunt Cup an unprecedented four times. Bobbie Janney had grown up jumping and fox-hunting in an era when females still had to ride sidesaddle over the same perilous courses as the men. They had both known all the thrills and risks inherent in a life so intertwined with horses. Now in their sixties, they had made numerous trips to the winner's circle, had shelves overflowing with trophies and ribbons and plaques. Yet here they were, quietly glowing, as if this were the first prize they had ever received.

After a moment Bill Rudy approached the couple. Rudy was the local correspondent for *The Blood-Horse* and the racing columnist for the New York *Post*, where he also served full-time as a political reporter. He was widely regarded as one of the outstanding turf writers of the day, and Mrs. Janney backed off a half step to let her husband field the questions. Her face, in repose, had the kind of beauty that allowed you to see straight past all the years to the child she had once been. Her glance could be either sweet or piercingly direct, but there was no mistaking her smile: A slight gap between her front teeth suggested something downright mischievous when she smiled.

Rudy asked a few questions about the race and then brought up the subject of the filly's name.

"Ruffian?" Mr. Janney glanced after the two-year-old as she disappeared into the tunnel. "Well, we had initially reserved that name for a Rambunctious colt, one that I had bred. But we ended up selling that one early on. So, when the filly was born, we decided to go ahead and give it to her."

"But I meant, why that name for a *filly?*"

Stuart Janney hesitated a moment, and his wife couldn't resist. She leaned over towards Bill Rudy and smiled. "Girls can be ruffians, too, you know!"

8

Off in the distance the ocean was engulfed in a shimmering haze. The heat was building up beneath it; when it lifted, the day would be stifling, but for now the breeze that floated in from the shore kept the backstretch bearable.

Vince Bracciale was in a great mood. He had gotten up at five to make the two-hour drive to Monmouth Park, in Oceanport, New Jersey, so he could work a horse. Not just any horse, either, but the horse who had finished second in the Kentucky Derby. His name was Hudson County, and he was a tiny colt, barely 800 pounds. He was being pointed for a stakes race in the near future, and the work had gone beautifully. Now Bracciale was relaxing back at the barn, shooting the breeze. He had a lot of friends at this track. Three years earlier, when he was still a bugboy, Bracciale had captured the riding title there, the only apprentice ever to accomplish that feat.

A little before nine the quiet of the backside was interrupted by the harsh static of the loudspeaker. *"Vince Bracciale! Vince Bracciale! Come to Security for a message! Vince Bracciale to Security!"*

For an instant his face clouded over. His wife Terri and the baby had been sleeping when he left. Everything had been fine. He forced himself to stride calmly over to the office, where a guard handed him a message with a phone number on it. "Frank Whiteley just called here from New York. Wants you to call him at the barn."

Whiteley got right to the point. "If you can be here by eleven, I might put you on a horse."

Bracciale didn't hesitate. "I'll be there." He was relieved and excited as he hung up the phone.

He hadn't asked who or why or what race. He didn't have to. In the first place, Whiteley wouldn't have told him. In the second place, he already knew.

Frank Whiteley's regular, first-call rider was Jacinto. Everybody knew that Jacinto was sitting out a ten-day suspension. Everybody also knew that later on that afternoon—Jacinto or no Jacinto—the 68th running of the Astoria Stakes was going off at Aqueduct, and Frank Whiteley had entered Ruffian.

Maneuvering with the tail end of rush-hour traffic into the city was easy for a man who spent the better part of his life negotiating fields of thoroughbreds. Bracciale stepped on the gas. He had seen the race they got Jacinto for. It was a maiden race for two-year-olds, and a couple of jumps out of the gate Jacinto had hit his horse. His mount then ducked to the inside, bumping another horse, and that colt had caused a little trouble. Jacinto had gone on to finish second. The stewards didn't disqualify him, saying he had not affected the outcome of the race, but what they did was much worse: They had given him ten days for careless riding.

Bracciale checked his watch as he entered the barn. He had made the drive in record time. It was a good thing they didn't have stewards patrolling the Garden State Parkway!

"Well?" Whiteley snapped. "You want to ride the filly this afternoon?"

Bracciale glanced over at Ruffian. "I'd love to!"

"I got another horse in the seventh race. You want to get on him, too?"

"Yes, sir. Which horse is that?"

"Loud. In that turf race. Mile and an eighth."

"Great. That'd be great."

"Yates'll van them over there pretty soon. I'll see you over there."

That was that. Whiteley wasn't the kind of trainer who would dog his rider all day in the jocks' room with a million instructions. He'd say what he had to say in the morning, at the barn, or briefly out in the paddock. And, after all, what was there to say about Ruffian? "Don't fall off"?

Bracciale burst into the jocks' room at Aqueduct and dropped his bag in front of his locker. "Where's Hole?"

"Greasing up." One of the valets nodded towards the steam-room.

Mike Hole was dipping into an industrial-size jar of Albolene when Bracciale grabbed him.

"Hey, Mike, guess what? I'm riding Ruffian in the Astoria!"

Mike's freckled face lit up. "No kidding, Jimbo! That's great! That's terrific! You know I'm riding in that race, too. You better watch it out there, I'll be after you. I'm going to make you work!"

They looked at each other and laughed. In spite of their age difference—Hole was thirty-three, Bracciale only twenty-one—they were great friends; had been ever since Hole arrived from Canterbury, England, and started riding on the Maryland/Delaware circuit several years earlier. They had both shifted to New York at the same time, only a few months before.

"You got to take off weight?" Mike asked.

"Not really. She's carrying 118. I got to check my other horses, though. And I'm riding another one of Whiteley's in the seventh." Bracciale hoped he wouldn't have to spend the rest of the morning in the hotbox. He didn't mind heaving—he did that all the time—but the sweatbox could really sap your strength, and the one thing he knew he was going to need with Ruffian was his strength. She was powerful, and Whiteley didn't even give his rider a break by sending out a pony—"I pay the damn jock to ride the horse!"—to take you to the gate.

"Well." Hole hitched up the towel around his waist. "I got to go in. But that is really great, Jimbo. Riding Ruffian! Good luck to you. Good luck."

He meant it, too. Nobody understood better than another rider what it meant to get on a truly outstanding horse. Mike Hole was an honest jock and would give the race his best shot, but he was hoping that the luck would go with Ruffian, because as long as her luck held out, there was no way she could lose.

Yates hopped out of the cab of the van. "You ready to go?"

Frank nodded. They loaded up Sled Dog, then Loud, then Ruffian. Frank had requested that Yates be the driver, and he paid Ralph Smith vans extra to ship the filly over "private"—that is, with no other horses but his own. Trainers could pay less and get their horses transported with a full load, but Frank would never take a chance like that with Ruffian. If someone sent along one studdish horse and he started acting up, the best grooms in the world would be powerless to prevent trouble.

They'd spend the next few hours over at the receiving barn. All the horses who shipped in were stabled there. Frank wanted to get Ruffian settled early so she could get used to everything. Then, later, he could take her out of the stall, like he did at Belmont. The fewer changes in schedule, the better, though Frank was becoming convinced that the filly could adjust to anything without batting an eyelash.

He'd test her today. This would be her first trip over a different track. She trained at Belmont, and her first two races had been there, but Whiteley had always been a gypsy when it came to racing. He traveled to wherever the best races were, convinced that a good horse shouldn't have to carry his racetrack around with him. Or her.

When Ruffian was installed in the holding barn, the horse identifier came over and rolled back her upper lip. Every thoroughbred was tattooed there with a number, and that number went on file with the Jockey Club. It had to be officially verified before every race. Along with the specific recorded markings of each horse, this provided insurance against "ringers," horses running under another horse's name.

By one-thirty everything had been taken care of. The filly was outside, nibbling on a pitiful patch of grass, and Frank was chewing on his Gelusil. He was not entirely surprised when he looked up a short while later and saw Jacinto walking towards him, wearing neatly pressed slacks and a sport shirt.

"What the hell are you doing here?" Whiteley had a big grin on his face.

"Oh, I just come by say hello."

They spoke quietly for a while, then the conversation grew increasingly animated. Finally, Jacinto just shrugged and walked away. Whiteley was chuckling to himself.

Loud's race was nothing special. The seven-year-old gelding trailed the field almost the whole way. When he made his move at the head of the stretch, he cut the distance between himself and the leaders in half, but it was too late. He managed to finish fourth, and so picked up a small check in the process. When Bracciale jumped off, he was sweating as much as his horse. If he hurried, he could shower before changing into the Janneys' silks. He wanted to look good when he got on Ruffian.

The paddock at Aqueduct was out front, between the stands and the track, with the saddling enclosures partially blocked by a concrete overhang. Whiteley had slipped into a clean shirt and a sport coat, and Minnor had donned the regulation blue cotton NYRA jacket that the track handed out to grooms for the stakes races. They both looked fresh and cool.

Also looking his usual cool self was Braulio Baeza as he walked, slim and erect, over to the stall where his mount, Laughing Bridge, was getting saddled by Al Scotti. Baeza was particularly respected for his incredible patience. He could sit chilly on a horse, waiting, waiting, until everyone thought he had fallen hopelessly behind—then he would make his move, having saved so much that his horse pulled easily ahead. It was a dazzling display of both skill and nerve. He had arrived in the United States in 1959, one year before Jacinto. Also from Panama, around the same time, had come Heliodoro Gustines, Laffit Pincay, and Jorge Velasquez. A well-planned guerrilla invasion could not have been more dramatically executed: Within a decade, these five men, plus a handful of other Latin American jocks, had forever changed the face of raceriding in the United States. But as good as they all were, so far only one of them—Braulio Baeza—had achieved every jockey's ultimate dream: In 1963, on a colt named Chateaugay, he had won the Kentucky Derby.

Baeza's appearance made him easily distinguishable. At five feet, four inches, he was taller than the average rider, and the features of his long, gaunt face—painfully chiseled through years of rigorous dieting—hovered between Oriental and Indian. His natural reserve contributed to his ascetic demeanor, a bearing that racetrackers would characterize as either regal or arrogant, depending on whether they had won or lost money on him in the last race. He didn't interact with the crowds; never acknowledged their boos or cheers, never scanned the faces that called out to him. Other jockeys strolled into the paddock snapping their gum and joking with each other; Baeza simply appeared, ghostlike, and materialized at the trainer's side. So the fact that he pointedly avoided so much as a glance at Frank

Whiteley was not a slight that the average observer would have
noticed.

Whiteley didn't say anything as he shook hands with his
rider, so, as they walked over towards the filly, Bracciale asked
him what his instructions were.

"Don't get her hurt," the trainer said, "and don't get her
beat."

Minnor led them once around the ring. At the last minute,
to Bracciale's total surprise, a ponyboy rode up on Sled Dog and
took hold of the reins. There was something vaguely familiar
about the boy. Bracciale peered under his helmet and tried to
figure out what it was.

"Jacinto!" he cried. "What the hell are you doing?"

Jacinto gave him a little smile. "I make a mistake."

"What are you talking about?"

"I go by the barn early, see Mr. Whiteley, and he say, 'Take
this bitch to the post on the pony or I'm taking you off the
mount.' "

"You gotta be kidding!"

"No, I swear to God. I thought maybe he joking with me, so
I say, 'Okay, I go.' And he say, 'You don't got the guts to get on
that pony,' and I say, 'If you threaten me, I do. I don't want to
lose the mount on Ruffian.' So he say, 'Okay, go on.' He serious!
So, here I am!"

By now people in the crowd were starting to recognize him.
They pointed and laughed. "Hey, Vasquez, get a real horse!"

"I trying!" he called back. There were a few hisses and boos,
but mostly good-natured greetings. No one could remember ever
seeing a jockey—let alone one of the leading riders at the meet—
pony a horse to the post. Especially a horse he himself was supposed to be riding. Especially a horse like Ruffian. And Jacinto
looked so different in street clothes! So *ordinary*, almost, compared to the flash of racing silks.

"Well, damn," Bracciale said, "as long as you're out here,
anything I should know about her?"

Jacinto shook his head. He knew Bracciale had watched her
in the mornings, on the backstretch, and had seen her races.
There wasn't much to add. "You be okay. Watch coming out of
the gate, though. She break a little bit slow, but in one jump she
be right up there."

Sled Dog started fighting Jacinto as they headed for the turn. He was tossing his head and dancing sideways. Jacinto didn't mind being out there; he had a good sense of humor, and he knew that Frank Whiteley was getting the biggest kick in the world seeing him in public on the pony. But all of a sudden Jacinto got the feeling that the little bastard was getting ready to put a hump in his back. A joke was a joke, but Jacinto wasn't about to be dumped by a common son-of-a-bitch pony in front of 17,000 people. As Ruffian began to warm up, galloping along the turn, Jacinto let go of her reins and said good-bye. "You be okay," he called to Bracciale. And, in spite of the butterflies swarming in his stomach, Bracciale knew that he was right.

Mike Hole rode past on Our Dancing Girl. "Remember," he teased, "you better hope you get off good or I'm going to catch you!" He made a face. They both knew that Hole had about as much chance of winning the race on Our Dancing Girl as he would have had on foot.

Ruffian went into the gate and pointed her nose straight ahead. Her ears were flicking back and forth, attentive to everything, but she concentrated on the door. When the bell rang, Ruffian made a perfect break. Not a step or two behind, as she had been in her previous races, but right up there with Our Dancing Girl as they leaped from the gate. In that one instant, while they were still shoulder to shoulder, Hole raised his whip in a fleeting tribute to Ruffian. "All *right!*" he screamed at Bracciale. Before his words had faded in the wind, the black filly was pulling away. Like a cat relaxing in the sun, she had simply stretched out into the lead.

Bracciale had a snug hold on the reins. He could feel the filly's strength, but at the same time sensed her kindness—that is, her willingness to respond to his commands. That was crucial. If a horse and rider listened to each other, they could do just about anything together. There were plenty of horses, rich with speed, who overspent themselves early in a race and came up empty-handed in the stretch. Ruffian was so awesome, Bracciale got the feeling she could go on burning up the track forever, start to finish, full speed ahead—but he sure as hell didn't want to find out. Not if he didn't have to.

Even under wraps, her speed was astonishing. She did the first quarter in :21⅘. That was too much for Mike Hole's filly, who rapidly dropped back. Baeza had moved easily into second place, and for a few strides Laughing Bridge actually managed to stay close to Ruffian. But Ruffian was only playing. As soon as Bracciale asked for a little more—a slight movement of his fingers on the reins—she drew away. By the flash of the red and white stripes that marked the quarter pole, Ruffian led by three lengths.

Laughing Bridge had made a genuine effort, but she began slipping farther and farther back. After the race, even Baeza complimented Ruffian. "I could have cut through the center field," he said, "and she still would have beaten me!"

Ruffian won by nine lengths, in 1:02⅘. That was a new stakes record and only one-fifth of a second off the track record set by Raise A Native in 1963. Immediately the crowd started to complain: If only the boy had let her run! She could have broken that record easily! She could have smashed it to bits!

Bracciale didn't waste any time with second thoughts. He knew that Mr. Whiteley didn't give a damn about setting records. He cared about winning races and keeping his horses sound for the long haul. Bracciale had done exactly the right thing. He hadn't gotten the filly beat, and he hadn't taken any chances that might have gotten her hurt.

This time Frank led Ruffian into the winner's circle himself. Mr. and Mrs. Janney, it had been officially reported, were off in Canada at an important business meeting. That was nonsense, as Mr. Janney would later laughingly admit. They weren't away on business at all; months before, he and his wife had arranged a fishing vacation with another couple. They had missed the filly's race because they didn't want to disappoint their friends. Nor did they want to embarrass them by explaining the real story to the press. But it only happened that once. From then on, no matter how much rearranging was involved, every time the filly went to the post, the Janneys were there to cheer her on.

9

The screen door swung wide, letting in more flies, but before it had a chance to slam shut, Yates caught it with his heel and muted the noise. Not that he cared about disturbing Weston, his dispatcher—as a matter of fact, the idea appealed to him—but he was negotiating now, and he didn't want to waste time getting sidetracked. He cleared the smile off his face and entered the office.

He stood quietly, waiting, while Weston finished up on the phone. "Morning," Yates nodded. "Frank Whiteley says he's going down to Jersey tomorrow with Ruffian and he'd like to have me take her down."

Weston didn't even stop to look over the schedule. "I don't think we can arrange it. You gotta take the last race home." His tone was flat, closed. There was nothing to discuss.

Yates rapped his knuckles against the desk a few times—tock-tock-*tock*-tock—deciding whether or not to argue, then shrugged and left without another word.

He found Frank sitting in front of the barn, grazing Ruffian. Some people hated grazing horses more than anything in the world, but not Frank Whiteley. He never seemed more at peace than when he sat back in his rickety old lawn chair holding a thoroughbred on a shank.

Yates bummed a light from him and the two men smoked in silence for a while, watching the filly. After a few minutes Yates repeated his conversation with Weston.

"There won't be any problem," Frank said. "Take the day off tomorrow."

"Okay. I'll take the day off."

"I'll call Mills." Frank lit another cigarette and tossed the stub of the first one away. "Mills will have a van up here and you will drive her to Monmouth."

"Okay," Yates said. His blue eyes danced with pleasure. Frank Whiteley was one smart son of a bitch. Yates stayed long enough to enjoy the last drag on his cigarette, then he strolled back between the barns to Weston's office. This time he pulled up a chair and made himself at home.

"You just lost yourself a big account."

Weston looked up. "What are you talking about?"

"You said I can't take Frank's filly to Monmouth, so he's gonna call Mills up here to do it."

"Mills! Mills's vans are over in Maryland! He ain't gonna have them come all the way up here to—"

"Oh yes he is."

Weston glared at him.

"By the way," Yates added, scraping a speck of sand off his jeans, "I'm taking the day off tomorrow."

"What for?"

"To drive Mills's van."

Weston jumped up from behind the desk. "You can't do that, you son of a bitch!"

"The hell I can't! Don't tell me I can't! I'm doing it!"

"Well, goddamn it! Goddamn it! Who the hell does Whiteley think he is anyway? You—You— Okay, now just be cool. We'll call up the boss, see if he wants to work it out. We'll try to work something out."

"Well, you better, if you don't want to lose that account."

Weston shuffled through some papers. "All right. All right. You got to take the fifth race home, then you can take her."

"Uh-uh." Yates shook his head. "That's gonna be too late."

"Well, what the hell race you want to take home?"

Yates thought for a minute, trying to recall what horses Whiteley had entered locally for the next day, and how early he'd have to leave for Jersey to avoid the rush hour. "I'll take the second race," he said.

When Weston didn't answer, Yates knew it was all settled. He got up, grinning like a hyena, and walked out of the office. The screen door banged shut behind him. Hard.

"Why you gotta put me on all those horses? I don't wanna ride all day down there! I going down ride Mr. Whiteley's filly. I don't want to get on those other ones, break my neck riding all that shit you put me on!" Jacinto was standing in front of Fats, in the vestibule outside the jockeys' room. He had on clean whites, a sleeveless T-shirt, and a towel draped around his neck. His hair was dripping from the shower, his face still mottled an angry red from the sweatbox, where he'd spent the better part of the morning.

Fats hiked up his trouser leg and crossed one massive knee atop the other. He was wearing one green sock and one brown, and his white sneakers were coming untied. Even sitting down, he towered over Jacinto.

"I want a race over the track," Fats replied. "I can't take any chances riding Frank's filly, so don't start with me!"

"Hell with you! I ain't gettin' on all those cheap sumbitches! Take me off or I quit! You fired! I get me a new agent!"

"I'm not taking off anything, so shut your goddamn mouth! Why the hell you think I was on the phone all goddamn night? You'll ride some horses, make some money while you're down there."

"If I don't get kill!" Jacinto sat down, tight-lipped.

Fats reached into the pocket of his plaid jacket—sometimes Jacinto had to wonder where the hell the guy got his clothes from—and produced a handful of pills: green and pink and red and white; tiny round pills and big fat capsules that would have choked a horse. "Look at this, you little bastard," he said, displaying the pills in his huge, pale hand. "Which one of us you think is gonna die first? Huh? I'll be pushing up daisies, and you'll be running around crying for an agent who can put you on live mounts!"

"Okay, okay! One horse! But take me off those other ones."

"I ain't taking off nothing." Fats started to cough. "Get me some water, will you?"

Jacinto walked over to the lunch counter—slap, slap, slap, went his flip-flops on the linoleum—and asked for a glass of water. Jack O'Hara, the Clerk of Scales, was very strict. He rarely allowed the agents inside the actual jockeys' quarters; they had to meet with their riders in the vestibule. From there they could see through the open doorway into the rec room, the kitchen, the weighing-out room, but they couldn't simply walk in. Seated inside that doorway was a security guard—a plainclothes Pinkerton with a .38 strapped to his hip. To the right, behind their desks, sat O'Hara and his assistant. Without their permission, no one could enter that room but the riders and their valets.

Jacinto returned and handed the paper cup to Fats. He sat down beside him on the edge of the bench. "Don't die on me now," he pleaded. "You die now, Mr. Whiteley gonna kill me!"

Jacinto stretched out his legs, studied his toes, then let them swing back. If he sat all the way back on the bench, his feet could not have reached the floor. For a moment the two men were silent. Then Fats turned to Jacinto.

"Tell me the truth, you little son of a bitch." He lowered his voice. "You okay for Saturday?"

Jacinto's hand flew involuntarily to the left side of his face. "I fine," he said. "Fine."

The accident had been unavoidable, one of the hundreds of spills that was nobody's fault. Jacinto had been coming out of the gate when his horse stumbled, pitching him overhead. The fall itself hadn't hurt him, but the horse had kicked him in the face as it ran off, and in those first few terrifying seconds, as he lay curled up in a ball while hoofbeats thundered all around him, Jacinto was afraid he had lost an eye. Later, in the hospital, when he was cleaned up and feeling better, the first thing on his mind was the Sorority, less than a week away. He wasn't taking off the filly again, not after being forced to miss the Astoria. When Ruffian went to the gate on Saturday, he would be the guy on her back. He didn't care who he had to lie to.

So far, that list had included his wife, his in-laws, the doctors, the stewards, the Clerk of Scales, Frank Whiteley, and now Fats. He could have used a few more days of rest—his nose had been broken, it was still swollen—but he had to get back and test himself before the filly's race. He insisted to the track doctor that his vision was perfect and received permission to ride. It was true that, more than once, a horse in front of him had blurred back and forth from one image to two, but it was manageable. He even won a couple of races. He was actually more worried about an extended blind spot that had developed, a whole area off to one side that disappeared when he shifted his gaze. But even that could wait. If it didn't come back—after Saturday—he would see a specialist. For now, he had to trust his instincts. He'd ridden plenty of races when he was less than a hundred percent; every rider did. As long as he could see, he could stay on the horse. And with a horse like Ruffian, that was just about all he needed to do.

Dan Lasater had a gift for making money. He had parlayed his interest in the Ponderosa Steak House restaurants into a chain of franchises that was so successful he had been able to retire at twenty-eight. Now he pursued his love of racing full-time. He had breeding operations in Florida and Kentucky, and the year before he had captured the Eclipse Award for top money-winning owner in the country. He was well on his way to repeating that accomplishment in 1974. When he arrived at Monmouth for that year's Sorority, he had three things going for him: He had an excellent trainer, Gordon Potter, handling the East Coast division of his stable. He had the services of one of the hottest young jockeys in the country, a nineteen-year-old Oklahoma City boy named Darrel McHargue. And, most important, he had a two-year-old filly named Hot n Nasty. Hot n Nasty was a little bay by Reflected Glory out of Lady Maggie, and, like Ruffian, she was undefeated. She had romped home by thirteen lengths in her maiden race, then gone on to capture the Schuylkill at Liberty Bell and the prestigious Hollywood Lassie, on July 13, defeating the favored Miss Tokyo by 2½ lengths, in 1:09 flat. When Lasater decided to enter her in the Sorority, he wasn't going after second-place purse money. He thought his filly could win.

Of course he had read about Whiteley's wonder filly, and he respected Whiteley. But he let a few reporters know that he thought some of the things he had been reading might be just a bit overblown. Reporters were writing about Ruffian as if she were the second coming of Secretariat. Clockers in the *Form* were saying they had never in their lives seen works like hers, incredible times with no apparent effort. Stories were making the rounds that spectators spoke in hushed voices as they gathered behind her saddling enclosure in the paddock, awed by her mere presence.

The way Lasater saw it, the two fillies were, at the very least, equal: both easy winners of their maiden outings plus two juvenile filly stakes. They were both going into this contest with perfect records, but by the evening of July 27 that would no longer be the case. One of those records would be spoiled. One of those fillies would go down in defeat.

Dan Lasater didn't think it would be his. In fact, he was so confident, he had already gone out and bought the champagne. On race day a case of it was chilling over at his barn.

In every aspect of training, as far as he could control it, Frank Whiteley believed in consistency. Keep the same people and the same basic routine, and you had taken a big step towards reducing the possibility of error or accident. There was no guarantee, of course; that word didn't exist on the racetrack. But you did what you could. That's why Yates drove the filly down to Monmouth Wednesday evening and Yates returned fourteen hours later to gallop her. With an ordinary horse, you could always round up a decent freelance exercise rider for a couple of days, but Frank wasn't about to let a stranger get near Ruffian, much less on her back.

If a stranger had galloped her that Thursday morning, two days before the race, he would probably have come away respecting her strength and swiftness, aware that there was no struggle when she ran, only her own pleasure in her performance. Yates knew her too well; he came away with a different impression.

When he hopped off the filly, he shook his head. "I don't know, Frank. There's nothing wrong, exactly. She just didn't seem quite herself. Maybe it's the track."

Whiteley nodded. "We'll blow her out tomorrow, see how she does." But there was something left unspoken between them.

Yates did not envy Frank Whiteley. There was no doubt that the filly was a blessing. Everyone connected to her was going to reap rewards: money, renown, prestige. Plus all the things that couldn't be put into words—the excitement of being around her, and the way knowing a horse like her made everything else worthwhile. But Frank was the one responsible for her, and anyone who dealt with horses, especially top horses, knew how difficult that could be. You couldn't stop training or scratch a horse every time it wasn't absolutely, perfectly all right. Horses ran with torn frogs and quarter cracks and minor splints; they ran with sore shoulders and toothaches and cut heels. The good ones ran. If you demanded the most from your body in any sport, your body paid a price. It was the same with horses. Everyone on the backstretch understood that, everyone who actually handled horses. But you could never, ever, say that to the outside world. To them, everything had to be either black or white, right or wrong. They didn't live inside the world of running horses, where the fitness of a thoroughbred was often a vast gray area, interrupted at times by clear-cut injuries, or illness, or fever, but more frequently muddied over with ambiguous realities and indecipherable situations. Only years of experience and attention allowed you to interpret these signs. To a great extent, the horses themselves told you what they needed: They needed to rest or they needed to run. The best trainers listened to their horses. They knew everything about every single horse in their barn, and they knew it before anyone else had to tell them. Then they made their decisions. But it wasn't easy. And they could never be sure.

Yates returned the next morning to blow out Ruffian. Three furlongs for speed, a "tightener" the day before the race. Frank watched from the rail, clocking her for himself as he always did.

"How'd she do, Frank?" Yates asked after they got back to the barn.

For once, Frank gave him a straight answer. "Went :36 and change. How'd she feel?"

"Well, she went pretty easy." Yates hesitated. For Ruffian, that was a decidedly slow time. "I don't know, Frank. She went all right, she just didn't feel quite as strong or something. She didn't grab hold of me the way she usually does." His voice trailed off. It was hard to describe. She didn't act as if she were in pain or distress, she was just the slightest bit off.

"We'll cool her out, see how she's going." Frank didn't appear too worried, but Yates knew that he wouldn't show it even if he was. If something was wrong, Frank would *do* something, but he sure as hell wasn't gonna sit around and *talk* about it.

Later that afternoon, Frank strolled over to the Racing Secretary's office. He had picked up the overnights and was about to leave when Dan Lasater appeared. Although Whiteley didn't know him very well, he was always ready for a little good-natured sparring with the opposition. It was a way of fooling around, really, like Mack Miller, back in June, trying to get Frank to enter

Ruffian in the Colleen instead of the Fashion Stakes and leave his little one-eyed filly alone. Whiteley smiled at Lasater.

"Maybe you ought not to run your filly here tomorrow. Might get herself hurt."

Lasater smiled back. "We'll take our chances," he said.

Supper was over. Ruffian had devoured every oat Minnor had given her and licked the tub clean. When she was finished, Frank went off to get himself a bite to eat, and when he came back it was Minnor's turn. The filly stood with her head out of the stall, as she did at Belmont; always curious, always eager to know what was going on. Frank pulled up a chair and settled in, and the slow summer evening gradually deepened into a violet dusk. Before he left for the night, he tore the plastic off a Gelusil tablet and gave it to the filly for a bedtime snack. Then he took a few himself.

Frank knew exactly what was going on. He had been through this kind of thing many times over the years, and he had decided to leave it up to Ruffian. He would watch, and wait, and keep his mouth shut, and tomorrow the filly herself would tell him whether or not to send her to the post.

The crowd of 26,000 was larger than expected, and before the eighth race a large part of it had gathered around the paddock, waiting. The press corps was also inflated, with reporters drifting in from all over New Jersey as well as Pennsylvania and New York. The only thing there weren't too many of was horses. Wee Bit of Irish and Stream Across were being led around by their handlers; then Hot n Nasty entered the paddock and was walked back and forth before being saddled. Finally, accompanied by a growing murmur from the crowd, Minnor appeared with Ruffian. Bareback, with nothing to identify her but the small post position number 3 dangling from her bridle, she was still immediately recognizable. She was not as composed as usual, and she had uncharacteristically worked up a bit of a sweat, but it was, after all, a hot afternoon, and she had been spending the last two days in unfamiliar quarters. The crowd had no doubts about selecting her as the favorite: They sent her off at 3-to-10.

As soon as he pulled on his helmet, Jacinto forgot about his eye. He walked out to the paddock, shook hands with the Janneys, exchanged a few words with Whiteley, then was up in the saddle and heading for the track. Sitting on Ruffian's back, he was easily the tallest man at Monmouth.

If there was any weak spot, however small, in the filly's performance, it was that first step out of the gate. Jacinto tried to anticipate her hesitation just as he would the acceleration that followed a split second later. He knew the two horses on the inside were not really contenders for anything but show money. On paper, though, the outside horse, Hot n Nasty, looked like she had some speed. She'd run 1:09 at Hollywood Park. Of course, everyone knew that the California tracks were always fast. Jacinto would take the race one step at a time. First he'd worry about the break, then he'd worry about McHargue's filly—if he had to.

Just as the gate snapped open, Hot n Nasty half stumbled, then recovered immediately and took off in front. It was an impressive move. The two inside horses also got away slightly in front of Ruffian. Jacinto didn't panic. He knew he could pass them all in a couple of jumps, so he let his filly gather herself together and start rolling. As soon as she got into gear, she pulled ahead. She was staying well out from the rail, half a length in front, but McHargue's filly was pressing, not giving way. This was a new experience, to have another horse at her flank, refusing to drop back. Ruffian responded to the pressure of Jacinto's hands and pushed through a blazing first quarter in :21⅗. It was her fastest quarter-mile so far, and none of the other fillies she had encountered could keep going after fractions like that. But Hot n Nasty wasn't those other fillies. She was fighting Ruffian for the lead. She was actually trying to take it away! And even though Ruffian pulled ahead as much as a full length, Hot n Nasty refused to buckle. She was dogging the big filly, not capable of passing her but not allowing her to rest either.

And then it happened. For an instant, at the point of the stretch turn, Hot n Nasty tried to stick her nose in front. The crowd gasped. Ruffian had never been headed before! No one had ever looked her in the eye! She had simply zipped past her rivals in her first three races and that had been the end of that.

What was happening? What was going wrong? Even Minnor, watching from the rail, shook his head in disbelief. "My filly's gonna lose this race," he said out loud.

Jacinto had a few questions of his own, but no time to wait for answers. He hit the filly four or five times, right-handed, and Ruffian responded with an acceleration so sudden, so powerful, that within two strides she had sprinted away from Hot n Nasty.

The crowd breathed its relief. Hot n Nasty had been tough, she had gone an eighth of a mile with Ruffian, both fillies running in very fast time; two-year-olds, practically still babies, fighting it out with all the guts and determination of seasoned veterans. It had been a show, a real battle, much more than the crowd had bargained for—but at the point of call, Ruffian was in front, her perfect record still intact: In all her races, at every call, she had always been on the lead. Now she was pulling farther and farther ahead, so that the cheers had once more become confident, then jubilant, as she crossed the wire 2¼ lengths in front and still drawing away. The final time was 1:09. It was a new stakes record.

But while the filly galloped out, while the spectators continued their wild ovation, Jacinto felt a knot twisting in his stomach. *Something was wrong.* At the same time she had been fending off her first real challenge from another horse, Ruffian had also been fighting something else, something her rider couldn't see. He didn't know yet what it was, but he did know how his filly had responded: She had come right back, driven by her desire to stay in front, and that desire had outstripped whatever pain or problem had been plaguing her.

Whiteley had come onto the track with Minnor and they escorted Ruffian, who was now being led by Mr. Janney, over to the winner's circle. Whiteley saw the question on Jacinto's face but ignored him and said nothing. The reporters were already approaching, pencils out.

Jacinto handed them the standard jock line comparing his filly to a gold-plated Cadillac.

"Were you getting worried out there today?" someone asked.

"No. This was the first time I whip her," he lied, "and you saw how she responded, like a Caddy when you ask for more gas."

"Was the filly okay?"

"Fine," he lied again. "She was maybe a little nervous going to the gate, so I don't think she gonna break too good. But I knew she was the best horse out there." This was not a lie. This was the truest thing he had ever said. "The *best* horse, and she proved that today."

McHargue had weighed in and gone directly back to the jocks' room. He was followed by one lone turf writer, Russ Harris, who was working for a Philadelphia newspaper. Harris was tall and stoop-shouldered, and he had almost twenty-five years' experience covering racing.

"Darrel," he asked gently, "can you tell me what happened out there?"

McHargue whirled on him, and Harris saw instantly how disappointed the boy was.

"My filly quit on me, that's what happened! The bitch quit on me!"

"Darrel." Harris lowered his voice. "Darrel, listen to me a minute. I've been around this game longer than you've been alive. If you tell those reporters"—he motioned to indicate the newspapermen who would soon be trailing in, when they finished with Jacinto—"that your filly quit, they'll plaster it all over the papers and the owner'll never ride you back. Don't use that word. Hot n Nasty ran a great race! You didn't get beat by any old horse, you know; you just got beat by the fastest filly that was ever born! You know that, don't you? Hot n Nasty's a terrific filly, and if you go blasting her to the press, Lasater's never going to put you on her again. I'm only saying this to help. I mean it."

McHargue glared at him with his dark eyes. He had come so close! And it wasn't his fault! Why couldn't he just say what he felt and the hell with the damn press and everyone else! Why couldn't he tell the truth?

The reporters were gathering now. *The Blood-Horse*, the *Racing Form*, the New York dailies. Everybody. They surrounded him. Darrel, they all asked, what happened to your filly out there?

McHargue took a deep breath and instantly composed himself. "My filly did everything I asked," he told them. "She ran a hard race. She never gave it up."

Russ Harris smiled to himself, and made a point of taking down this last quote for his paper.

" 'Scuse me. The boss says you're the ones that deserve this."
One of Lasater's stablehands set down a case of champagne in
front of Frank Whiteley. "And congratulations."

Whiteley wasn't a champagne drinker, but he could recognize a sporting gesture when he saw one. "You tell Mr. Lasater
thanks." He even smiled at the messenger. "We sure do appreciate it."

After Jacinto had showered and dressed, he went looking for
Whiteley at the barn. As soon as they were alone, he turned to
the trainer. "That bitch give me a hard time out there! She don't
change leads, and she trying to get out after the first quarter-
mile!"

Whiteley nodded. "I know."

"She don't run her race today! She don't change leads at all!
What happen?"

"Don't worry. She's fine. She's just got a little splint. I kept
her cool enough to run. Her next race won't be till the Spinaway, and that's not for a month. She'll be fine. Wouldn't run her
if she wasn't."

"I know that." Jacinto stared after the filly. Minnor had
bathed her, slipped a fly net over her, and was walking her under the shedrow. Splints were not unusual. They would heal with
time and rest. But this was not an ordinary race that Ruffian
had just won. She had gone six furlongs in 1:09, set a stakes
record, and come back when that other filly tried to jam her
nose in front. To do all that when she was even a little bit off
was the mark of a truly gutsy horse.

And Jacinto couldn't even brag about her to the press! He
couldn't tell anyone! If he tried to tell the truth, things got too
complicated. He had learned that years ago. Truth could seldom
be reduced to a single paragraph, let alone a headline. Especially
by people who didn't understand, people who had never worked
around horses. They would distort whatever he said, twist it into
something ugly, something that it wasn't. It was better to keep
quiet. It was better, if necessary, to lie.

PART THREE

1

NYRA press aides and officials mingled with a group of turf writers who had come to witness the first of several spectacles promoting the Great Match Race. This was the weighing-in of the colt and the filly, on June 25, and the horses were being treated as if they were contenders for the heavyweight crown.

A special equine scale had been set up in one of the paddocks on the Belmont backstretch. Two years earlier, when Secretariat was being weighed in front of the press, he had become unexpectedly skittish; as a result, both the ramp and the scale were now covered with special rubberized mats to provide traction and prevent slipping.

No one said a word as Frank Whiteley rode up first on Sled Dog. He clucked once to the pony, who proceeded to walk up the ramp and stand atop the scale for a moment. Squeaky appeared a few feet behind, leading Ruffian. It was all very casual, but the point had been made: Sled Dog had demonstrated to the filly that it was okay to do this, and Ruffian then took her turn on the scale as if she had been getting weighed every day of her life. Chances are she would not have objected to the scale under any circumstances, but to Whiteley, those chances were like flies in the summer heat—just because you could never kill them all didn't mean you stopped swatting.

As Ruffian gazed calmly at the crowd, the needle on the scale pointed to 1125 pounds.

"She sure is a big one," laughed LeRoy Jolley.

Then it was the colt's turn. His groom, Frank Morris, led him up and he, too, stood placidly. The scale registered 1061 pounds. Before Foolish Pleasure even stepped off the ramp, peo-

115

ple had turned away to debate the significance of this weight differential. Suddenly, with no warning, the colt ducked his head down between his knees and kicked his hind legs high into the air, scattering the onlookers. They stumbled over each other in their haste to avoid his powerful hooves.

"He's okay, he's okay," Jolley said, stepping up next to the groom. "He's just feeling good." The colt settled right back down as Frank Morris talked to him and played with his shank.

The colt's exuberance caused some tense moments among the NYRA officials. If Foolish Pleasure sustained even the slightest injury before the Match, the deal would be off. That would be a disaster. Apart from the Triple Crown races, the sport itself rarely received any national attention. For New York in particular, where NYRA was still reeling from the recent one-two financial punch of the State Lottery in 1969 and Off-Track Betting in '71, the chance to make a huge splash with a special event like a match race—especially one that so perfectly captured the mood of the moment—was a dream come true. But along with the unique glamour of a match race came a unique risk. When you ran a race with a full field of horses, even if the star attraction had to bail out, the event itself could go on; some angle could always be found to promote it. With a match race, there was no margin of error. Thoroughbreds might be fragile animals, but if they forced an hour-long network special to be canceled at this late date, it was unlikely that racing would get a second chance.

The weighing-in ceremony was only the beginning of the program that morning. Like boxers, these two were going to be measured and compared down to the smallest details. Dr. Manuel Gilman, the track veterinarian, brought out the special metal instruments with which every dimension of a horse could be officially ascertained. Both the filly and the colt remained docile and well-mannered throughout their documentation. Then the numbers were announced. Even though everyone could see with their naked eye that the filly was the more imposing of the two competitors, the results were still surprising: Ruffian stood at 16 hands, 2 inches; Foolish Pleasure at 15 hands, 3¼ inches. Ruffian measured 75½ inches around her girth, Foolish Pleasure, 73. From hip to hock the filly was 43 inches and the colt 41. From shoulder to buttock she was one inch longer,

69 to 68. And from point of buttock to the ground, Ruffian was 57 inches and Foolish Pleasure 54.

There was, however, one area where Foolish Pleasure put up bigger numbers, and that was his shoe size. He wore number 6 plates, and Ruffian wore number 5. She was taller, broader, longer, and heavier—and she bore all that weight, crashing down at record-breaking speeds, one leg at a time, on a foot that was a full size smaller than Foolish Pleasure's.

2

Most of the big outfits sent their good stock up to Saratoga Springs—the "Spa," as it was called, famous for its mineral waters—for the month-long race meeting in August every year. Frank Whiteley was an exception. He didn't like Saratoga. He resented the inflated rents and the high prices common to all tourist towns in peak season. He had no patience for crowds or the long lines at restaurants. And the hectic social scene was not his cup of tea.

They wrote good races, though; outstanding races. So when Frank had a horse ready to start, he would ship him up a few days early, run him, and go home. That system had worked well in the past. Even with Damascus, back in '67, when everyone urged him to go up for the entire meet, Frank had refused. He'd shipped the colt up from his home base, Laurel Race Course, only a few days before the Travers, and he had won by 22 lengths—the largest margin in the history of the race.

Frank would do the same with Ruffian. He could have sent her up anytime. David had stalls at Saratoga; he was spending the whole month there. Frank, however, preferred to keep her at home, where life on the backstretch became less congested for the month but remained otherwise unchanged.

Ruffian had been given a little rest after the Sorority, and then she'd started galloping again. Frank had never worked her too often, but whenever he did, she drew a crowd. So when word got around that he was sending her five furlongs on August 13, a number of other trainers lined up along the rail. The glint of their stopwatches was unmistakable in the morning sun.

She went in :59⅕ and came back ready to do it again. When

other horses went that fast, observers praised their bullet works; when Ruffian went over :58, they raised their eyebrows and wondered if she was hurt.

Rumors circulated: The filly was sore. She had taken a funny step. She had tried to throw her rider. She had run off. She was flattening out.

Frank paid no attention to the rumors. As long as there had been racehorses, there had been rumors. A year earlier, when Secretariat was heading for Louisville and the Kentucky Derby, there was a sudden flurry of reports about his "bad" knees. He would never make it to the wire, according to anonymous insiders, let alone finish in the money. These reports were given credibility and published in newspapers, most notably by oddsmaker Jimmy "The Greek" Snyder. Once the colt arrived in Kentucky, even wilder rumors surfaced—the colt was bleeding; he was going to be scratched. Then, when Secretariat not only won the Derby but smashed the old record for the mile and a quarter race, everyone grew silent. Had there been even a grain of truth to any of the rumors? Only a handful of people would ever know for sure—the colt's trainer, Lucien Laurin; his groom, Eddie Sweat; and maybe one or two others who worked at the barn. But anyone who wanted could talk to the press.

Whiteley probably hurt his own cause. He was so close-mouthed, so evasive, that people sometimes got the wrong idea. Because he tended to answer questions about his plans by saying, "If everything goes okay ..." some people assumed that things were not going okay. But that *if* was meant in the genuinely speculative sense; it came from a lifetime of dealing with the uncertainty of horses. That *if* was the gate to Frank Whiteley's mind, and you had to pass through it to get to everything else.

Meanwhile, some people were suggesting that Whiteley wasn't going to ship Ruffian to Saratoga after all, not after this work. The competition was looking tougher than expected up there, especially a filly named Laughing Bridge. Under Braulio Baeza, Laughing Bridge had finished nine lengths behind Ruffian in the Astoria, but she had been twelve lengths ahead of the next horse. Since then she had shown steady improvement. Her trainer, Al Scotti, had brought her up to the Spa early and she had immediately displayed a liking for the deep track. She had already won two juvenile filly stakes up there: the Schuylerville on July 29 and the Adirondack on August 12. Her owner, Neil Hellman, was a movie impresario, originally from nearby Albany, so it was especially thrilling to have his filly win before a "hometown" crowd. If she held her form, she might be the one to end Ruffian's winning streak.

And even if the vague rumors about Ruffian weren't true, Saratoga had long been known as the "Graveyard of Favorites," the place where the chalk—the favorites—got buried. Secretariat had suffered one of the few losses of his career there. Man o' War, arguably the greatest racehorse of the century, was beaten only once in his entire life, by a horse with the uncanny name of Upset. That had happened in the Sanford Memorial Stakes— at Saratoga.

Every trainer who had ever had a top horse in his barn knew how little control he had over what other people said or wrote. You could issue statements refuting the claims that got published, or you could ignore them. Frank Whiteley chose to ignore them. People believed what they wanted to believe. There wasn't much you could do about it.

Yates steered the van down Union Avenue and turned off onto the dirt roads of the Saratoga backstretch. As he pulled up over by Barn 10, he spotted Frank sitting in front of an empty stall, his hat pulled down on his forehead as though he were taking a nap. Yates, of course, knew better. Frank had driven himself up earlier in the day, and the last thing he was going to do before the filly arrived was to fall asleep.

"Ho, there!" Yates called out. "Everything's fine, Frank. Just relax."

"Better be fine, goddamn son of a bitch." He joined Yates at the back of the trailer and they opened the doors and let down the ramp. Minnor greeted them and led Ruffian out. Her legs were wrapped in thick cotton traveling bandages.

"Walk her around once, let's take a look," Whiteley said.

Minnor nodded. He glanced over his shoulder, beyond the barn, at the clusters of elm trees. Their heavy branches were swaying in the breeze, and everything was drenched in green. The filly flared her nostrils as she was led around the barn. Minnor chuckled at her. "It smells good up here, don't it?" he said. "Enjoy it while you can, girl, 'cause we're only staying till you win that race on Friday."

"How you know she'll win?" Yates teased him.

"What else?" Minnor answered. "If she win that last one down at Monmouth, who you think can beat her up here?"

Minnor was in his usual ebullient mood when a reporter stopped by a little later on and caught him by surprise.

"How *much* you think your filly's gonna win by?" the man asked him.

Without stopping to consider, Minnor blurted out the first thing that came to his mind. "Thirteen lengths," he said.

The reporter wrote it down on his spiral pad and moved on.

Oh, shoot, Minnor thought immediately. Why had he gone and said that? They'd write it up in the papers and he'd look like a fool, bragging on his filly like that. Thirteen lengths! Good lord, what was he thinking? Next time, he told himself, he would keep his mouth shut.

The afternoon's races were still going on when Jacinto drove over to the barn. He stood before Mr. Whiteley in a tailored sport coat, creased tan slacks, and shiny brown dress boots.

"Well, what've you got to say for yourself, Por-ta Rican?"

"Those goddamn sumbitches give me seven days. I already appeal the decision."

"Hell! They ain't gonna reverse it. You know that well as I do. Now listen to me and listen good. You want to keep riding this horse, stop getting yourself suspended, you understand me?"

Jacinto tugged on the visor of his camel's hair cap. He was only confirming, in person, what they both already knew, for he had called Mr. Whiteley in New York on Saturday, immediately after the decision had been announced.

The announcement had appeared with all the other news releases, hung up on pegs on the left-hand wall just inside the door of the NYRA press office. But this was Travers Day, the biggest day of the Saratoga meeting, and it was not surprising that the reporters passed over the small paragraph concerning Jacinto. It simply stated that each of the three jockeys disqualified from, respectively, the previous day's fifth, sixth, and seventh races had been set down for one full week, from Tuesday the twentieth through Monday the twenty-sixth of August.

Jacinto was furious. He didn't think any of their actions warranted such severe punishment, but he knew why it had happened. The day before they were disqualified, another rider, Angel Santiago, had been thrown from his mount and was in serious condition, partially paralyzed, at Ellis Hospital in Albany. That accident had stunned the crowd. Unlike the two downstate tracks, Saratoga attracted large numbers of families, tourists, and college kids. These infrequent racegoers viewed an outing at the track much as they did a trip to the ball park; danger was the last thing on their minds.

But danger was a part of the racetrack. Riders risked their lives every day, and you could not move inside this world for long without witnessing spills, breakdowns, injuries. The three jocks who were disqualified the following day had not been involved in any accidents, but Jacinto was convinced that they were being used as scapegoats, suspended for seven days in an attempt to reassure the public that rough riding would not be tolerated. It was all a show. It added to the illusion that if everyone just followed the rules and did the right thing, the "problems" would all go away.

Jacinto couldn't take any action until Monday, when he filed the appeal. He knew the stewards' decision would never be overturned; strategically, all he was hoping to achieve was a postponement of the suspension so he could ride that final week of Saratoga.

Those seven days were crucial to him. Saratoga concluded its meeting with two of the crowning races for juveniles, the 6½-furlong Hopeful for colts, and the six-furlong Spinaway for fillies. This year, for the first time in seventy runnings, the Hopeful had so many entrants that it had been split into two divisions, and Jacinto had been named on the favorite for both: The Bagel Prince, who had finished second in the Sapling; and Foolish Pleasure, the colt who had beaten him. Jacinto had ridden Foolish Pleasure in that race; it was the first time he'd been aboard the colt, and if he got replaced at this stage of the game, LeRoy Jolley might not ride him back. Jacinto also had the mount on Ruffian for the Spinaway. In those two days, for those three races, he stood to lose almost $12,000—his share of the $120,000 purse money. Worse, it would be the second time he had missed a turn on Ruffian. Mr. Whiteley was going to be pissed.

The 1¼-mile Travers was the oldest stakes race in the country. It was important not just because of its history and prestige, but also because of its timing. It served as a prelude to the major fall races, where, traditionally, the three-year-olds began facing older horses. When it came to awarding Horse of the Year honors and divisional championships, a horse who stood out from Saratoga through the fall could displace a horse who had made a showing only in the spring. For those who had not competed or done well in the Triple Crown events, the Travers was a chance for redemption; for those who had proved themselves early, it was a chance to solidify their reputation.

Rains fell off and on throughout the day, but they did not deter the crowds that gathered to watch a three-year-old filly named Chris Evert challenge the colts in the main event. Earlier in the year, Chris Evert had captured all three jewels of the Filly Triple Crown—the Acorn, the Mother Goose, and the Coaching Club American Oaks. She had also won a well-publicized match race against Miss Musket, a California filly, at Hollywood Park on July 20, in what had been highly touted as an East Coast vs. West Coast duel. As a sporting event, it was a disappointment— Miss Musket tired on the far turn and was eased to a canter for the final three-sixteenths of a mile, allowing Chris Evert to beat her by a humiliating fifty lengths. Still, the race had commanded a lot of attention; it was not broadcast on network television, but it got enough print coverage to give the equine Chris Evert a national reputation.

At Saratoga her trainer, Joe Trovato, had been talking about her to the press all week and showing them some of her fan letters. When a reporter asked how the filly compared to the teenage tennis star after whom she had been named, Trovato smiled.

"You should compare her to that other one, Billie Jean King!"

That got a big laugh; during the past winter, Billie Jean King had trounced Bobby Riggs in the first "Battle of the Sexes" match between professional tennis stars.

"In fact," Trovato went on, "my filly's got it even tougher

than Billie Jean King in this race, because King just had to beat one male, and this filly's taking on a whole field!"

Chris Evert was, in fact, the second choice in the race; given a reasonable chance by the professionals, she also had a number of supporters who came out solely to see her beat the boys. Likewise, Little Current, a colt, had a contingent of supporters who were there just to see him whip the filly. He had won both the Preakness and the Belmont in convincing style and was the even-money favorite for the Travers, which had experienced a mild surge of publicity based on the "boy vs. girl" angle, which was always good for selling newspapers. Whenever management attached a gimmick to a race, they could hook in customers, because no matter what people said—even hardcore handicappers—in a race like this, some part of them identified with the horses on the track. Certain dramatic themes could be counted on to attract an audience—David vs. Goliath, North vs. South, Girl vs. Boy. In real life these conflicts were not so easy to resolve, but in sporting events you always got an answer.

On Travers Day the answer came a little after five-thirty in the afternoon. Chris Evert took over the lead after the first half-mile, and the crowd broke into wild cheers. But she began to tire and was challenged by Holding Pattern, an unprepossessing little horse known around the backstretch as "Shorty." Meanwhile, Little Current was battling courageously through the sloppy track, steadily moving up between horses. He finished with a tremendous rush, but it was not quite enough. Little Current finished second; Chris Evert held on for third. The surprise winner turned out to be Holding Pattern.

Those looking for a symbolic victory in this event went home somewhat abashed, for Holding Pattern was a gelding. What that signified in terms of the battle of the sexes was something most people preferred not to think about.

Jacinto shifted from one foot to the other. He was sorry to have let Mr. Whiteley down, because he knew the trainer didn't like switching riders. Not because the filly couldn't adjust; she was the least temperamental filly Whiteley had ever had in his barn. Any decent jock could ride her. But familiarity with a horse gave you an edge. It was not just about winning. Whiteley used to point to a little dog running around the stables and say he could put that dog on Ruffian and the filly would still win. It was something more important than that. The better you knew the horse, the better chance you had of avoiding trouble, of noticing any slight change in her way of going, of recognizing even the most subtle signs of distress. This was the edge Whiteley wanted to preserve.

Jacinto could do nothing about his current suspension, but he swore to himself that after the Spinaway, no one else would ever ride the filly in a race. Part of that decision was purely selfish. The filly had a great future—maybe the greatest future of any filly in the history of the sport. For Jacinto that meant purses and prestige and a shot at the true superstar recognition he was just short of achieving. Part of it, though, was more personal.

That part was harder to describe. It was the way he felt about Ruffian herself. He wanted to be specific, to explain to people why she was different from every other horse he had ever ridden, but he didn't know how. The filly could not be reduced to words.

Jacinto kicked the dirt around in front of Mr. Whiteley's chair. "You breezing her tomorrow?"

"Nope. Probably Thursday. Yates'll be on her."

"Okay. You got my number here, right? Gimme a call you want anything."

"Give my best to Patty. Don't go getting on her nerves now just 'cause you ain't riding."

"Nah. I hardly there anyhow. Houseful of damn people all the time."

"Well, stop by here anytime you want. I'll let you muck out a few stalls, keep you busy."

Jacinto smiled and climbed back into his Cadillac. "I already done that once. Long time ago."

"Well, I'm warning you," Whiteley called after him. This time there was an edge to his voice. "Keep getting yourself suspended and you're gonna end up doing it again!"

Ruffian finished lunch and pushed her nose around the feed tub to make sure she hadn't missed anything. Reporters had been stopping by all morning, though they knew that Whiteley did not welcome their visits. That was just too bad, they thought. It was the day before the Spinaway, and he had the overwhelming favorite in the race. Only a few hours earlier Ruffian had breezed three furlongs in :33⅘. If Whiteley didn't want attention, he shouldn't allow horses like that in his barn.

There was nothing wrong with the trainer's hearing, but often the writers had to repeat their questions two or three times. Frank's answers were short, understated, usually polite. He didn't encourage anyone to stick around.

Then, when the strangers were gone, he sat alone in front of the filly's stall, alternating cigarettes and Gelusil. From time to time he would look over his shoulder. These were private looks, unguarded, full of a feeling that went beyond the obvious love and pride. That feeling was fear: fear that the filly was just too fast, that she couldn't go on like this, that she would use herself too much. It was a fear that everyone on the backside understood. When a horse came along with speed like Ruffian's—pure, effortless, unearthly speed—they asked themselves: Was it a gift from God, or a bargain with the Devil?

When Vince Bracciale received the unexpected long-distance call from Frank Whiteley, the jockey's heart started to pound.

"I hear you've been going over the jumps," Whiteley said.

"Yeah, yeah," Bracciale answered. He couldn't believe it! How had Whiteley heard about his good luck? He had been asked to ride one of the top steeplechase horses in an upcoming race at the Spa. He had been schooling the horse in the mornings, learning as he went along. Flat riders rarely made the transition to jumpers, but a good jockey could give it a try. Bracciale loved the challenge.

"Well, you know you got second call on my filly," the trainer continued.

"Yes, sir, I'm glad of that."

"Well, then, goddamn it! I better not ever hear of you getting on any more jumping horses if you want to keep it that way!"

For a split second Bracciale was too stunned to grasp the meaning of those words. Then he understood.

"All right, Mr. Whiteley. No, sir. You won't."

Whiteley didn't want him getting hurt. It wasn't even personal, but just in case something should happen to Jacinto, he

wanted Bracciale whole and healthy. There was always some risk
when you worked any kind of horses, but there were definitely
more spills going over the jumps than there were on the flat.
Protecting a first-call rider was one thing; restricting a backup
boy like that was practically unheard of.

And yet, Bracciale felt no resentment. Although he knew that
his chances of getting another ride on the filly were slim, he
willingly agreed to the conditions that the trainer laid down. His
reason for doing so was simple: He had been aboard Ruffian
one time, and he would do whatever was necessary to get up
there again.

At a quarter past five on the afternoon of August 23, due to
Jacinto's suspension, Bracciale's second chance arrived. He left
the jockeys' room with Mike Hole, who was once again facing
Ruffian aboard a long shot, Scottish Melody; just behind them
came Jorge Velasquez and Braulio Baeza. Velasquez was the rider
for Some Swinger, and he was known to be a big fan of Whiteley's filly; when someone asked what it was like to ride against
her, he joked that he really couldn't say—the only part of her
he'd ever seen in a race was "her beautiful black butt" moving
off into the distance. The fourth horse in the Spinaway was
Baeza's mount, Laughing Bridge, the filly who had already captured two stakes over the track.

The riders strolled over to the saddling area flanked by Pinkertons. Children held out their programs for autographs; the
jockeys scribbled their names as they entered the unfenced paddock where the horses were being walked under trees marked
with their post positions. Bracciale headed for the elm with a
big number 2 on it.

It had rained heavily that morning, but now the sun was out
and the track, which had been a swamp, was officially listed as
"Fast." Not one rider who had been over it agreed with that
designation, but at least it had begun to dry out. It would be a
decent surface to run over.

When Ruffian stepped out in front of the stands, she was
rewarded with that rarest of tributes: a round of applause *before*
the race. Surprised, Bracciale glanced up. There were people
everywhere—packed into the grandstand and the clubhouse,
jammed together all along the rail—and every one of them was

looking at his filly. She had riveted their attention. Then, as he broke her from a walk into her stately trot, something happened that Bracciale had never experienced before. The crowd started to chant: *"Ruffian! Ruffian! Ruffian!"* It sent a chill up his spine.

The track had been slow that year at Saratoga. Good horses were going in 1:12, 1:13 for six furlongs; the very best were getting only 1:11 and change. The single exception had been the four-year-old filly La Prevoyante, who had regained her outstanding early form after a mediocre sophomore year. She had captured three straight sprints at the Spa. In the last, on Travers Day, she had beaten one other filly and six colts going three-quarters of a mile, and she had done it in 1:08⅖. No one else had come close to that all month.

The riders circled once as they approached the gate, and Ruffian loaded up with no problem. Although she had broken perfectly for him in the Astoria, Bracciale remembered Jacinto's warning that she could be a little bit nasty in the gate and that she sometimes broke a step slow. Today she tipped her head slightly to the side as if she were actually watching the doors, waiting for them to open. When the bell rang, she hit them perfectly. It almost seemed as if she had gathered herself up a fraction of a second too soon and was going to slam into the metal barrier in spite of her jockey's firm hold; if the gate had not opened just then, she might well have crashed right through. But her timing was perfect. She didn't need the first two or three jumps—those effortless lunges that were becoming her trademark start—to pass her rivals, for she had broken a full length in front.

Some Swinger had immediately fallen back into fourth, where she would remain for the entire race. Mike Hole had Scottish Melody tucked into second place, but she was being pressured by Baeza aboard Laughing Bridge.

At any moment Ruffian could have pulled away, but Bracciale refused to allow her more than a length on her nearest rival. He kept her under wraps all down the backstretch and had no idea that she still got the first quarter in :22⅕. As they rounded the far turn, Laughing Bridge mounted her challenge. It was good enough to move her into second, but it was costing her something. Baeza was making her work. Ruffian was just playing.

Ruffian was waiting, and Bracciale could feel it. She was primed for the signal that would allow her to run. She stayed close to the rail now, losing no ground, making everything look easy. Then, at the top of the stretch, Bracciale moved his hands a tiny bit and the filly exploded. He thought he was prepared for her, but once again she took his breath away. In three jumps she had widened her lead from one length to seven. How had she opened up like that? Bracciale, on her back, was as mystified as the 19,000 people in the stands. It wasn't possible! The filly was a freak! She had descended from another planet; that was the only explanation. Horses on Earth just didn't run like that.

Suddenly, a sobering thought struck Bracciale: Mr. Whiteley would blame him for making Ruffian run too hard! If she kept pulling away like this, Mr. Whiteley would crucify him.

Bracciale drew on all of his considerable strength. He felt like he was strangling his horse, but he had no choice. She was so powerful! She would get away from him if he didn't bear down. No one was threatening them, they could take it nice and easy the rest of the way—but the filly didn't want that. She wanted to run.

He knew better than to fight her. Instead, he tightened his hold little by little, all the way down the stretch. He judged, by her easy-striding manner, that she was finally reduced to a comfortable gallop as they crossed the wire. He was even ready to joke that, during the last sixteenth of a mile, he had actually pulled her up into a trot.

Although Bracciale was convinced he had just won a very slow Spinaway, the time didn't seem to matter to the crowd. They were hysterical as the filly swept under the wire. Ruffian's perfect record was intact, and she had won by a large margin. Bracciale didn't know exactly how large, but he suspected that in spite of all his efforts through the stretch, she had continued to pull away.

He galloped out around the clubhouse turn, the shouts echoing in his ears. Jimmy Dailey, the outrider, pulled up alongside the filly.

"Nice race!" Dailey called. "How fast you think you ran?"

"Gee, Jim." Bracciale was still catching his breath. "I never really let her run, you know. Maybe eleven, ten and change, something like that." He shook his head. "I was strangling down on her all the way, and that would be a good race."

"It sure would." Dailey had a big grin on his face. They took their time heading back towards the stands. Everyone was whistling and clapping and waving their programs in the air. Bracciale had never heard a crowd so ecstatic. When they got around the turn, Bracciale looked over at the tote board.

"That can't be right, Jim! Look at that!"

Dailey just kept grinning.

"What does that say?" Bracciale demanded.

Dailey laughed out loud. "You can read, can't you?"

"That says eight and three! How can it, Jim? You saw me, I was choking her the last eighth! I was pulling her up all the way home!"

"Well, she fooled you, Jimbo! She sure fooled you."

"But that'd be a record! That'd be a new stakes record, wouldn't it?"

"So? What else is new? That filly's been setting records every time she runs!"

What neither of them realized at the time, what the crowd had no way of knowing, what the turf writers and publicists and officials didn't even think to check until much later, when they had all returned to New York, was the fact that Ruffian's 1:08⅗ was not just the fastest time ever for the Spinaway, not just the fastest time for any two-year-old all season at the Spa—but the fastest six furlongs ever run by any two-year-old of either sex in the history of Saratoga. That included, in chronological order, such all-time greats as Colin, Man o' War, Equipoise, Tom Fool, Native Dancer, Nashua, and Secretariat.

At Saratoga Race Course there was no separate enclosure where the victory ceremonies took place. Instead, each day at the beginning of the card, a chalk circle was spread on the track itself, near the finish line, along the outside rail. Usually, after the first few races, the line was no longer visible, but everybody knew where to go when they won. The Janneys and their four children joined Frank and Minnor there. Bracciale tossed his whip to his valet and took another long look at the crowd.

Ruffian stood still, poised and regal, and gradually the crowd grew quiet. Then the filly tossed her head and pranced sideways a few steps and the audience screamed its approval. She wanted to get back on the track! She wanted to keep running! Bracciale took up the reins a little more. Mr. Janney had a hold of the shank, and Minnor was waiting a few feet away. But Ruffian didn't want to go back to the barn. She wanted to run. She repeated this little performance several times. First, she settled down and the crowd would hush; then up came her knees and she'd start to dance away. Each time she did this, the people in the stands erupted, stomping and cheering, as if they were calling her back for an encore. It happened four or five times. Nobody wanted the show to end.

Finally, at a signal from Whiteley, Minnor took the shank and Bracciale jumped down. He undid her girth, slid off her saddle, and walked over to weigh in beneath the green-and-white-striped awning. Yates joined Minnor and together they led the filly off to the spit-box, where winning horses were taken for mandatory blood and urine testing.

The two were silent as they followed the dirt path past the paddock and around the white frame buildings towards the backstretch. They nodded politely as people called out congratulations. They were cool. They were very cool. But as soon as they were out of sight of the public, they turned to each other, wide-eyed.

"My God, Minnor, can you believe it! This horse didn't even have to catch her breath! Look at her! Goddamn! Did you ever see a race like that? Did you see how much this filly won by?"

"Oooooh, baby! Did I see? Did I *see*?" Minnor shook his head slowly back and forth, as if he couldn't quite believe it himself. "I can't wait for that reporter to come around the barn tomorrow. Man, I can't wait to see his face!"

The two men laughed. Ruffian had won the Spinaway by exactly thirteen lengths.

3

The soundman adjusted the knobs on his tape recorder. He slipped the foam cover over his microphone and aimed it at the eaves, where the cooing of pigeons tumbled down like a waterfall. He gathered the background noises on tape one by one: the slithering of straw off a pitchfork; the squeak of saddles; the thud of hooves; the occasional sharp command, "Hold back! Hold back!" as someone crossed unexpectedly in front of a line of horses.

The producer checked his watch one more time. Whiteley had told him to come around eight-thirty, and the television crew had assumed they would catch the filly's work. No one had explained to them that the track was closed then for a half-hour break so it could be reharrowed and watered. By the time they drove up to the barn, Ruffian had already finished cooling off. "Run her early," Whiteley chuckled when he saw them unloading their gear.

He hadn't exactly lied to them. They had said they wanted to see her work; he had told them when to come. Why should he let them bother her? He didn't care that they were from a big network. Maybe the press office and the Association enjoyed all the attention his filly was starting to attract, but Whiteley did not. He didn't want any distractions, especially on a day like this. It was the morning before the Frizette, a $100,000 stakes race. There was no way he would permit a TV crew to follow her around. Let them go over and film Jolley's colt. He was running in the seven-furlong Cowdin that very afternoon. Nobody had beaten him, either.

"You can take your pictures while she grazes, over there."

That was Whiteley's concession to the disappointed crew. He pointed to the grassy area where Mike Bell stood holding the filly's shank.

He was being generous. When he really wanted to get rid of someone, he sent them over to Loud's stall, at the far end of the barn, and told them it was Ruffian. It was amazing to Whiteley how few people could tell one horse from another. And even more amazing that they never thought to look at the nameplate that was affixed to the halter of every horse in the barn.

Certain writers, who knew something about horses or had taken the trouble to learn, Whiteley didn't mind too much. There were even a couple he actually liked: Bill Rudy, of *The Blood-Horse* and the *Post*, and Teddy Cox, who had a column in the *Daily Racing Form*. And Barney Nagler was okay, too. Nagler was a small, birdlike man who'd been writing for the *Form* almost thirty-five years. He was there that morning, watching Whiteley supervise the film crew. He had his pad and pencil out, but Whiteley didn't feel like this was a formal interview. Still, he was careful what he said.

"Come on." He motioned for Nagler to follow him over to where the television people had congregated. The producer grabbed Frank for a few minutes, to talk to him on camera, and Frank consented so that the filly could graze in peace. Then the producer turned back to Bell and asked him to walk Ruffian around a minute more. Bell tried to cooperate without upsetting the filly, who preferred to keep munching on her grass. She was wearing a ratty red blanket that Frank had acquired years ago at Shenandoah Downs. They had a stakes there called the Tri-State Futurity, and they used to give every horse that ran in it one of these blankets, or "coolers" as they were called. Frank didn't know how many years he'd had that thing—it was no prize even when it was brand new—but this was the kind of private joke he enjoyed: covering the most talked-about horse on the grounds with a worn-out blanket from a third-rate track.

There had been plenty of third-rate tracks in the old days. Half-mile tracks with five-day meetings. Whiteley had followed the races from Marlboro to Timonium to Hagerstown to Cumberland to Bel Air, long before he could afford any help. He served not only as the trainer, but also as the groom, hotwalker, exercise rider, and errand boy. He owned one or two or three horses at any given time—cheap horses, hundred-dollar horses. Sometimes he had to go without dinner so that they could have their oats. He slept in the back of his truck or bedded down in one of the stalls, and it was a long time between baths.

This was already one step up from the fair circuit where he'd started. At the fairs, things were really wild. He might run the same horse five-eighths of a mile twice in one day; fourteen or fifteen starters would go off in a tangle, risking life and limb, all for a fifty-dollar purse.

And in the winter, when there was no racing, he lived off what he'd earned, if he was lucky, or he went out and got another job.

Frank had worked at only three jobs outside the track. After he quit high school, he waited on customers at the local A & P. That was during the Depression, and he took home six dollars a week. At twenty-three he had married, and for three years he worked with draft horses—Belgians—on another man's farm. It was steady, but it wasn't what he wanted. Then his uncle Harmon, who also trained in the minor league circuits, sent a horse to Frank to help him get started on his own.

From then on the only thing that ever interfered with his career at the racetrack was the Second World War. Farmers were needed to raise vital crops, so Frank spent the war years on a rented farm in Maryland working with his brother-in-law.

Afterwards, as soon as he could, he returned to training and never looked back. He had started at the bottom of the barrel, working with cheap, broken-down horses. It was his ability to get them in shape again and place them in spots where they had a chance to win that had first gained him attention. People noticed that he was totally dedicated to his horses. Owners started sending him stock, and he had moved up little by little till he had reached the pinnacle of the game: He'd been named Trainer of the Year in 1967, and he had trained two champions, Tom Rolfe and Damascus. Now, with the filly, it looked like he had a third.

"Okay. You got enough." Frank abruptly dismissed the TV crew. Barney Nagler had just asked him to compare Ruffian and Damascus. People always wanted to compare top horses, and you couldn't really do it. The only horses you could truly compare were those that had faced each other on a track. But the question set him thinking.

The colt and the filly were such different types of horses. Damascus hadn't started his career as a two-year-old until September 28, and here it was September 25 and Ruffian was getting ready for her sixth start—five of them stakes. The colt had come in second in his maiden race, and the filly had dominated from the first furlong of her career. Then, too, Damascus had been a handful. He wasn't mean; he just didn't care to work hard in the mornings. Even Squeaky had trouble getting the colt to move when Whiteley had him in Camden. He had to put his son David on to thump the colt around the track.

But once Damascus got to racing, once Shoemaker, his regular jock, had figured out how to ride him—or, as he would later say, how *not* to ride him—there was nothing that horse couldn't do. Sure, there had been a couple of disappointments, notably the '67 Kentucky Derby. Damascus had gone off as the 3-to-5 favorite but had come in third. Frank kicked himself for letting the horse go to the paddock before the race; it was always such a madhouse for the Derby, and that year the crowds and the loud music had rattled the usually calm Damascus. On that crucial afternoon, he was so rank that even Shoemaker had not been able to get him to relax and run his race. After that, Frank got him a pony named Duffy for company, and that settled him down. Damascus came right back to score in the Preakness and the Belmont, and then stole just about every stakes that wasn't nailed down: the Dwyer, the Travers, the Aqueduct, the Jockey Club Gold Cup, and that unforgettable Woodward, where he came out of nowhere to defeat Buckpasser and Dr. Fager. He stacked up so many trophies that by the end of the year he was named Best-Three-Year-Old Male, Best Handicap Horse, and Horse of the Year. He had earned every one of those titles.

His style enhanced the drama of his races. He was a come-from-behind horse with a powerful burst of speed. When he started picking up horses along the turn for home, he was like a tornado gathering strength, destroying everything in his path.

Ruffian was different. With her, there had been no disappointments, no failed opportunities. Her style was dazzling rather than dramatic, for she had hardly ever been challenged, and she had never come from behind. She went right to the lead and opened up daylight all the way to the wire. Her place was in front. She owned it, and she would not give it up.

Damascus had been awesome, and Frank would always have a soft spot in his heart for him, but Ruffian was damn near perfect.

Damn near. Take that morning's work, for example. She had been carrying 130 pounds, counting Yates and the heavier training saddle that he used, and Frenchy had timed her in :33⅖ for the three furlongs. What more could you ask? But even those fractions didn't tell the whole story. There was an intangible, unmeasurable aspect to her, and this time the clocker's less objective reactions were also noted in the *Form*.

"She's sharp as ever!" Frenchy raved. "She isn't real! She's invincible!"

As soon as he entered the barn the next morning, Frank knew something was wrong. Hamp didn't say a word; he just turned his head in the direction of the filly's stall. Frank was over there in three strides and saw immediately what Hamp was unhappy about. For the first time since he'd had her, the filly had failed to polish off her oats.

Frank looked her over carefully. Her head was up, her eyes were clear, there were no bumps or bruises, no bleeding, no discharge, he couldn't feel any heat in her legs—but she hadn't cleaned up her feed. That was something you never ignored in a racehorse. Frank went to the tackroom and got the thermometer. A few minutes later he reemerged from the filly's stall.

"Don't tack her up," he told Minnor. "We'll just leave her inside for now." He made his usual check on the other horses and went over the set list with Barclay. Then he telephoned Stuart Janney.

Frank wasted few words. The filly was running a slight temperature, he said; 101.6, and she'd left a few oats in the tub. Better not run her till they found out what was wrong. Mr. Janney agreed. He was as disappointed as anyone to have his horse scratched on the morning of a big stakes, but this was a game where the people adjusted to the horses' needs, not the other way around. At least, that's the way he and Frank played it.

Frank then called Kenny Noe, the Racing Secretary. There was a brief silence while the news sank in.

"I'm sorry to hear that, Frank. What can I say is wrong?"

"Don't know for sure. She's running a little temperature."

"And what are you doing for her?"

"Not much. Just aspirin, till we know what's wrong."

"Well, that's a shame, you know. We're gonna have 25,000 people out there this afternoon that's gonna be mighty disappointed." He waited, but Frank didn't say anything. "But that's the way it goes I guess."

"Might have to scratch her from the next one, too. Depends what we come up with."

Noe's heart sank. The next one was a big one, the Champagne. A mile stakes race, it was the climax of the fall series for juveniles. Though it was contested almost exclusively by colts, fillies were eligible to enter, and Frank had indicated he was going to try Ruffian against the undefeated Foolish Pleasure in that race. It was an irresistible matchup, one the press had been calling for since Saratoga. Very big box office. Kenny Noe's job was writing nine races a day, six days a week, and it was always a challenge, but the real reward was getting the superstars to lock horns. Personally and professionally, he hated to see the filly miss that race.

The crowds would start arriving in a few hours for the afternoon's card, many drawn specifically by Ruffian's presence in the Frizette. Her name was already printed in the program; she was still listed in the *Form* and all the morning papers. The groans wouldn't start until people looked up at the chalkboards where late scratches were written out by hand, or when they heard Dave Johnson, the track announcer, intoning those same names through the loudspeakers before the first race. The only people who wouldn't be sorry were the six other horsemen who had entered their fillies in the race. Now, instead of competing for place and show money, they had a chance to win.

Ruffian was glad to get out of her stall. Because Minnor had to care for his other horses, Frank asked Yates to lead the filly

around the makeshift walking ring, a path worn in the dirt behind the barn. She took one funny step when she first came out
under the shedrow, then eased right out of it. It was very slight,
but both men noticed. Something with the right hind. But what?
Yates led her forward and backward, then paused and started
up again. They could see nothing wrong.

"Back her up again." Frank lit another cigarette. "Now bring
her over this way." He studied every move, eliminating one possibility after another. She didn't seem stiff. Her range of motion
didn't appear limited. All they really had to go on was that one
funny step.

The most likely problem would be with the stifle or the hock.
That was difficult to detect, and like many minor injuries, it
could have happened anytime—turning around in the stall, lying down, getting up. It didn't take much to throw off the legs
of an animal as finely tuned as a thoroughbred.

"All right, that's enough," Frank said at last. "I'll get Prendergast over here and have him take pictures."

Jim Prendergast was the attending vet for Whiteley's stable
in New York. He was only twenty-eight years old, and in certain
areas he lacked experience, but he was smart and honest and
Frank had taken a liking to him right away. Though he stopped
by two or three times a day to see if there was anything he could
do, he'd grown used to the fact that his services were not needed
very often. Few trainers relied less on veterinary expertise than
Frank Whiteley.

Prendergast examined the filly and could detect no heat or
effusion in the leg. He took a series of X rays, and before they
could be developed, Frank suggested they call Alex Harthill in
Kentucky and ask him what he thought.

Dr. Harthill was widely recognized as one of the most brilliant—and controversial—equine veterinarians in the country.
He was an especially astute diagnostician, and, over the years,
Frank had depended on him for help when serious problems
arose. Harthill said he'd have to see the filly.

There was one slight problem. Harthill was not allowed to
practice in New York. He had been ruled off one of the other
East Coast tracks for some infraction, and the New York Racing
Association was honoring that ruling. Frank Whiteley wasn't.

Harthill took the next flight out.

By the time he arrived that afternoon, Prendergast had lo-
cated a little cloud in one of the X rays. That gave him the
location of the problem. Further pictures confirmed that there
was a hairline fracture of the phalanx bone in Ruffian's right
hind ankle. It was a very minor injury, probably not career
threatening, but to ensure the stability of the area, Harthill fitted
her with a plaster of paris cast.

At first Ruffian accepted it with her usual equanimity. Then,
less than two hours after Harthill had finished, she had a change
of heart. She began kicking her hind leg against the metal screen
at the front of her stall, trying to knock off the cast. Whiteley
and the vets waited a few minutes to see if she would relax.
When she kept kicking, they had no choice. If the cast wasn't
removed, the filly would smash her foot to bits.

Prendergast watched her with renewed respect. Ruffian was
the boss here; she was calling all the shots. If she could speak,
she couldn't have made herself any clearer.

Harthill cut off the cast, which now had a noticeable dent in
it, and handed it to the younger vet. Prendergast started to throw
it away, then changed his mind and locked it up inside his truck.
He was going to take it home. It would be his keepsake from
the filly.

The hard cast was replaced with a pillow cast, which was really
just elastic tape over very thick, absorbent cotton. This immo-
bilized the joint almost as well as the plaster of paris, and what
was more important, the filly tolerated it. It would have to be
changed every four or five days, when the cotton became com-
pressed, but that was no problem for Prendergast.

Early that evening, with everything under control, Harthill
flew back to Louisville.

Ruffian's 1974 campaign had come to an abrupt end. She would
spend the next eight weeks confined to her stall, her foot in a
pillow cast. There would be no Champagne Stakes for her, no
Foolish Pleasure, no chance to meet the colts. But, provided
everything went well, she would have something much more
valuable: a three-year-old season.

4

LeRoy Jolley, like all trainers, was free to change riders whenever it suited him. That's why Jacinto was worried. After missing
the Hopeful because of his suspension, he wondered if the trainer
would give someone else the mount on Foolish Pleasure. Jacinto
had ridden him only once, and two other riders had also brought
him home in front. But fortunately, Jacinto had Fats as his agent,
and when the colt's next race, the Cowdin, rolled around on September 25, he had once again been named as the rider.

Although Foolish Pleasure had not been so dominant in his
races as Ruffian had been in hers, he did have the same record—
five victories in five starts—and it was hard to argue with an
undefeated horse. In the Cowdin he was once again the favorite.
The track was listed as fast that afternoon, but the skies grew
threatening as the horses went to the post. All of a sudden the
clouds burst, and the field took off under fierce and pounding
rains.

A brutal wind lashed against them down the backstretch.
Mud kicked up by the horses in front pelted those who followed.
Jacinto kept his colt tucked into fourth, letting him feel his way
over the sloppy track, making sure he could handle the footing
before asking for any real speed. Then, on the turn, he began
to emerge. From between the sheets of rain, far out from the
rail, he moved steadily towards the front, sure-footed and drawing away. He won by 6½ lengths, in 1:22⅗ seconds. Considering
the conditions, it was an excellent time. The colt had shown
maturity and assurance in the face of difficulties. Jacinto was
impressed.

Ten days later the two were paired once again for the Champagne. This time the bettors sent Foolish Pleasure off as the 3-to-10 choice. He had been the favorite in every one of his starts, and he had not yet shown the public any reason to bet against him.

But before the feature went off, a colt named Wajima attracted more than a little attention running in a sprint. This late-blooming son of Bold Ruler was making only the second start of his career, but even before he began racing, he had garnered headlines: The year before, at the Keeneland Sales, he had brought a record price for a yearling when he was sold for $600,000. He was sent to Claiborne to be broken, which made him a member of Ruffian's yearling class—the class of '73—though they were never anywhere near each other on the farm.

Wajima won his race that afternoon, but he had a long way to go to prove himself, and as soon as he was led off the track, everyone's attention returned to the afternoon's big draw: Foolish Pleasure and his six-race winning streak. Foolish Pleasure's owner, John L. Greer, took great pride in pointing out that his colt, purchased at the Saratoga Yearling Sales, had cost only $20,000.

Jacinto felt confident as he steered the colt into the gate. Confident, but not overconfident. There was always pressure in a race, especially aboard a horse who had never lost. Jacinto had been feeling that unusual pressure all year, with the filly; it doubled when he became the regular rider for Foolish Pleasure as well. One of the ironies of life was that a jockey could go for years and never get a mount who ran up a long unbeaten streak. Now, in the same season, Jacinto had two of them.

Though the last thing in the world Jacinto wanted was for Ruffian to be hurt, part of him was relieved that her minor injury had prevented a head-on confrontation between the two undefeated juveniles. Up at Saratoga, reporters had started asking him which horse he would choose, if he had to choose. Jacinto, who was generally too outspoken for his own good, was unusually circumspect. "*If* I ever have to choose, then I'll make my choice." That was all he would say.

Unlike the Cowdin, run in a sudden downpour, the Champagne took place under ideal conditions: a crisp autumn afternoon, clear skies, a fast track. Foolish Pleasure was way outside in post 9. When the bell rang, he got off beautifully and remained slightly behind the front-runners until they reached the turn. Then Jacinto steered him towards the rail, and with a rush he started making up ground. With little effort he managed to stick his head in front of Bombay Duck and Lefty, the horses who had led the field from the start.

As they headed for home, Foolish Pleasure had a solid lead, so solid that the colt began acting like the race was over: He started to relax and look around. Not taking anything—even seven lengths—for granted, Jacinto lit into him with the whip. That got his attention, and even though a colt named Harvard Man made a good run down the stretch, he couldn't catch Foolish Pleasure, who crossed the wire six lengths in front. The crowd gave Foolish Pleasure a thundering ovation. They were saluting not only this one race, but his entire juvenile season. Foolish Pleasure deserved every clap and whistle. He had beaten everything they had thrown at him from April to October. He had been tested over six different tracks, at six different distances, under all types of conditions. He had won under pressure and he had won with ease.

Jacinto was proud of him. He didn't have the brilliance or the presence of Ruffian. He didn't set records every time out or make the hair on the back of your neck stand on end. But he was a terrific horse; a gutsy athlete who did everything you asked; a fighter with a big heart. Best of all, he constantly improved, winning with more authority each time out.

In addition to training Foolish Pleasure for John Greer, LeRoy Jolley conditioned horses for Bert and Diana Firestone, who had recently built a training facility near Leesburg, Virginia. Now, after conferring with Greer, Jolley announced that he would be taking Foolish Pleasure down there, along with the rest of his stable, for the winter.

"What else has he got to prove?" Jolley asked the group of reporters that gathered after the Champagne. The answer was simple: nothing.

Nobody asked him, but Jacinto, too, thought it was a good idea to rest the colt over the winter. Let him grow a bit more, let him relax, let him mature. They could test him in Florida, bringing him along in the prep races, stretching him out gradually over longer and longer distances. Then, if the colt stayed healthy and didn't get into trouble, when the first Saturday in May rolled around, Jacinto would have himself a horse for the Kentucky Derby.

5

The predawn frost was scattered like silver pebbles across the paddocks at the Training Center. The breath of horses and riders formed pale clouds that stood out for a moment against the dark green background of the pines before vanishing into the air.

Ruffian stood quietly at the back of her stall, gazing out the window. She had been an exceptionally good patient. Apart from rejecting the initial cast, she had not paid much attention to the injured ankle. She sometimes pushed around her feed tub in disgust—her rations had to be reduced since she wasn't getting exercise—but she had surprised everyone at the barn by her overall acceptance of confinement. It was, they felt, as if she understood what was necessary to help herself along.

Since arriving at Camden in the middle of November, she had experienced only one minor setback. A local vet, who stopped by every few days to change the pillow cast, had inadvertently wrapped it too tight. Minnor noticed right away and called Whiteley's attention to it. The bandage was replaced, but the irritation caused a knot to form on the front of the filly's ankle. This inflammation erupted into a small, pus-filled blister that Minnor treated with Furacin. It was nothing serious, but the incident worried Frank enough that, after speaking with Stuart Janney, he decided it would be best to fly Harthill in from Kentucky every few weeks to supervise the filly's recovery.

Minnor had been with the filly constantly, tending to her morning and afternoon, but by December, when Ruffian was finally allowed out of her stall to start walking under the shed-

row, Minnor was no longer the man leading her by the shank—
he had quit.

The reason he gave for this decision was simply that he was
tired of traveling each year and wanted to stay put. He had a
wife and kids in Camden, he was thirty-five years old, and he
wanted a more settled life. All that may have been true, but
rumors around the barn suggested he was less than pleased with
Whiteley's year-end bonuses. Some trainers followed an old tra-
dition of filtering down one percent of the purse—which
amounted to ten percent of the trainer's cut—to the groom who
cared for the winning horse. Other trainers felt this system pe-
nalized hard workers who happened to be assigned to less successful horses, and so handed out fixed bonuses to everyone
when the time came. This was generally the method Whiteley
favored, and since he was widely known for conservative behavior when it came to spending money, there were always some
stablehands who felt undervalued at the end of the year.

Minnor, being a proud man, wasn't going to go begging, but
others in the barn guessed he had felt slighted by what Whiteley
offered him. He had, after all, had the filly. And it was hard not
to look around at other barns and see that the grooms who had
the big horses were duly rewarded.

Minnor himself never uttered a word in public that even
remotely sounded like a complaint. He gave two weeks notice,
and when Whiteley handed him his final paycheck, the trainer
asked him if he wanted to reconsider. Minnor shook his head,
and Whiteley assured him that any time he wanted a job he was
welcome back.

Minnor's departure was not the only change around the barn
in the last few months. Both Ric Martin and John Bruno had
quit while they were still at Belmont. Barclay Tagg had not traveled with Whiteley to South Carolina, having decided it was time
to go out on his own again. He returned to Maryland to begin
training a public stable, and Mike Bell took over his duties. Then,
in November, Frank made a more personal change as well. After
having been divorced for several years, Frank got married for
the second time, to a woman he had met in Camden. The marriage did not alter his routine at the barn.

With Minnor gone, Dan Williams was assigned to Ruffian.

His experience, patience, and devotion were just what the filly required. In fact, she required so much of it, Frank took the unusual step of assigning Dan to care for her full-time. Generally, each groom had three horses, but Frank had a feeling this was a fair trade.

The next morning—after shaking out her stall, wiping her empty feed tub, picking her feet, and rubbing her down—Dan led Ruffian out for a long walk around the barn. Soon he was handwalking her for an hour and a half in the morning and an hour and a half in the early afternoon. The aim of these leisurely strolls was to have her ready for a rider after New Year's, when Frank planned to start sending her over to the track.

He had hoped she could be let out into one of the Porta-paddocks that were set up behind the barns. Horses were animals of freedom. Frank had always believed that, and he tried to let his horses spend as much unrestricted time as possible outside. There were also large permanent paddocks where he released horses overnight or for several hours during the day, but he would never let Ruffian into one of these because he didn't want to encourage any all-out running on her part. The Porta-paddocks were small, and he thought they would be safe.

One morning, he had Dan lead her out into one and unhook her shank. The first thing she did, out of sheer exuberance at this taste of freedom, was to kick up her back legs and then rear up and paw the air. That was no problem in itself; under the circumstances, rearing and bucking were just signs of feeling good. But Ruffian was so big and so frisky that the third time she stood straight up, she hoisted a foreleg right over the edge of the high fence, and Frank's heart skidded into his throat. Her half brother, Icecapade, had smashed right through a Porta-paddock one winter when he'd been down there and run off all the way to Wrenfield before they could catch him.

"Ain't gonna work, Dan." Whiteley shook his head. "Ain't gonna work. You're gonna have to handwalk her even out here."

Dan nodded. They both preferred to give the filly her freedom, but the risks were too great. The spirit that worked to her advantage on the track, that made her such an extraordinary runner, would work against her under these conditions. Those carefree yearling days, loose in a paddock in the sun and rain and snow, were gone. Perhaps when Ruffian was retired from the racetrack and sent to breed, when she was ready to have free-running foals of her own, she would once again know the pleasure of being turned out between green earth and blue sky. But until that day arrived, she would never again be allowed outside her stall unless she was attached to a human being.

6

The fourth annual Eclipse Awards banquet was held on January 31, 1975, at the Fairmont Hotel in San Francisco. The Janneys could not attend, so Frank had flown out in their place to accept Ruffian's statuette for Best Two-Year-Old Filly.

Eleven hundred people had gathered in the ballroom for the presentation ceremonies. Historians had conferred retrospective honors on thoroughbreds dating back to the 1800s, but it was only since 1936 that various organized groups had begun voting for the champions in each division. This sometimes resulted in conflicting or "shared" championship titles, and it was not until 1971, with the creation of the Eclipse Awards—voted on by the *Daily Racing Form*, Thoroughbred Racing Associations, and the National Turf Writers Association—that the process had finally been consolidated into one unified effort.

The announcement of the winners contained no real surprises that year. Undefeated Foolish Pleasure, who looked better and better as the year wore on, captured the Best Two-Year-Old Colt award. Chris Evert, who had won four of her seven starts, including the Filly Triple Crown and the match—or, more accurately, the mis-match—race against Miss Musket, and had finished in the money in each of her other outings, was the overwhelming choice for Best Three-Year-Old Filly. The Best Three-Year-Old Colt was the only category that generated any argument. The title went to Little Current, who had won the Preakness and the Belmont after finishing fifth in the Kentucky Derby. He had then lost two big races—the Monmouth Invitational and the Travers—to Holding Pattern. Still, the consensus was that, on the whole, Holding Pattern's victories had not come in the same caliber of races as Little Current's, and that ultimately settled that issue.

After the Spinaway, there had been some talk that Ruffian might be a contender for the overall Horse-of-the-Year Award if she faced—and beat—colts in the fall. That would have been an extraordinary honor, for a juvenile almost never displayed the talent to be rated higher than an older horse. Secretariat had been the only recent exception, in 1972, and that was because of his own outstanding performance and the fact that the older horses that year did not have one clear-cut leader to attract the votes.

In 1974 they did, and his name was Forego. Forego was a huge bay gelding, seventeen hands high, 77 inches around the girth, who weighed over 1200 pounds. He was owned and bred in the name of the Lazy F Ranch and trained by Sherrill Ward, one of the grand old masters of the game.

That year Forego had won eight of thirteen starts and finished out of the money only once. He had succeeded at everything from seven-furlong sprints to the two-mile Jockey Club Gold Cup. He carried over 130 pounds on four occasions and appeared just as strong at the end of the year as he had at the beginning. So it was fitting that his owner, Martha Gerry, had to make three trips from her table to the speaker's platform, to receive awards for Best Sprinter, Best Handicap Horse, and the ultimate championship award, Horse of the Year.

Even Frank agreed that Forego deserved it. He respected a hardknocking horse and a trainer who could keep him sound and interested in running ten months a year. And he had enjoyed watching the gelding flash some brilliant speed in his sprints, the last time carrying 131 pounds while covering seven furlongs in 1:21⅗. That was horseracing.

But Frank wouldn't have traded any horse in the world for Ruffian. Although she had been forced prematurely to shorten her season because of the hairline fracture, what she had shown Frank in her first five starts was more than enough to convince him. Reporters had quoted him saying things that seemed completely out of character. Frank had actually told them that Ruffian was the best horse he had ever trained—not the best two-year-old, or the best filly, but the best horse, period.

In November, when the editor of *The Blood-Horse* had visited

Camden and asked the trainer about those highly unlikely
quotes, Frank sheepishly confessed that they were accurate. He
even went a step further: Ruffian, he asserted, was not only the
best horse he had ever trained, but the best horse he had ever
seen.

There was only one part of the evening that Frank Whiteley
didn't look forward to, and that was making the acceptance
speech on behalf of the Janneys. When Ruffian's award was announced, everybody could see why Frank had been so successful
running track as a boy. He leaped from his chair and was at the
podium in the blink of an eye. There had been several noticeably short speeches that evening, but Frank's was the shortest of
them all: "Weappreciateitandwe'rerealproudofherandwethank
you." He lowered his eyes and charged back towards his table
as if he were hurrying to get in out of the rain. He almost equaled
his record for the 50-yard dash.

Frank returned to Camden the morning after the awards ceremony.
    "Where you been?" Jackie asked him.
    "What do you care?"
    "I don't," she laughed. "We enjoyed the break from you and
your grumbling these past two days!"
    "Is that right? I was out grumbling in San Francisco, matter
of fact."
    "San Francisco?" Then Jackie made the connection. "Did you
pick up the filly's award?"
    "What if I did?"
    "Oh, Frank! Why didn't you tell us?"
    "Goddamn, Jackie, there's a lotta things I don't tell you!"
    It was Jackie's turn to sound smug. "Oh, yeah? Like the fact
that yesterday was your birthday?"
    Frank was tapping out a cigarette as he moved off down the
barn. "Hell, that don't matter. It's a day like any other day."
    "Well, Happy Birthday anyway, Frank!"
    He shook his head at her and tried not to smile. But it had
been a pleasant coincidence—that on the day the filly got her
first Eclipse Award, he had turned sixty years old.

7

A good blacksmith was essential to a successful stable. That's why Jarboe Talbott was still shoeing Frank's horses after thirty years.

At six feet, two inches, Jarboe was a massive man, with a broad back, powerful legs, and huge hands rough with calluses. He was almost Frank's age, but his hair was still sandy-blond, and the mischief had never faded from his clear blue eyes.

The two men had come up together, in Maryland, and they could set the barn rocking with tales of the old days. When Frank shifted from Laurel to New York, in 1972, he insisted that Jarboe continue shoeing his stock. That was fine with Jarboe. He didn't like to fly, but he'd drive up every few weeks, take care of business, and drive home. Technically, he wasn't permitted to shoe horses in New York. Jarboe belonged to the Blacksmiths Union, and when he'd joined, shortly after the Second World War, union blacksmiths could work anywhere in the country. Then New York began its own system, requiring state licenses. Jarboe thought that was nonsense; he wasn't about to go take a test from some upstart who hadn't even been born when he'd started shoeing horses. He and Frank just ignored all that red tape, and since Jarboe wasn't trying to set up there permanently, nobody had ever complained.

During the winter, from the last of October till the first of April, Jarboe lived in Aiken, South Carolina, about a hundred miles from Camden. He drove over to the Training Center—it didn't take long if there weren't too many cops on the highway—two or three times a week, depending on how much work

Frank needed, but this last visit had been the result of a specific concern.

Not about Ruffian. The filly was doing fine. It was early February, and she'd been galloping since the start of the year. Yates had come down for the two months that the New York tracks were closed, and he'd been getting on the filly's back. In another month Frank planned to start breezing her. Everyone was cautiously optimistic. She seemed stronger than ever, and, for the time being, she was not the one Frank was worried about. He was concerned about the filly in the next stall, his other favorite, Honorable Miss.

Honorable Miss had recently been flown back from California, where David Whiteley had taken her for the winter. After failing dismally in several starts, she had been returned to Frank to figure out what was wrong.

The first thing Frank did was call in Jarboe. "Take a look at that mare, will you?" Frank asked. "David couldn't find anything the matter, but she just wasn't acting like herself out there on the coast. Rooster!" he hollered. "Bring that goddamn mare out here, will you? Walk her around for Jarboe."

The groom led Honorable Miss up and back under the shedrow while Jarboe studied her in silence. The subtleties of equine locomotion were the focus of the blacksmith's art. Anybody with half a brain could nail in a shoe. The challenge was figuring out how to compensate for imbalances or quirky strides or a whole host of foot problems that could keep a horse from reaching its potential. A blacksmith had to understand the way a horse traveled, because the way it moved affected everything it did. "No foot, no horse"—that was the bottom line in racing. As Rooster led Honorable Miss up and down the shedrow, Jarboe watched from every angle.

Finally, the blacksmith shook his head. "Ain't nothing wrong, Frank!" he boomed. "Come on, let me get my box." It didn't take him long to pull off the old shoes and replace them with new ones. "This old gal is fine, Frank. Just fine." He kept talking while he worked, without looking up. He knew Frank was standing right outside the stall. "Some old fool out there just shoed her wrong, that's all! She'll be good as new, you'll see."

When he was done, he stood up and scratched the mare's

oversized ears. She lowered her head and bumped her nose in-
sistently against his chest.

"Here." Frank reached into his shirt pocket. "Wants one of
these." He ripped the plastic off a Gelusil tablet.

"Goddamn it, Frank, you know, your horses are 'bout as
screwed up as you are!" Jarboe gathered up his stuff. "Who's
next?"

8

The yellow jessamine had climbed high up along the outside of the fence that circled the training track. Its delicate, horn-shaped blossoms had long since trumpeted the arrival of spring, and its thin sweet smell, something like honeysuckle, filled the air with hope.

This was to be Ruffian's last breeze in Camden. It was April 8, and if everything went well she'd be shipped up to New York in a few days with the remainder of the stable. Whiteley sat watching from Sled Dog's back.

He felt safe working her at Wrenfield. The track was much deeper than those in New York, which was one reason he liked bringing young horses along down there. A soft track was easier on immature bones, especially those recovering from fractures.

Frank pressed his thumb against the button of his stopwatch as Ruffian took off at the five-eighths pole. As usual, trainers and stablehands from the other barns had lined up along the rail to watch the filly make her move. When Frank pressed the button a second time, the watch read 1:02⅕. He wasn't the only observer who had timed her. Word would get back to Belmont— eight hundred miles away—before the filly finished cooling out. A work like that would start scaring off the competition: 1:02 at the training track translated into :57 and change in New York. That would convince just about everybody that the filly was back in shape.

Now Frank had to figure out the right spot for her first start of the year—the right distance, the right conditions, even the right competition. His main concern for her comeback was that Ruffian not immediately face the toughest of her rivals. This was a filly who did not want to get beat. Not only that, she didn't even want to let another horse stick its nose in front of her. Frank knew she would push herself as hard as she needed to, no matter how she felt, and he didn't want any all-out effort from her until she had at least tested the mended leg under racing conditions.

After he had chosen his spot, he would need to hide it from the rest of the world until the last possible moment. Otherwise, trainers could avoid that race. Kenny Noe might put a little friendly pressure on them, but nobody could force them to enter a race. If the race didn't fill and was canceled, the filly could be stuck at the last minute without a solid prep before the spring stakes began. Hiding the 1975 debut of the most eagerly awaited horse in New York might have seemed a daunting task to most trainers, but not Frank Whiteley. He had succeeded in camouflaging Ruffian's maiden appearance the year before, allowing her to sneak off at odds of better than 4 to 1. He took it as a personal challenge to succeed again this year.

After all, in this particular art he was the acknowledged master. They hadn't dubbed him the "Fox of Laurel" for nothing. He had a reputation to uphold. More important, he had a filly to protect.

Frank had once again been assigned to Barn 34 at Belmont Park, and when he arrived with the bulk of his stable, Ruffian was led into Stall 34, the place of honor next to the breezeway. A small crowd had gathered to catch a glimpse of the filly, but all they could see was that she was as gleaming and self-possessed as she had been the year before. They couldn't tell anything about the injury that had shortened her two-year-old campaign because her legs were still encased in the thick, standing bandages that all horses traveled in. Dan Williams was at her side, looking drawn and serious.

Friends stopped by during the day to greet Frank, and a few even ventured to ask about his plans for the filly. He repeated what he had told the *Form* the week before: The filly was coming along faster than he'd anticipated; he'd probably have to find something for her before the Comely at the end of the month; he didn't think she could wait that long. It would probably be the Prioress, a six-furlong race on the twenty-first. The leg seemed good, the doc was pleased. Matter of fact, Doc Harthill couldn't quite believe the progress she'd made; couldn't even find a trace of the fracture in the latest X rays. But it was rare that a horse ever healed up completely from any kind of break. They would just have to wait and see.

The next day Dan was walking Ruffian under the shedrow when Jacinto and Fats stopped by to say hello. The first thing they noticed was the filly's attitude. She was bouncing on her toes, practically jumping out of her skin. When the reporters asked about her next race, though, Frank shrugged. Oh, maybe in a week or ten days, he told them, if she breezed well at Belmont, she'd be ready to go.

Alone in the tackroom, Frank pulled out the condition book and once more went over all the upcoming races. There was no way in the world he could wait another week or ten days to put this filly in a race. Ruffian was ready. Now.

PART FOUR

1

"The Match is off." Frank Whiteley folded his arms across his chest and stared straight ahead. "I mean it. I'll take her out of the race."

An uncomfortable silence settled over the informal gathering of officials. Finally someone spoke. "Frank, he's got to have a New York license to shoe here. That's the rule. It's impossible to work here without one."

"Is that a fact? Who the hell you think's been shoeing her all along? Her and all my other horses, too?"

"Well, we didn't know about it before. There was no complaint before. It wasn't in the newspapers. Be reasonable, Frank. All he's got to do is take the exam."

"The hell with the goddamn exam! This man knows more about shoeing horses than anyone I've ever met. I ain't asking him to take no exam."

"But, Frank, it's not even an exam really, he just has to make a shoe for them."

"Look, damn it." Frank stood up. "I got a barnful of horses to get back to. Make any damn rule you want. Do whatever the hell you please. I'm just telling you one thing. Either Jarboe Talbott shoes my filly or there'll be no match race."

Frank was so angry he refused to talk to any reporters that afternoon. He had enough worries without new hassles from the Association. The outside pressures were building as the Match approached. Frank tried to ignore them, but they were unlike anything he'd seen before, and he had been through it all: two Kentucky Derbys; Preaknesses and Belmonts; even the Arc de

Triomphe. The coverage of those events had been intense and, in many ways, more demanding, but they had remained horse-races. This wasn't just a horserace anymore. His filly was being turned into a symbol and the whole thing was getting out of control.

It was the male-female angle that had stirred everybody up. Boy against Girl. Colt versus Filly. It was a big publicity stunt. Everybody knew that. To draw attention to racing, to give a popular, timely image to the sport; to put people in the stands and at the betting windows. To help out the New York Racing Association. To sell newspapers. That was all. And yet . . .

And yet, Frank had to admit, it had touched a nerve. The response had been unbelievable. People who had never followed the sport, who had never watched a horserace in their lives, had gotten caught up in this event. Even people who had been in the game forever, who should have known better, were acting as if something bigger were at stake, as if this race would really prove something about the world in general: that women were better than men, or men were better than women. The whole thing was ridiculous. Horseraces proved only one thing: who the fastest horse was on a given day.

They could call it whatever they liked—the Great Match Race or the Battle of the Sexes—but the confrontation between Ruffian and Foolish Pleasure was a horserace. A big race, to be sure. An important race. But still, just a race.

That's what Frank Whiteley believed. Or wanted to believe. But Frank Whiteley was in the minority.

Frank had been training for the Janneys since 1969, and they allowed him to make all the decisions concerning their horses. He determined how fast they were to be brought along, when and where they raced, who would ride them, everything. Everything, that is, until the Match itself.

Even then, Stuart Janney had conferred with Frank before giving his consent. He asked Frank if he thought the filly had a chance, and Frank told him honestly he thought that she could win. He had, however, expressed some reservations about the timing—he had planned to rest Ruffian after the Filly Triple Crown, a series of three stakes races at increasing distances, run on May 10, May 30, and June 21. He wanted to keep her out of competition during the hottest part of the summer, then test her against the colts later in August, probably in the Travers up at Saratoga. In the fall she would be ready to take on older horses.

Mr. Janney agreed it was an excellent plan, but sometime that spring other factors intervened. The clamor for a confrontation between Ruffian and the colts—specifically Foolish Pleasure, whose undefeated two-year-old season had paralleled her own—grew to such proportions, mainly in the press, but also from various track managements, that Mr. Janney felt they could no longer avoid it. If they refused, they'd be made to appear selfish and unsporting, the worst criticism you could level at a genuine old-school horseman who sincerely believed he owed something to the game. It would also imply a lack of faith in their filly.

"Frank, I don't see how we can get out of it," Janney confessed in a phone call one night. "They've got us up against the wall. The newspapers won't let go of it, and if we're going to have to do it, we may as well do it here in New York." He hesitated. "It would be a big boost to the Association, you know."

Frank knew then that it would take place. Dinny Phipps, Barbara Janney's nephew, had recently been named vice-president of the board of trustees of the New York Racing Association. No one ever directly referred to the family connection, but Frank understood. The Association could use the help. Something to attract attention and generate good publicity.

It wasn't necessarily a bad thing, nor was Frank opposed to it outright. However, like many trainers, he thought head-to-head confrontations, where both horses had to give everything over the entire distance, were awfully wearing on a horse. He would have preferred to follow his original schedule and leave any confrontation with the colts—match race or full field—till the fall.

Stuart Janney also had one major reservation: You could not scratch a horse from a match race. If your horse was not one hundred percent that day, it was too bad. You ran anyway. In regular stakes races, you could withdraw up to the last minute; in a match, too many people—in this case, millions of people— were counting on you. Once you had committed yourself, you could not let them down. He had no reason to think the filly would be less than fit, but he was a horseman. He knew about the thousand little things that could go wrong.

He also knew that Frank wasn't thrilled with this decision, but the trainer had accepted it and would have the filly ready for the race. He assured Frank that once the Match was over, Ruffian's schedule would once again be entirely up to him, and she could have all the rest she needed.

2

Jacinto usually spent his winters in Florida, riding at Gulfstream and Hialeah, but in the fall of '74 David Whiteley decided to ship his stable to California for a few months, and Jacinto followed him out West. He knew that after Foolish Pleasure had been rested in Virginia, Jolley planned to bring him along via the Florida route. Jacinto made it clear to the trainer that distance was no problem; he would travel anywhere to ride a colt like that.

Foolish Pleasure began his three-year-old campaign in February with an easy victory in a seven-furlong allowance race. Jacinto was aboard, and he returned a few weeks later to ride him in the Flamingo, where the colt extended his winning streak to nine races.

Then, on March 29, Foolish Pleasure went off as the favorite in the Florida Derby and lost for the first time in his career. Afterwards, it was discovered that he had torn the frogs of both forefeet, an injury Jolley compared to having your fingernails ripped out. He was completely rested for the next five days and put on round-the-clock iodine treatments for his feet. Jacinto wasn't worried. He had complete faith in the colt. Foolish Pleasure had a terrific spirit and he was being well cared for. He would ship to New York for his final preparations, but there was no reason to think that he would not return to form in time for the Kentucky Derby.

Jacinto looked forward to the coming year, but he was also something of a fatalist. Things didn't always work out the way you thought they would. Racing was a precarious profession. He couldn't forget that even if he wanted to.

He had been reminded all too clearly out in California.

Santa Anita was one of the most beautiful racetracks in the world. The San Gabriel mountains towered in the background, stark and majestic, providing a dramatic setting for each day's performance.

It was the afternoon of January 18. The race was nothing special—three-year-old maidens—one of the bread and butter events that made up every program in the country, and Jacinto was on the type of horse he would forget as soon as he crossed the wire. Next to him in the starting gate was Alvaro Pineda, an excellent rider and one of the most popular jockeys on the Southern California circuit. Originally from Mexico, Pineda, like Jacinto, was married and had two young children. He was twenty-nine years old.

Pineda's colt was making only the second start of his career and was very nervous going into the gate. As soon as the doors closed behind him, the colt panicked and charged forward, ramming the front. It was a wild move, and Pineda barely managed to scramble off and hop onto the narrow metal ledge along the inside wall. He balanced himself there while the assistant starter tried to settle the frantic colt.

Jacinto, poised in the adjoining stall, his horse under control, glanced over at the very instant that Pineda's colt lunged sideways in a frenzy, rearing up and whipping his head around at the same time.

Later, all Jacinto would remember was the explosive sound of the crack as the colt smashed Pineda's head against the upright steel bar at the back of the stall; that sound, and the horrifying sight of Pineda's skull split open just below the rim of his helmet, his brains oozing out onto his silks. He was dead even before the assistant starter got his arms around him and pulled him from the gate.

3

Spring had been on the cool side that year, which suited Frank Whiteley just fine. Hot weather could really take something out of a thoroughbred, especially the fast ones.

Yates got to the barn early and glanced in at Dan, who was cleaning Ruffian's feet with his hoof pick. She'd been pushier and a little less patient since returning to Belmont a few days earlier, and Dan was glad when Frank appeared and signaled him to start walking her around the shedrow.

A new routine was established for the filly that year: Squeaky was going to be the one riding her every day for her regular gallops, and Yates was getting on her only when she breezed. Frank had made a deal with Squeaky, paying him extra—unheard of for Whiteley—so that he'd skip Delaware and stay in New York. Squeaky's ability to steady the filly and keep her calm was more important than ever, because she had changed a little over the winter. She was tougher and stronger and more competitive. Even when exercising in the morning, she wanted to race everything in sight.

Yates was almost forty pounds lighter than Squeaky and he had a shorter fuse. That was okay for certain horses, but it had become clear that the filly would fight back against too much control. Squeaky was more willing to humor her, and he never tired of playing her favorite game: Ruffian would drop her head, challenging Squeaky to pick the reins up and get her in hand, and he would refuse the bait. She'd drop her head lower. Squeaky would still refuse. Sometimes, he joked, her head was so close to the ground he could hear her knees knocking against her chin. But if he gave in and picked her head up, she could run off,

which was what she wanted to do. This way, she continued galloping peacefully around the track, which was what Mr. Whiteley
wanted her to do. When Mike Bell teased him, saying he was
putting Ruffian to sleep instead of exercising her, Squeaky
smiled. "She just like a little schoolgirl, you know. Like a little
sister. She don't want nobody bossing her around."

Yates still hopped on the filly when Frank wanted some
speed, which was every six to ten days unless a race was coming
up; then Ruffian breezed more frequently. She had quickly made
the connection between what she was going to do with each of
her main riders, and she geared herself up accordingly as they
headed for the track.

The first time Yates rode Ruffian at Belmont that spring, Frank
warned him to be careful. Her mended hind leg had not been
tested over the track.

He repeated his instructions at the gap. "Take her three-
eighths, see how she feels."

Yates tossed out his half-finished cigarette. The muscles in
his shoulders and arms tensed as he wrapped the reins around
his fist. Ruffian snorted and kicked out as they entered the main
track.

"But take it easy, hear? Thirty-five and change. If she don't
feel a hundred percent, pull her up right away!"

Yates nodded. The track was in good shape, harder than the
one at Camden, but nice and even. The filly always went out
early, before it got too choppy from the morning's traffic. As he
jogged her around to warm up, Yates collected himself, took his
bearings to make sure of a clear path, then pressed his heels
against the filly's side.

Frank tried to signal him to slow down as soon as possible,
but the filly galloped out a half-mile in just a little over :47. She
had gone the three furlongs in :33⅘. Frank could see Frenchy
up in the stands, shaking his head, so he knew the clocker had
got her under :34 as well.

Frank grinned. This time Frenchy could rave all he wanted;
it was a Sunday morning, so the workout would not make it into
the *Form* until Tuesday. By then it wouldn't matter too much.
Frank had led everyone to believe he wasn't running Ruffian
until the Prioress on April 21. Word of her workout might get

around the backstretch, of course, but other trainers would assume Frank was just giving her a test over the surface. They had no idea he would go right back to his tackroom and dial the Racing Secretary.

"Mr. Noe!"

"Yes, Frank?"

"Got a horse for the eighth race tomorrow."

"Who's that, Frank?"

Frank leaned back, enjoying himself. "Name's Ruffian," he said.

"Please note the following late scratches." The voice of Dave Johnson was clear and strong as it carried through the loudspeakers to all corners of the track. "Please check your program." It was noon on Monday, April 14, time for him to bring the public up to date on jockey changes, overweights, and scratches before the first race went off at one-thirty. Any information that was received after the programs were printed, Johnson included in his prerace announcements. When he got to the feature, a six-furlong allowance race known as the Caltha Purse, he said, "Ladies and gentlemen, no scratches in the eighth race. No scratches in the eighth race. Please note, however, we do have a late workout time for Ruffian. The 1974 Juvenile Filly Champion went three furlongs yesterday morning on the main track in 33⅘ seconds. Three furlongs in :33 and four." If there was any doubt among the betting public, this workout was all the proof they needed that the filly was back in force. They lined up at the windows and sent her off at 1-to-10.

"You know what to do out there." Whiteley reached down as Jacinto bent his left knee, and in one fluid motion he lifted the jockey into the saddle. "Don't put pressure on her 'less you have to."

Jacinto adjusted his stirrups and smoothed out the reins. This was the first time he'd been on Ruffian since the Sorority, last July, and he felt the change immediately. It was not a question of size, but of power. Everything she had shown him the year before had been impressive, but now, in a single instant, he realized that what he had seen so far was only the beginning.

The other four fillies, all decent horses, were practically ignored. Their owners and trainers took it well. Whiteley had fooled everyone into thinking Ruffian would not run for another week, and because this was an allowance race, rather than a stakes, they were not permitted to scratch their horses without good cause. They smiled ruefully and shook their heads as reporters asked them the same question over and over. Yes, they conceded, one after the other. Whiteley had trapped them. He certainly had.

Frank walked alongside as Dan led Ruffian to the gap. "Listen, Por-ta Rican." Frank rarely talked to the rider once he was aboard. They both kept staring straight ahead. "Don't try to set any records out there."

Jacinto would have liked the reassuring presence of Squeaky and Sled Dog as he warmed up the filly, for Ruffian was ready to explode. She was not acting nasty, but she was full of reckless energy. She put her head down, took a few hops, skittered back and forth. She was enjoying every minute of her return, but under the circumstances, Jacinto couldn't afford to let her play. It was one thing to let her goof off in the morning: Squeaky was a lot heftier than Jacinto; he rode with a regular saddle, not a two-pound postage stamp; and he had the benefit of a martingale to give him a little more control of her head. He didn't have to worry about getting her into a starting gate and keeping her calm. Jacinto had his hands full.

Ruffian knew she was going to race again. After all those weeks confined to her stall, after all those weeks of nothing but walking, after all those weeks of slow, easy gallops—she was ready to get out there and run. It was the one thing Jacinto could not possibly let her do.

Unlike most trainers, Frank never used binoculars to watch a race. With his regular glasses he saw so well that the stablehands used to say he could pick out a grain of sand in a pile of sawdust. But he couldn't see through steel; once Jacinto got the filly into the gate, she was hidden from Whiteley's gaze. Ruffian had never needed a twitch or any kind of restraint at the start, but today she was acting up, putting her head down and laying up against the side of the gate. The assistant starter leaned in and reached for her bridle. There was nothing Whiteley could do but hope they quickly got her settled down. It was out of his hands. Then the bell rang and the gates opened.

Jacinto would have liked for Ruffian to relax immediately, but Ruffian had other ideas. She dragged him to the front, not giving him any choice, and only after she had established herself as the leader did she give in to his wishes and slow down. That was the compromise she offered. Jacinto had no choice but to accept.

As they coasted down the backstretch, Jacinto's efforts began to pay off: Ruffian ran the slowest first quarter of her career—23 seconds flat. Whiteley saw the time flash on the tote board and felt slightly relieved. Ruffian had settled down. She was going to cooperate.

Daryl Montoya, tagging along behind on Sir Ivor's Sorrow, knew that this was the moment to test the champion. He asked his filly to run.

Jacinto did nothing. He didn't shift his hands, he didn't show the whip, he didn't chirp to his horse. Montoya took note. Riders always watched each other, trying to pick up clues, like baserunners checking out the pitcher on the mound. The smallest signal could alert them to the fact that another horse was tiring, or preparing to make a move. As Montoya's horse approached, Ruffian simply picked up the pace and drew off. Catch me if you can, she seemed to say. It was a game, and Ruffian knew exactly how to play.

Montoya realized he was outclassed. He couldn't take anything away from his own filly, but she was no match for Ruffian. Ruffian didn't even need a rider! By the top of the stretch Montoya's objective had become more realistic: to hang on for second place.

Alone on the front end, just inside the eighth pole, Jacinto finally let Ruffian go. Suddenly she was ahead by 4¾ lengths, and already they were at the wire.

The time was relatively slow for her—1:09⅖. It was the only outing of her career when she did not break or equal a record. It was, nevertheless, a fast time over the track at that point in the season. The fact that she had achieved it while hardly breaking a gallop made it more impressive than the stopwatch alone indicated.

The reporters moved in at their first opportunity.

"She looked good, Frank."

"Yep, she did."

"Any difference from before her injury?"

"Not really. She's a little rougher now. Not in the stall, but when you work around her."

"Any particular reason for the bandages?" Ruffian had run for the first time wearing long elastic run-down bandages on her hind legs. They were quite common, especially at the sandier tracks like Belmont, which tended to abrade the skin on a horse's fetlocks, and elicited questions only because the year before she had worn nothing but the small, patchlike stickers.

"Nope. Just protective. She runs hard, you know."

The reporters smiled at the understatement.

"What's next, Frank?"

The trainer shook his head. "We're still aiming for the Comely, end of the month."

"Not going to Kentucky?"

Frank looked disgusted. "We were never going to Kentucky. I told you guys that six months ago."

"But a lot of people are saying she's got it all over the colts this year, that she's by far the best of either sex. They say your filly is the three-year-old to beat. What do you think, Frank?"

"She may be. I don't know." Whiteley tapped out a cigarette. "But they ain't gonna beat her in the Derby 'cause I ain't running her there."

4

Monday morning sessions in the hotbox were particularly painful. Sunday was still the dark day at the track, and jockeys had a tendency to eat more than usual on their one day off.

Most riders learned not to let their weight balloon beyond a manageable margin; the backstretch was full of ex-jocks who had eaten themselves out of promising careers. For many riders, like Jacinto, controlling their weight was simply a matter of eating moderately and sweating off one or two pounds every morning. For others, like Braulio Baeza, sweating was not enough; he engaged in a constant struggle to maintain himself on a diet that reportedly consisted of nothing but lettuce or celery for days at a time. Still others, like Vince Bracciale, had mastered the art of heaving. They ate whatever they wanted several times a day; afterwards, they emptied the contents of their stomachs into the porcelain heaving bowl that occupied its own little stall, right in the middle of the row of toilets.

The hotbox itself was debilitating. Temperatures hovered around 180 degrees. If you stayed inside too long, you could become too weak to stand up, let alone control a thousand pounds of horseflesh. A small glass window had been cut into the wall so the masseurs in the next room could keep watch: A lone jockey sitting inside would be in big trouble if he collapsed and no one knew about it. A tank of oxygen was mounted by the door in case of emergencies.

On this Monday, though, the room was crowded and everyone was complaining. They had all overdone it, and now they were regretting the price they had to pay. Even if they devoted the entire morning to this torture, a number of riders were not going to make weight. That would infuriate the trainers, because no one wanted his horse to carry more than the assigned load.

Jacinto listened for a long time, eyes closed, as one after another of his colleagues moaned about their predicament. Jacinto was thinking. There were no major races that afternoon, and he was not riding anything for either Mr. Whiteley or LeRoy Jolley. What was the harm? Finally, he spoke up.

"I got a idea."

Everybody turned to him.

He opened his eyes. "None of us gonna make weight today, right?"

They nodded.

"I can fix it so we don't got to."

"How? O'Hara would never let us get away with anything!"

"Leave it to me. Only thing is, you all got to agree with whatever I say, okay? You got to go along, no matter what."

There were a few raised eyebrows and some skeptical remarks, but they all agreed. If anybody could cook up a scheme, it would be Jacinto.

"Okay. Wait here." Jacinto hitched up his towel, left the room, and marched up to the Clerk of Scales' desk.

"Mr. O'Hara!" he burst out indignantly. "You gotta get José Amy out of the sweatbox! I saw with my own eyes! That guy got crabs! They crawling all over the place! If I go home with crabs, my wife gonna give me a divorce! I can't stay in there!"

"What are you talking about?" Jack O'Hara looked incredulous.

"In the sweatbox! You come look! They crawling all over Amy! I not going back there!" Jacinto's face, red and blotchy from the heat, added to his outraged appearance. He was so vigorous in his protest that his towel kept slipping and he had to clutch at his waist to prevent it from falling down.

"All right. Let's take a look." O'Hara called over one of his assistants, and Jacinto trailed after them through the long hallway back to the sauna.

Some officials would have insisted on examining José Amy directly, but not Mr. O'Hara. Jacinto was counting on the fact that he was too proper for that. Still, until the Clerk of Scales actually opened the door to the hotbox and ordered everyone out, Jacinto did not fully relax.

"What's going on?" the jocks muttered as they cinched their towels and trooped out, glancing at Jacinto.

O'Hara, impeccable as always in jacket and tie, did not go in and inspect the room. He accepted Jacinto's report at face value. Quietly, he ordered his assistant to shut off the heat and have the room scrubbed and disinfected. The riders stared at each other, jaws hanging open.

Finally, in a voice full of contrition, Jacinto burst out, "I sorry, but I had to tell about Amy!" José Amy tried to look innocent of whatever disaster he had caused. He, too, stared expectantly at Jacinto, waiting for him to go on. "I had to tell about the crabs." Jacinto risked a quick smile while O'Hara's attention was diverted. "I said I saw them, and we don't want to stay in there when you got the crabs, cause they might get on everybody else and cause lotta trouble!"

One by one the riders started to catch on. "Yeah," someone whined, "that's true, but now how're we gonna make weight?"

"I'm sorry, gentlemen." O'Hara motioned for them to move out of the narrow corridor where they stood crowded together. They inched past the massage tables and gathered in the hallway by the whirlpool and the ice machine. "Due to a health hazard of which I have just been informed, the sauna will be closed for the remainder of the day. And José," he turned to the dumbfounded jockey, "please give this matter your immediate medical attention or I will bar you from this locker room indefinitely."

"But what about our weight?" the riders demanded. "We gotta take off weight before this afternoon!" Never had a bunch of jockeys sounded so disappointed about missing a morning's sweat session.

"Unfortunately, this is a circumstance beyond our control." O'Hara spoke with his usual dignity. "I trust I will have your full cooperation in keeping this matter private?"

Everyone nodded. They would never tell a soul. Whatever he decided would be completely confidential. After all, there were the trainers, the owners, the betting public; their responsibilities, etc., etc. . . .

"Very well, gentlemen. You may rest assured that you will all make weight this afternoon."

The sweaty group dispersed to the showers.

Hours later, when weighing out, the jocks stepped up to the

scales and jumped off again, one by one, perhaps a bit more quickly than usual. They had to go through the motions. There were forms to be filled out, and reporters wandering in and out of the vestibule. O'Hara stood with his clipboard in hand and carefully recorded an official weight for each jockey. If the needle on the scale indicated 120, O'Hara wrote down 115.

Once O'Hara had given his word, Jacinto knew there would be no problem. He spent a leisurely morning playing cards and telling jokes and briefly considering a Hollywood career. But the first thing he did after showering was to go back to the kitchen and order a second helping of bacon and eggs.

5

The mile and a quarter Kentucky Derby was too great a distance for Ruffian to try so early in her comeback season. That was Frank's decision, and the Janneys deferred to him completely in this matter. They had, however, kept the filly nominated for the race, and perhaps, if everything had gone smoothly as a two-year-old—if there had been no hairline fracture— Ruffian would have run for the roses in 1975.

Frank denied he had even considered it. He belonged to a respected minority of horsemen who believed the Derby distance was generally too far to test any three-year-old at that stage of their development, let alone one who was returning from an injury. No single race—not even the Derby—took precedence over a long, productive career. The Janneys agreed. Frank would bring the filly back gradually. She had come out of the six-furlong Caltha just fine. Two weeks later he would try her back at seven.

The Comely Stakes took place on April 30, three days before the Kentucky Derby. Interest in the sport always ran high that time of year, and even on a Wednesday afternoon, 20,000 people showed up at Aqueduct to watch Ruffian run.

"Hey, Jacinto, better fasten your seat belt!"

Jacinto looked over as Jorge Velasquez jogged alongside him on Point in Time. They were rounding the turn, heading for the starting gate.

"You think I gonna crash?" Jacinto smiled.

"You might! She too fast for you! You might fall off! Buckle up!"

175

A moment later Angel Cordero rode by on Aunt Jin, but he said nothing. He was the leading rider at the Aqueduct meeting, and he hadn't gotten there by admiring other people's horses. On the contrary—he was considered one of the toughest and most ruthless riders in the New York jockey colony. He'd try anything if he thought he could get away with it.

George Cassidy, the starter, climbed up into his tower and watched the five fillies load into the gate. When a horse was fractious, rearing up or banging on the walls, Cassidy refrained from springing the gates, but he had to walk a fine line. Every single horse was not going to be standing perfectly still, nose pointed straight ahead, at the same instant. So it was just bad luck that when Cassidy squeezed the prongs of his starter's gun together, releasing the gates, Ruffian had her head way down and was not ready for the break. Everyone else got off ahead of her.

Jacinto remained cool. Although his filly's start was so poor that some people in the stands actually thought she had stumbled, he knew she was fine. His only concern was to let her gather herself together, find her stride, and go on. She had done it before, every time. And now, as the crowd held its breath, she did it once again. Before they had gone half a dozen jumps, Ruffian was out in front.

Jacinto's goal for the season was teaching Ruffian to relax. The longer races were coming up, and it would be necessary for the filly to start stretching out her speed over a distance of ground. The kind of fractions she routinely turned in—first quarters in :21 or :22 and change—were breathtaking, but when you started running more than a mile, you needed to be realistic.

Jacinto wanted to slow down the pace right away, but Cordero had something else in mind. He wasn't so naive as to believe his filly could wear out Ruffian, so his plan was to make Ruffian wear herself out. He was on the inside, having broken from the number 1 spot, and as they took off down the backstretch, Cordero managed to stay within a length of the black filly. When he got as close as he could, he started screeching like a maniac. "Yeeeaaaaaaaaahhhhhhhh!" he howled at the top of his top of his lungs. "Eeeeeeaaaaiiiii! Hey! Hey! Hey! Hey! Heyaaaaaaahhhhhhh!"

Startled, Ruffian tried to take off, and Jacinto had to use every ounce of his strength to keep her under control. He understood instantly what was happening. If Cordero could spook Ruffian and make her sprint away early, maybe she would run out of steam before the wire. After all, she had never gone seven furlongs before. Maybe she couldn't extend her speed over the distance. Maybe, if she tired herself out, Cordero's much slower filly could overtake her.

Jacinto would deal with Cordero later. Now, Ruffian was fighting to open up a lead that Jacinto didn't want. In spite of the bit tearing against the sides of her mouth, Ruffian was easing away. As they approached the top of the stretch, she was six lengths in front and showing no sign of fatigue, whereas a tiring Aunt Jin had already started to drift out.

Then, even as he crossed the finish line, Jacinto knuckled his filly to keep going. He didn't rise in his stirrups to pull her up. It took only a second for the crowd to realize what he was doing, why he continued to let her run when there was no need, after she had already won by 7¾ lengths—he was galloping her out a final eighth. The clockers alertly kept their watches going and caught Ruffian in 1:35⅖ for the mile. That was more than respectable for the distance, especially since she was under no pressure. Her time for the seven furlongs of the race was a stakes record of 1:21⅕.

A brief ceremony took place in the winner's circle, with the Janneys receiving a small silver trophy. Jacinto was in no mood to chat. He stalked off towards the jockeys' quarters, ignoring the reporters; once inside, he wasted no time before cornering Cordero. Jacinto started screaming at him in Spanish, and Cordero screamed back. They exchanged a string of insults and threats that attracted a circle of onlookers, but they stopped short of actual blows. Jack O'Hara would throw them both out for a week if they started swinging, and neither was hotheaded enough to risk a suspension with the Kentucky Derby only three days away.

Teddy Cox witnessed the confrontation but had no idea what it was about. Later he grabbed Jacinto off to the side and the

the jockey explained what had happened on the backstretch, which had not been obvious from the press box or the stands.

"I don't really blame him, though," added Jacinto, who had finally calmed down. "Shit. It's part of the game. I done the same thing myself many times." His brown eyes lit up. "But it don't work for him because my filly can run all day! Did you see I let her gallop out an extra eighth and they caught her in :35 and two? Don't make no difference to her, she can run ten miles! She don't never want to stop!"

Ruffian had done something even more unusual than setting a stakes record or winning by a very large margin. She had created a minus pool across the board, both on-track and at OTB. That meant that in every category—win, place, and show—such a high percentage of the money was wagered on Ruffian, rather than being spread out among several horses, that the track was in the almost unheard-of position of having to pay out more money on the race than it had taken in.

This happened occasionally in the show pool, where heavy hitters often wagered substantial sums on what they considered a sure thing. Ruffian had already caused this twice as a two-year-old, in the Astoria and the Spinaway, triggering minus place pools (there had been too few entries to allow show betting in those races). These gamblers won only a small percentage on their dollar, but they bet a lot of dollars. However, betting to show was one thing. There was a degree of caution involved; it was a kind of "saver" of a bet. But to put all that money in the win pool—that was an extraordinary testament to their belief in Ruffian's ability. Such popular favorites as Count Fleet, Citation, Kelso, and Secretariat had failed their entire careers to spark a minus win pool in New York.

After the race, Yates and Mike accompanied Dan over to the spit-box with the filly. The urine test never bothered her—the man just stuck a cup underneath her when she started to urinate—but she didn't like to have blood taken. The quick sting of a needle in her neck did not hurt, but she did not like people fussing around her head, especially strangers. Dan mumbled to her and held tight to her shank until the two small vials were filled with her blood.

During this procedure, one of the agents from the van company caught Frank off to the side for a minute.

"Say, Frank, we're kind of tight on vans right now. Would it be all right if I put another horse in with you going back?"

Frank hesitated. Then he figured, what the hell. The race was over, they'd be going straight home. "Sure," he agreed. "If it'd help you out, go ahead."

Yates had gone back to double-check the van and get it ready. The agent found him inside, testing the hooks where the horses were tied up. "You got two horses going back," he said, handing Yates the corrected trip sheet.

"No way, unless you clear it with Frank."

"Frank says it's all right to put him on."

"Okay, if Frank says so."

Dan loaded Ruffian in first. Always good about traveling, she settled right down inside the stall.

Then the other horse appeared from around the corner. As soon as Yates saw him, he knew there was going to be trouble. The colt had his head down and was swinging it from side to side, snorting, blowing, and generally acting studdish. The way the compartments were set up inside the van, the colt was going to have to be led in with his head up by Ruffian's hindquarters and then turned around into his separate enclosure only a few feet away.

Frank had been talking to Mike off to one side when he looked up and realized what was happening. "Hold on right there!" he hollered at the groom. In two jumps Frank was up by the horse's head. "Where the hell do you think you're going with this goddamn colt?"

The groom, who barely had the colt under control, shrugged helplessly. "I told to bring him here, load him up!"

Frank jerked the shank firmly to settle the colt down. "Yates!" he cried. "Go get that damn agent over here now!"

Yates hopped down from the cab and cut through the walkway into the office. "You better get out there," he told the man behind the desk. "Frank Whiteley's pissed as hell!"

The agent barged out and headed for Frank. "You just said I could send the horse back with you, Frank! What the hell's the matter now?"

"You goddamn lyin' son of a bitch! You never said you was

sending back some old rank stud colt to get in there with my filly! I oughta have your job for this! Get him out of here before I run him over with the van! Get the hell away from here and don't ever ask to put another horse in with me, you hear, you goddamn fool! Yates! Get up there and get her out of here! Right now!"

The other groom was desperately trying to lead his colt under the shedrow, but now that the colt had got a whiff of Ruffian, he was even wilder than before. Mike felt sorry for the groom and went over to give him a hand. Together they managed to lead the colt kicking and snorting back to the receiving barn.

Red-faced and furious, Frank peered inside the van for a quick check. Dan was sitting on an overturned water bucket, and the filly was standing quietly in her box, one foreleg idly riffling through the straw.

"She fine," Dan frowned. "Don't worry none, let's go." The commotion all around her, the screaming, the unruly colt—none of it had bothered Ruffian. She had other things on her mind. She nickered once at Dan. "I know, I know," he answered. The filly wanted to get home. It had been a long time between meals, and she was hungry.

6

The Kentucky Derby was the hardest race in the country to win. Not just because of the distance or the competition, but because of the circumstances under which it was run. It was a circus, a constant crush of cameras and microphones and pushing and noise. There was a long wait in the paddock with nothing for a horse to do but get worked up into a lather. There was the tension of people taking once-in-a-lifetime chances. And there was always a big field.

Fifteen colts were entered in the 1975 Derby. That was big, but not enormous. Foolish Pleasure had raced in fields that large more than once. The first time Jacinto had ridden him, in August of '74, he had won the Sapling coming out of the 13 hole in a fifteen-horse field. Two weeks ago, at Aqueduct, he had electrified the crowds in his final prep, the Wood Memorial, breaking from post 15, the far outside, giving away lots of ground into the first turn, then gradually working his way over near the rail, digging in past the eighth pole, and hanging on until he thundered past the wire a head in front. He had raced the mile and an eighth in 1:48⅘, equaling Bold Ruler's 1957 stakes record.

It had been the high point of his career, especially coming after his only loss. Jacinto flew off to Kentucky with all the confidence in the world. His colt had speed and he had heart. There was nothing more he could ask for, except a little luck on Saturday afternoon.

The crowds at Churchill Downs had grown rowdier in recent years, and security was constantly increased, but it was impossible to exert complete control over the crush of people mobbing the infield. They saw little of the races on Derby Day, but that wasn't why they came. They came to party. They brought coolers and picnic blankets, beer and bourbon, and, increasingly, marijuana, speed, and acid. They began drinking and getting high early in the morning and were wasted long before the band played "My Old Kentucky Home." But afterwards, they could always say they had witnessed what the media referred to as the most exciting two minutes in American sports.

The post parade was uneventful. The horses loaded easily, fourteen into the main gate, one into the fifteenth position in the auxiliary gate. Everything went smoothly, which was a sharp contrast to the race about to be run.

As predicted, Bombay Duck went right to the lead. He was the speed, and had been expected to set the pace, but not even his rider had anticipated that he would blaze the first quarter in a record-breaking 22 seconds flat. Whether he was riled up by the prerace commotion or just feeling his oats, that was the fastest first quarter ever in 101 runnings of the Kentucky Derby. By the half, he was three lengths in front. His time was :45⅖, also a record for the Derby. But the colt was tiring badly, and there were still six furlongs left to go.

Meanwhile, Jacinto had taken hold of Foolish Pleasure and tucked him in near the rail, towards the back of the pack. The colt was not grabbing the track particularly well, and the best thing Jacinto could do was let him take his time and settle into his stride. Jacinto had a good sense of pace; at this rate, he knew something had to give. There would be some burnouts along the way. Slowly he let his colt pick off horses, and by the time they had gone three-quarters, Foolish Pleasure had moved up to sixth. At the back of the pack Braulio Baeza was sitting patiently on Prince Thou Art, the colt who had beaten Foolish Pleasure in the Florida Derby.

Suddenly there was a movement from the crowd, and a flash of silver hurtled through the air towards the horses. Someone had thrown a beer can at the field. There was no time to ponder the stupidity of the act. Fifteen horses and riders were thundering around the track, under the most intense pressure of their professional lives, and one idiot had just put them all at risk.

The can caught Bombay Duck on the hip while the entire field was strung out behind him. If he had bolted, or stumbled from the blow, there could have been an epic disaster. As it was, he stayed calm and didn't disturb anyone else. The beer can bounced away. Bombay Duck eventually faded to last and came out of the race with a swelling the size of an apple on his hip, but a miracle had spared him and everyone else from a much more horrifying outcome.

The incident didn't affect Jacinto and his colt, but about that same time something else did. Angel Cordero, on Sylvan Place, swerved sharply, knocking a third colt over towards the rail in front of Foolish Pleasure; for an instant Jacinto was in a box. He could have been trapped there, but he refused to panic and soon a space opened up for him. His colt was ready to run, he could feel it, but there was still a quarter-mile left in the race. Not yet! he thought. Not yet! Not yet!

At that point a California horse named Diabolo, who had been rushing up from the outside, took the lead. He was immediately challenged by Avatar, and the first mile was completed in 1:36. Now Master Derby also moved into contention, while Foolish Pleasure continued gaining ground along the rail. As they entered the top of the stretch, it looked like a four-horse race: Only 3½ lengths separated Avatar, Diabolo, Foolish Pleasure, and Master Derby.

Nearing the eighth pole Diabolo unexpectedly ducked in, bumping Avatar so hard it knocked his back end sideways. Avatar bumped back. The jostling continued between the two, and, determined to avoid it, Jacinto steered his colt out from the rail and went three wide. Foolish Pleasure had gotten up a head of steam, and nothing was going to stop him now. It was Jacinto's job to make sure the colt avoided the trouble just ahead; it was the colt's job to run. In the middle of the stretch Foolish Pleasure charged through between Diabolo and Master Derby and took the lead.

Ahead was a clear path to the wire! They were going to win the Kentucky Derby! If luck stayed with them, they were going to win!

So it came as a huge shock to Jacinto to hear the voice of the race-caller, Chic Anderson, announcing to everyone present and to millions more watching on TV that Prince Thou Art was in front and drawing away! Jacinto could see straight ahead, and there was no one between him and the wire. Then he heard Anderson a second time. "Prince Thou Art in front!" It gave Jacinto an eerie feeling. He was not a superstitious person, but he did get feelings sometimes, feelings that certain things were fated, things he could have no rational way of knowing. Had someone snuck in front of him? Was he going to lose at the last jump?

He glanced around and the feeling vanished. Nobody was beside him, and, unless he had gone blind, nobody was in front. The hell with the announcer! Jacinto thought. Let him call whoever he wants!

The wire was getting close, and for those final seconds Jacinto shut out all sounds, all sensations, until there was nothing left in the world but him and his colt. He urged Foolish Pleasure on, hitting him once or twice more to make sure he didn't stop, and then a huge roar rose up from the crowd. Now he could hear again, as he rose in his stirrups and eased the colt into a steady gallop, as reality began to settle on his shoulders.

He had won the Kentucky Derby! He had won! Later he would find out that Chic Anderson had corrected his call before the colt hit the wire, and so, except for a few seconds of confusion, there had been no doubt in the crowd that the plucky little colt they had picked as the favorite had indeed come home in front.

Into the winner's circle descended all the colt's connections: his owner, John L. Greer, and his wife; LeRoy and Myrna Jolley; Patty Vasquez; the stablehands; friends and relatives; plus the mayor of Louisville and the governor of Kentucky. The press surrounded them all, and after they had draped Foolish Pleasure in his blanket of roses, and everyone had crowded together for the victory photographs, and Jacinto had looked this way and that for the cameras, the jockey jumped down and was hustled off with LeRoy Jolley and John Greer for the awards ceremony.

Foolish Pleasure's time for the mile and a quarter was 2:02; decent, nothing extraordinary—nowhere near Secretariat's record of 1:59⅖—but time was not the point here. Time, any trainer would tell you, only mattered in jail. On the racetrack, what counted was who came home first.

A week later no one would remember Foolish Pleasure's

time, but they would remember that he had won the Derby. A hundred years later his name would still be in the record books.

Jacinto and his wife had dinner with friends, but there were no wild parties or all-night celebrations for him—he had to be up at seven the next morning to catch a nine o'clock plane to Boston, where he was riding in the Bay State Handicap at Suffolk Downs. Racing went on, every day, and if you were a rider who wanted to remain competitive, you went on with it.

So when an out-of-town reporter wanted to know how soon he'd be back in New York, Jacinto looked surprised.

"I be at the barn early Monday morning."

"What barn?" the baffled reporter asked.

"What barn?" Jacinto laughed. "Mr. Whiteley barn! I don't never like to stay too far away from Ruffian!"

7

At six o'clock Monday morning Jacinto pulled into a parking space in the horsemen's lot at Belmont Park. When he entered the Racing Secretary's office to meet Fats, he was surprised to find a small group of reporters waiting for him.

"What's the matter with you guys, you don't hear who won the Derby yet?" With Jacinto, there was a fine line between his scorching sarcasm and his very dry sense of humor. The writers were caught off guard for a second, unsure how to read his mood.

"Uh, how was Boston?" someone ventured. They knew he had not won the race, but it didn't matter, because the Bay State Handicap was not what was on their minds.

Jacinto made a face. "How you think it was? You been to Suffolk Downs. It make this place look respectable!" That broke the ice, and they all laughed. Now they could relax. Jacinto was in a good mood.

"What do you think your chances are for a Triple Crown?"

As soon as the question was asked, everyone in the room felt the temperature drop. Reporters always, always, always asked jockeys if they thought they would win. Jacinto wondered at their ignorance. Did they really think any jockey in the world was going to tell them he thought he would lose? ("Well, I'll probably come in eighth or ninth. Unless a couple horses scratch. That ought to move me up a little.")

The first law of the jockey's jungle was that you had to ex-press confidence in your horse. If you didn't act like you were going to win, why the hell would a trainer put you up there in the first place?

For a moment he toyed with the idea of walking out on them. Frank Whiteley had done that at the Kentucky Derby in 1967, the year he arrived in Louisville with Damascus. Never fond of the press, especially on occasions like the Derby, when hundreds of papers sent out reporters who knew absolutely nothing about racing or horses, Whiteley tended to be either rude or silent. However, in the final days of preparation at Churchill Downs, track management had prevailed upon him to grant at least one major group interview. Reluctantly, Whiteley had agreed. A room was set aside, the press notified, and a huge crush of reporters jammed together for this single opportunity.

The first question was an unfortunate one.

"Mr. Whiteley, what are Damascus's sleeping habits?"

There was a brief silence before Whiteley answered. "How the hell do I know?" he snapped. "I ain't never slept with him!" The trainer turned and stomped out of the room, and that was the end of his interviews for the Derby.

Now Fats came to Jacinto's rescue. "If anybody can get this horse a Triple Crown," he said, "it's Jacinto. But you tell those damn stewards they gotta keep Cordero from banging into everybody like he did in Kentucky. He's not in Puerto Rico anymore. We're supposed to have rules here. Come on, let's go."

He took Jacinto in his car and they drove around to the backstretch. Their first stop, as always, was Frank Whiteley's barn. Ruffian had just come back from galloping, and Squeaky still had on his helmet. "Hey, champ," he called softly. "Congratulations! You done good out there."

"Thank you."

Whiteley was inside the next stall with Rooster, helping to bandage Honorable Miss. "Screw up a two-car funeral," he muttered without looking up. "Couldn't get this here mare loose in a race with three other horses, then goes out there in Kentucky and gets by fourteen colts. Don't know how the hell that son of a bugger managed to win!"

Jacinto smiled. This was the closest to a compliment he would get from Frank Whiteley. The trainer wasn't going to praise him for riding another man's horse, especially not one belonging to LeRoy Jolley. Jacinto didn't expect him to.

He also knew that just because Whiteley didn't discuss the Derby with him, or praise him for his ride, it didn't mean that

he had failed to take the measure of the colt. He had sized up
Foolish Pleasure and all the other good three-year-olds around.
Whiteley acted like he didn't follow any race he wasn't in. It was
true, he didn't watch them from the stands, but he studied the
charts in the *Racing Form* and he kept his eyes open in the morning. He was almost as aware of other people's horses as he
was of his own. That was part of the business. Finding spots
for your horses meant knowing who they would be likely to
face in each situation, and being able to evaluate the competition. And ever since Ruffian proved in her comeback race
that she was as sound and sharp as before, Whiteley had
known that he would not get through the year without his filly
facing the colts.

Jacinto knew it, too. Most likely, he would someday have to
choose between his Derby-winning colt and his perfect filly.
Someday, he thought. But not now.

In New York there were three major spring stakes for three-year-
old fillies: the Acorn, the Mother Goose, and the Coaching Club
American Oaks. They were run at progressively greater distances, culminating in the Oaks at a mile and a half, which was
just about as far as American horses of either sex ever raced.
The Oaks and the Mother Goose had been established for years
before someone came up with the idea of adding a third contest
to create a Filly Triple Crown. And since "Great oaks from little
acorns grow," an earlier, shorter race was initiated and chris-
tened the Acorn. It was run at a mile, and it was prestigious
enough to draw six other fillies even against such a prohibitive
favorite as Ruffian.

Ruffian's preparations for the race were similar to those before the Comely. For that race, she had breezed four furlongs
on the Tuesday before, and she had done it in :48⅕ on a sloppy
track. On Friday, the day before the Comely, Whiteley sent her
out again, and she covered three-eighths of a mile in :34⅗.

The Acorn itself was one furlong longer than the Comely,
so this time Frank sent Ruffian five furlongs on the Tuesday
before the race. She zipped that in :59⅖. Then, on Friday, she
again breezed three furlongs in :34⅗. Frank Whiteley had a reputation for consistency, but this was getting ridiculous.

Jim Prendergast continued to stop by the barn several times a day. It was a standing joke that any vet who worked for Whiteley was lucky to make a dollar a week; the trainer did almost every-thing himself, he avoided medications whenever possible, and he had always focused on prevention.

It was inevitable, though, that when horses began to cover greater distances, the wear and tear on their legs grew more pronounced. Prendergast was not surprised that as a three-year-old, Ruffian had developed some low-grade osselets, small bony deposits around her ankles. This was a common condition in racehorses, something to be dealt with but not worried over. Frank frequently stood her front legs in ice tubs and continued to hose her every day. She was never lame, and unlike many horses, she never had to have her ankles tapped, or drained, to remove excess fluid from the area. Still, periodically, rumors would spring up around the backstretch that Ruffian was hurt-ing, or Ruffian was sore. Every time she ran, she put all the rumors to rest.

When Ruffian loaded into the gate for the Acorn, she was not as keyed up as she had been for her last two starts. She wasn't calm exactly—she was too much of a racehorse to be calm inside the starting gate—but she was cool. She kept herself straight-ened out, and Jacinto kept her head up.

The bell rang.

Jacinto sat tight, and Ruffian bounded to the front on her own initiative. The subtle dance began, with Jacinto hoping she would follow his lead. He took her in hand, as firmly as he dared, and waltzed her through the first quarter. He had no idea till later, when he saw the fractions, how well he had succeeded: She ran even slower than in the Comely—:23²⁄₅. Ruffian was the perfect partner. She had learned the new dance.

Her mild start gave rise to a brief illusion on the part of jockey Ron Turcotte that he might actually have a chance in the race. The fact that his filly, Piece of Luck, was running only a head back at the quarter struck him as unusual. Except for her race with Hot n Nasty, Ruffian had never let anyone stay near her very long. She had always sprinted away and left them in the dust. It occurred to Turcotte that he may have caught the filly on a bad day. Usually she dragged Jacinto way out front; now, from the quarter to the half, she was allowing Piece of Luck to stay within a length. She was so relaxed, Turcotte began to wonder if she was a little off. Any athlete could have a bad day. No one knew that better than Ron Turcotte, whose greatest mount, Secretariat, had been defeated five times in his 21-race career. Maybe this was the day that Ruffian could be caught.

They cruised into the far turn. Jacinto barely shifted his hands, but the filly picked up the signal. It was her permission to accelerate. She had not liked having that other filly at her flank, and she quickly opened up three lengths on Piece of Luck before Turcotte realized that he'd been had. There was nothing wrong with Ruffian! Jacinto had been conserving her speed, but he had a delicate balance to maintain. He could restrain her only so long before she blew up in his face. Ruffian had submitted a little longer than before; Jacinto had relented when he sensed her tolerance was running out.

Ruffian picked up the tempo as she drew off. Heading into the stretch she was ahead by seven lengths. With such a comfortable lead, Jacinto wanted to slow her down. This filly could never be rated to come from behind; she had made that perfectly clear. However, if she could learn to relax once she was firmly in front, she could save some speed in case she ever needed it in a battle to the wire.

Jacinto was envisioning future contests. What would happen when a great, come-from-behind horse like Forego challenged her in the final sixteenth? That's when all these efforts might pay off.

For now, he was just hand-riding her home. He hadn't even shown her the whip since the Sorority, and against this level of competition there was no need for it. If he'd urged her, she could have picked up a second or more on her final time and challenged the track record for the mile, but that was not his goal. His goal in this race was to get her home safe and to slow down her usual fractions. He had been successful on both counts. She crossed the wire 8¼ lengths in front. It had been a magnificent exhibition, and the filly had set a new stakes record of 1:34⅖, but it had not been much of a contest for her.

Behind her, though, there had been a real race. Not with Piece of Luck, who had stayed with Ruffian for the half and then faded. But with two other very game fillies: Somethingregal, who had saved ground on the turn while in third place, then drifted out a little coming into the stretch and moved into second, and Gallant Trial, steadily gaining as they neared the wire. At the last second Somethingregal bravely plunged ahead and stuck her nose across the finish line. An instant later there was an audible gasp from the crowd as Somethingregal pulled up lame.

In the stands people tried to figure out what had happened. Drifting out was often a signal. Either she had taken a bad step, or was hurting, or was tired. Many people craned their necks as the horse ambulance pulled up near the clubhouse turn. People who normally couldn't take their eyes off Ruffian were torn between watching every step of her entrance into the winner's circle and checking out the progress of Somethingregal as she was dismounted and loaded into the ambulance.

Later, word filtered out through the backstretch that the filly would be okay. One of her shoes had twisted off and a nail had entered her foot. It was painful, but in no way threatening to her health or her career. Within a few days she would be as good as new.

Frank Whiteley was glad the filly would recover. He wanted to beat the competition clean and honest, but this kind of an injury annoyed him, too, because it was something that might have been—*should* have been—avoided. When he told people that his blacksmith had saved him—meaning his horses—many times out there on the track, he wasn't exaggerating. He meant it literally. And this was a good example of the kind of thing you needed to be saved *from*. An injury like that would never happen to a horse that Jarboe Talbott had shod.

8

The twenty-ton metal starting gate was driven up and positioned just behind the finish line. Because the Mother Goose was a mile and an eighth, exactly once around the Aqueduct oval, the seven fillies entered in the race would load directly in front of the spectators, many of whom pressed up against the chain-link fence to catch a close-up glimpse of Ruffian.

When a race started on the far side of the track, the crowd was removed from the reality of the gate. When it started a few yards away—starters and jockeys yelling, metal doors slamming, hooves knocking against steel—then people began to appreciate the power of volatile thoroughbreds and the fragility of their riders. The seven fillies for the Mother Goose loaded swiftly and without trouble, but when the doors flew open, only six sprang out. The seventh, Dan's Commander, stumbled badly and went to her knees, flipping her rider, Rudy Turcotte, brother of Ron, over her head. She took off by herself as Turcotte lay crumpled in front of the gate. There was no time to wait for the ambulance to collect the motionless jockey. The starting gate had to be re-moved immediately before the horses completed their circuit of the track. Realizing this, one of the assistant starters rushed for-ward, scooped up the jockey in his arms like a child, and got him safely out of the way.

Dan's Commander took off after the field, and Jacinto, who had been right next to her in the gate, worried for a few seconds how the race would unfold. You had to ride a little different with a loose horse in the field; they could be dangerous, and you had to exercise more caution. He had no time to think what might have happened to his own filly if Dan's Commander had stumbled a few inches to her left instead of her right.

Fortunately, Ruffian had broken well and gone straight to the lead. She was more relaxed than she had ever been at the beginning of a race. Jacinto could feel the difference immediately. Behind her the other horses were bunched together.

Ruffian continued to control the field, running the half effortlessly in :47⅗. That was almost two seconds slower than she had ever run the first four furlongs of a race. Jacinto had no way of knowing the exact fractions, but he could tell the pace was slow and he was overjoyed. It was just what Mr. Whiteley had ordered.

At the five-eighths pole, Sir Ivor's Sorrow, again ridden by Daryl Montoya, tried to come to Ruffian. Jacinto let out the reins a tiny bit and Ruffian leaped away. Perfect! She was playing the game just right: cat and mouse. The filly understood.

With three furlongs left to go, she had opened up two lengths. Jacinto still wasn't putting pressure on her. She rounded the far turn—two turns meant nothing to her, just as he had thought, she could run all day!—and somehow she had stretched her lead into eight lengths. All Jacinto wanted was a steady twelve-second clip, enough to keep her sharp for future competition. With such a long lead, there was no point in pressuring her, but even as she rolled off a final eighth in :12⅕, the field was dying behind her. Jacinto could do nothing about that. He wasn't trying to humiliate anybody, but his filly crossed the wire 13½ lengths in front.

She entered the winner's circle to another standing ovation. Her shoulders glistened like onyx, her fine-cut veins stood out along her neck, but if you wanted to see this filly sweat, it looked like you were going to have to throw her into the hotbox with Jacinto.

Her final time was 1:47⅘. It was a new stakes record, which surprised no one, and it was only four-fifths of a second slower than the track record set by the 1972 Kentucky Derby winner Riva Ridge. Once again racetrackers and turf writers shook their heads. Just how fast could the filly run if they ever let her go?

A reporter hurried over to Whiteley. "You gonna run her in the Belmont?" he asked.

"What in hell would I do that for?" Whiteley hardly broke stride as he responded. He stood alongside the Janneys while the picture was snapped. Then the track presented trophies to the owners, the trainer, and the jockey.

"Let's get this over with." Whiteley tugged at his tie and glanced around as Dan took the shank from Stuart Janney and led the filly off. "I'll be right over there'n a minute," Whiteley called after him.

Mr. and Mrs. Janney beamed as they shook hands with Jacinto. "That was a beautiful ride, Jacinto," Mr. Janney said. "Beautiful."

"Thank you." The jockey reached over and shook hands with Whiteley. He was probably the only man in the world whose opinion really mattered to Jacinto. "Well?" He looked up at the trainer. "How we play the game this time?"

Whiteley could not hold back a chuckle. "You didn't do too bad," he conceded. But he couldn't resist putting the emphasis on the "too."

9

The morning after the announcement of the Match, Jacinto and Fats stopped by to see Frank. The three of them disappeared briefly into the tackroom, and when they reemerged, Fats, as usual, was talking a mile a minute. Jacinto paid no attention. He was thinking about their next stop, which he dreaded—a trip to LeRoy Jolley's barn to give him the news: Jacinto had elected to stay with Ruffian for the Match.

They were long gone when Frank sent the filly over to the main track. Usually Ruffian went out with the first or second set, but today Frank had waited an extra hour because of the weather. The track itself was wet, and fog lingered over the entire area, thick enough in spots to blot out the horses, who moved around the oval like airplanes darting in and out of clouds. Yates had his hands full.

"She really wants to run, Frank," he panted, as they drew up alongside Sled Dog. "Damn near wore me out. I'll tell you one thing—you got to be sober to ride this filly!"

"Yeah?" Frank retorted. "How would you know?"

"What'd you catch her in?"

"Fifty-nine."

"She feels good." Yates rotated his shoulders, easing out the kinks. "Did you see her take off, Frank?"

"Yeah, I saw her. Went eleven and two before you got a hold of her."

"Is that right? Shit! And I was choking her, too."

"I might have to put Jacinto on her once more before the Oaks."

Yates nodded. Frank had kept the jock off her except for the

races themselves, but the Coaching Club American Oaks, one
week off, was a long haul—a mile and a half—and the filly took
off like a bullet. If you didn't get the hang of slowing her down
immediately, she might run off. And there was no way she could
blaze her typical fractions for a full mile and a half. Or, if there
was, Frank Whiteley didn't want to know about it. He liked to
win races as much as anybody, but he didn't believe in killing
good horses to do it.

By nine o'clock Frank had the hose out and was spraying the
filly's legs, when Teddy Cox stopped by.

"How'd the filly go this morning, Frank?"

"Hell, I couldn't see too much of it! Hardly see anything in
that damn fog! Managed to catch her at the poles though. She
did fine."

"Frenchy got her in :59," Cox said.

"That right? Well, if old Frenchy says so, I guess she did."

"Got the first eighth in eleven and two."

"Is that right?"

"You try to slow the boy down any?"

"He couldn't see me even if I did! But no, I didn't. You could
slow the boy down, maybe, but you can't slow the damn mare
down! That's the problem."

They laughed. "You gonna graze her when you get finished
with her legs?"

"We'll try to." Frank shifted the hose so he could reach in
his shirt pocket for his cigarettes. "She's picky, you know. Don't
like mud on her grass. Might be too wet for her today. We'll take
her over there and see. Keep her out for a while either way. Till
it's time for her lunch."

"Frank, are you going to go through any special preparations for the Match?"

"Hell, Teddy, she still got to run in the Coaching Club first!
Let's get through that one, okay? Then we'll see about the damn
match."

Jolley had refused to name the new rider for his colt, but he
told reporters that whoever rode Foolish Pleasure for his next
work would get the job for the Match. As a result, on the morning of June 17, when Foolish Pleasure was scheduled to breeze,

several reporters dragged themselves out of bed to see who it would be. Unfortunately for them, overnight rains had left the track a sea of mud, and at the last minute Jolley canceled the work. Under such sloppy conditions he felt safer having the colt's regular exercise rider, John Nazareth, gallop the colt his usual two miles.

The delay heightened the anticipation. The Match wasn't just another race. It was a once-in-a-lifetime event with huge rewards: Not only would both jocks have a guaranteed payday—the *loser* of the Match was taking home $125,000, ten percent of which would go to the rider—but, given the television coverage, which was being projected at somewhere between sixteen and twenty million, they would both emerge from the race as household names. And one would emerge as a hero.

Jolley publicly stated that he harbored no ill will towards Jacinto for his choice. The jockey had guided Foolish Pleasure to victory in the Derby and to second-place finishes in both the Preakness and the Belmont Stakes. Jolley assured the press that he would ride him back after the Match. He understood, he said, that Jacinto had been riding first call for Mr. Whiteley for a number of years, and he respected the jockey's sense of obligation.

That was not exactly the way Jacinto would have put it, but he wasn't going to contradict LeRoy Jolley. After all, Jolley had put him on a Kentucky Derby winner, and he had plenty of other good horses in his barn. Jacinto didn't want to lose those mounts. And though he had a reputation with reporters as someone who would always speak his mind, in those last few weeks before the Match, Jacinto transformed himself into a first-class diplomat.

What LeRoy Jolley said was partly true. Jacinto did feel a sense of loyalty to Frank Whiteley that he felt to no other trainer on the grounds, but that was not why he had chosen to ride Ruffian in the Match. He had chosen Ruffian because he thought she was the better horse, and he was in a uniquely qualified position to judge.

He chose her for another reason also. He thought she was just coming into her own. As astonishing as that might be, he believed that she had not yet approached the peak of her powers, and he wanted to be the one riding her in the months to come, when she really proved herself by beating older horses in the fall.

Still, Foolish Pleasure was a very good horse, and Jacinto could understand if Jolley was a bit insulted. How often did a rider take off a horse who had won the Kentucky Derby to ride a filly who had never faced a single colt? But then, how often did a horse like Ruffian come along?

That morning, while John Nazareth headed out with the colt, Ruffian and Squeaky were kicking up the slop as they made their usual rounds. The two exercise riders exchanged friendly challenges as they passed, each convinced his horse would win when they met up on July 6. They laughed and went their separate ways, forgetting all about each other as they concentrated on their horses and the slippery track.

The colt's last race had been the Belmont Stakes on June 7. Before the Match he would have a full month's rest, plenty of time for Jolley to sharpen his speed. Speed would be the determining factor in his battle with the filly: You didn't win a match race coming from behind.

Ruffian still had the mile and a half Oaks coming up that weekend. After that, she would have two weeks to rest and prepare for the Match.

The next morning, skies were clear and the racing surface was back to normal. LeRoy Jolley accompanied Foolish Pleasure over to the track to breeze six furlongs. Braulio Baeza was aboard the colt.

The track had just been harrowed, and the smell of dirt threaded its way into the warm air. It was the Thursday before the Oaks, and Jacinto was readying Ruffian for her final blowout. Her only real competition in that race, a King Ranch filly named Equal Change, had just breezed four furlongs in a respectable 50 seconds flat. Ruffian, under tight restraint by Jacinto, now covered the same distance in :46⅖. On the way back to the barn, she was as lively as ever, reaching her long neck up to snare a few leaves from the branches of a maple tree as they passed.

The next morning Jacinto was quoted as saying that his shoulders were so sore from holding the filly back, he wasn't sure he could contain her in the race. On Saturday, when he entered the barn, Whiteley stopped him.

"You still think you're gonna have trouble holding her back?" he asked. " 'Cause I can always get a rider who's in better shape, if I have to."

Jacinto grinned. "You know I just saying that to them reporters."

"Well, you better be. 'Cause that damn race is a mile and a half, and I don't want you running the bitch 'less you have to."

"Don't look like I gonna have to."

"I hope not. If the pace is nice and easy, you can let her run a little bit at the end. See how it goes."

Jacinto's face brightened. "How little bit?"

"Maybe the last sixteenth. You'll see once you're out there. You gotta remember something, Por-ta Rican. Hey, Squeaky!" Frank called out abruptly. "Walk her around one more time, then bring her over here and we'll stand her in some ice." He turned back to Jacinto. "She's running a mile and half today, and in two weeks she's got to go a mile and a quarter against that colt. And that's gonna be a tough race, 'cause they'll both be running right out of the gate. She'll use herself up out there if you don't stop her. You got to help her save something."

10

The cartoonist Pierre Bellocq, known professionally as "Peb," was to the world of horseracing what Bill Mauldin had been to the Second World War, and on the morning of the Coaching Club American Oaks, June 21, the *Daily Racing Form* carried one of his masterpieces on its front page. It showed Ruffian posing like a wrestler inside a roped-off ring. Lying comatose at her feet were two fillies labeled "Acorn" and "Mother Goose." In Ruffian's arms was a third, the "Oaks," about to be slammed down onto the mat with the others. Front row, ringside, watching nervously, was Foolish Pleasure, wearing a Derby hat, rumpled shirt, and loosened tie. He was chomping on a fat cigar and sweating profusely. Ruffian was looking at him from under long, curly eyelashes. "Be with you in a minute," read the caption.

By the time the feature race rolled around, Jacinto had been through the wringer. He had ridden in five of the first seven races and won two, one of them for LeRoy Jolley, on a colt named Honest Pleasure, who shared the same sire as Foolish Pleasure and appeared to be a promising prospect for the following year. Although Jacinto liked the colt a lot, he feared that, whatever the outcome of the Match, he would no longer be asked to ride Jolley's first-string horses. Jolley had promised this would not be so, but Jacinto would believe that when he saw it. In the meantime, as long as he was being asked, he was more than happy to jump on any decent horse. After all, except for that one time Jolley put up Baeza, Jacinto was still working Foolish Pleasure in the morning. Pragmatism rather than pride guided most of the choices that a jockey made; many became so skilled at it that they could easily have won political elections.

Jacinto captured the next race on a filly named Blade of Roses. He was almost caught at the last jump by Baeza on Tell Meno Lies, who made a remarkable late charge from the back of the pack to come in second by a neck.

The sixth race was for $40,000 claimers. Jacinto was riding a colt named Magic Lore, who started to fall back after less than half a mile. Sensing that something was not quite right, Jacinto eased the colt up, letting him practically jog along, but near the finish line, with the race over for everyone else, the colt suddenly tensed up, the muscles of his neck went hard, and he collapsed onto the track. When he hit the ground, he was already dead.

Jacinto managed to jump clear and was not hurt. His colt had suffered a heart attack, or possibly a stroke. It happened—not often, but it happened—just as it happened to people. A horse appeared fine one minute, and the next minute it was dead. Jacinto waited for the trainer and the vet, but there was nothing that could be done. It made him and everyone else sick to see something like that: a huge thoroughbred lying on its side, suddenly frozen in death. He shook his head and walked off. There was no time to dwell on what had happened. He had to change for the next race.

As soon as he donned the red and white silks of Locust Hill Farm, he put everything—victory and defeat and death—out of his mind. He stepped on the scale in the basement room, the lead weights secured in their slots in his saddle pad. Jack O'Hara marked down 121 on his clipboard and Jacinto handed his tack to Timmy. Then he returned to his locker, spit out the gum he'd been chewing, and took a fresh piece. A few minutes later he headed up the stairs alone.

It was a clear, warm day. A large crowd had gathered early at the paddock, and as he entered he was aware of people calling his name. He kept his face blank, his stick tapping against his boot, and joined Whiteley near the enclosure where Ruffian was to be saddled. Dan Williams was walking her back and forth along the dirt path, and the crowd outside the rail was already six deep. Squeaky stood guard aboard Sled Dog. Mike Bell had finished up over at the barn so he could come watch. As usual, now that he was there, he was sick with dread and couldn't wait until the filly's race was over.

Dan spoke quietly to the filly while Frank smoothed the blanket over her back. "Hold still, now, girl. Damn! You be good, hear? Don't bite, now, don't bite. Hey! Hey! You wanna run, don't you? You got to get your saddle on if you gonna run this race." While he was talking, he kept one eye on Frank, who centered the pad over the blanket, slipped on the saddle, then reached under her belly to tighten the girth. Predictably, she kicked out once with her near hind leg, curling her lips back and rolling her eyes to find the offender. Dan tugged at the shank. "Oh stop, you old baby! Hush! Hush now, girl, it's done already. Don't you want to go out there and beat them fillies? Well, all right, then. All right. All right. Yeah."

Whiteley leaned over and picked up Ruffian's foreleg, checked her hoof, then gently pulled the leg forward, like a runner stretching before a race. He repeated the procedure with her other front leg, double-checked the girths, the stirrups, the reins; then nodded to Dan, who led her out again to circle the walking ring.

Many in the crowd had bet early. They didn't have to see the filly in the paddock to decide where to put their money. If past performances meant anything, only a fool would have bet against her. On paper, anyway, there was no challenger in this field— and, in a way, it didn't matter. The people had shown up for the thrill of watching Ruffian run. If she galloped out there by herself, ten-to-one she would still have drawn an audience.

Sled Dog had taken her to the paddock, but Ruffian entered the track, as usual, without a lead pony. No one in the stands had to check their program to see which one she was. They didn't have to glance at the number on her racing blanket. She was immediately identifiable, and she was greeted by a round of applause. There was not an ugly filly in the post parade, but the others suffered in comparison to Ruffian. Once she became the point of reference, they were reduced to being merely ordinary.

Earlier in the day, Jacinto had looked over the race in the *Form*, but he could hardly focus his attention on the past performances of the other six fillies. It was not the other fillies he was worried about. The only filly that scared him was his own.

In each of her last two races Ruffian had gotten off smoothly, gliding out of the gate rather than bunching up and exploding. She did it again this time, seizing the lead immediately. She was now the consummate racehorse. She was doing everything just right.

Jacinto could have placed her anywhere he wanted, on any part of the track, and he chose to keep her out from the rail, aware that the track was deeper and slower, deader, on the inside. He was high up on her neck, grabbing as much rein as he could without pulling her over backwards, hoping to slow her down. As they headed around the first turn, Ruffian was three lengths ahead of the nearest horse.

"Save something! Save something!" He could hear Whiteley's voice giving him his instructions. He was doing his best, but he was only one side of the equation. The big filly felt relaxed; now all Jacinto had to do was keep her steady till it was time to make a move.

Even at a modest pace, Ruffian had stretched her lead to five lengths, and heading down the backstretch she started to open up even more. Jacinto clamped down. He wasn't interested in a big lead. He wanted the filly to play the game he'd been teaching her. He wanted her to wait at the front of the pack until someone came to her, then she could leap away from them. Not only would Ruffian save her own strength this way, she would discourage her opponents. It was a way of psyching them out. She would fool them into thinking they could overtake her, then she'd fly off and break their hearts.

Let Me Linger, who had been in second place all around the clubhouse turn, made up only one length by the time they had completed the first half-mile, and Ruffian was still loping along in :49 flat.

Meanwhile, Braulio Baeza, who had patiently rated Equal Change all along the backstretch, began moving up. When he was ready, he passed Let Me Linger with ease. As they entered the far turn, he had pulled within a length and a half of Ruffian. There was still a half-mile remaining in the race. Anything could happen.

Jacinto was no longer worried, though. He could feel Ruffian gathered beneath him, her power, all that energy waiting to be tapped. She was not quite so impatient as she'd been those first few races this year; she was more solid, more sure. There were no more questions left between them. For two seasons he had ridden her, in sprints and over distances. He had seen her courage when she was hurting, her spirit coming back from injury, her never-changing excitement at the chance to run. But what he marveled at the most was her dominance. From their very first encounter, she had been the most self-assured, confident, proud horse he had ever seen. She was, ultimately, always the one in charge.

He knew the pace for the Oaks had been unusually slow. The mile was timed in 1:38, and that left him with a fresh filly. She was ready to take off any time he asked, but he didn't want to ask. He wanted to get her home without the stick. There was a kind of authority in that, beating fillies in a major stakes without even cocking his whip. It emphasized the enormous gulf between Ruffian and everyone else.

The crowd might have had an anxious moment as Equal Change remained only a length and a half back around the huge arc of the far turn, but Jacinto knew he had a lot of horse left. When he chirped at Ruffian, she doubled her lead to three lengths. Racing down the stretch, Equal Change refused to fold, displaying her own kind of courage. Baeza was going to the whip, but several sound whacks could not induce his filly to move up on Ruffian.

The two front-runners widened their lead over the rest of the field, first to five lengths, then six, seven, eight, nine; they were nearing the finish, but try as she might, Equal Change could not close in on Ruffian. Jacinto and his filly crossed the wire almost three lengths in front.

Thirty thousand people remained on their feet, screaming, stamping, whistling, clapping. Ruffian had swept the Filly Triple Crown; for only the fourth time in history, one single horse had triumphed in the Acorn, the Mother Goose, and the Oaks. If there had been any doubters in the crowd, here was further proof of Ruffian's superiority over all the rest of her sex, perhaps over generations of fillies past and future. She had won the three races by an average margin of over eight lengths. She had set a new stakes record in each of the first two legs, and her time for the mile and a half Oaks was 2:27⅘, which tied the old record.

The time was the only disappointment for Ruffian's legions of fans, and like it or not, Jacinto took the responsibility for that. She had won easily. Jacinto had not urged her any more fervently than a few pushes with his hands. If he had let her go, even a little, if he had let her run more than the last eighth of a mile, which she covered in :11⅗, a remarkable time for the final furlong of a long race, she could undoubtedly have set a new record for the Oaks. Maybe, if he had pushed her at all, she could have at least approached Secretariat's phenomenal track record for the mile and a half. It wasn't out of the question. Secretariat's own trainer, Lucien Laurin, after seeing Ruffian's Spinaway, had been widely quoted in all the newspapers: "As God is my judge," he had told reporters, "she may even be better than Secretariat!"

But it was futile to ask "What if?" Record books didn't hold all the answers. In the end, no matter how astonishing their numbers, great horses were remembered for something more than numbers: It was a feeling that they gave you, a belief in something bigger than yourself. They were a reminder—if only for an instant—that some bright, wordless magic still existed in the world.

11

When Ruffian crossed the finish line in front, everyone at CBS breathed a sigh of relief. If she had lost the last leg of the Filly Triple Crown, the network would have been stuck promoting a match race between two horses who had each lost their previous start. Even with the boy-girl angle, that would have been a tough sell. The American public wasn't going to turn on their TVs to watch just any filly and a colt, but they would turn on their sets to watch an *undefeated* filly—a *perfect* filly—challenge a colt who had won the Kentucky Derby. That's what CBS had gambled on, and they had won.

One thing about the Oaks had surprised Frank: the fact that the race did not appear to have taken anything out of the filly. Over the years, he had sent out a lot of horses to run a mile and a half, and even the best of them—even the winners—came back with their tails dragging for at least a little while. Ruffian had come back wanting more. Just past the finish line, she had buck-jumped several times as Jacinto galloped her out. When she had finished over at the detention barn and was back in her stall, she tried to get a rise out of Dan by grabbing the rub rag from his back pocket. She hadn't played like that since her first winter out in Camden, when she was just a big fat baby that the stable-hands called Sofie, and Jackie Peacock thought she didn't want to run.

For the next two mornings, Ruffian's exercise was limited to long walks under the shedrow, with either Squeaky or Dan holding her shank. Physically, she was in fine shape, but like many athletes soaring on their own adrenaline, she was wound up and hyperactive. Whiteley wouldn't dare take her over to the track again until she calmed down.

"What you think, boss?" Jacinto was leaning on the rail with Whiteley, watching the filly walk by.

"What I think about what?"

"She run that last furlong in eleven and three, you know. She coulda went a lot faster in that race."

"She win it, didn't she?"

"Yeah, she win all right."

Squeaky stopped a few yards away to let Ruffian take a drink of water. "What you think, Squeaky?" Jacinto called.

"I think this filly just galloping in that race. She go out do it again today, it was that easy for her."

"Yeah, everything easy for *her*," Jacinto complained. "My back so sore from that race I can hardly move! You know why she just galloping out there? 'Cause I working my butt off she don't run away. Otherwise I prob'ly get fired off the horse, right?" He glanced sideways at Whiteley.

"Hell, I might fire you anyway! Put Squeaky on her for the Match."

Squeaky shook his head and smiled at the thought. He had been on the filly's back more than anyone else—more minutes, hours, days—but he could never ride in a race or even in a morning work. No thoroughbred carried 160 pounds when it was doing serious running. No, Jacinto would ride her in the Match, and she would beat Foolish Pleasure. She would beat everyone, because she was the best. There was not a doubt in Squeaky's mind. "Come on." He chirped to her and they moved off around the bend.

Jacinto turned back to Whiteley. "She look good, no?"

Whiteley nodded. "Looks fine. Came out just right. Better than you, from the looks of it!"

On the twenty-fourth Squeaky finally took Ruffian back to the track and galloped her two miles. She was like a puppy after her two-day absence—a powerful, 1100-pound puppy—and though she was well-behaved going around the oval, on her way back to the barn she unexpectedly reared up. Occasionally, the filly surprised Squeaky like that. She had never unseated him, which he modestly attributed to her excellent balance rather than his own superb skills, but he didn't like for her to do that. It made him nervous. She was tall enough with all four feet on the ground. When she rose straight up on her hind legs and started pawing the air—well, it was thrilling, on the one hand, to be way up on top of the world, but it was scary, also—one inch too far and she could tip over backwards and crash.

PART FIVE

1

"**H**orsemen, get your horses ready for the Match Race!"

The words everyone had waited for all afternoon crackled over the P.A. system that dotted the backstretch. Only two horses, in barns scarcely three hundred yards apart, were competing in this event, but there was not a shedrow in all of Belmont that did not feel the excitement.

Neither Frank Whiteley nor LeRoy Jolley showed emotion as they worked. They completed their usual preparations before heading to the paddock. They looked over their horses to make sure they were okay, double-checked their tack, nodded at the help as each man fell into place.

Squeaky led the short procession from Barn 34 astride Sled Dog. Dan held the filly's shank, and Frank walked out next to him. Yates would meet them by the saddling enclosure. Jacinto was in the jockeys' room changing into the silks of Locust Hill Farm.

Only Mike Bell was missing. He had gone with Rooster to take Honorable Miss over to the spit-box after the last race. The post-time favorite for the Nassau County Handicap, Honorable Miss had shocked the crowd by finishing next to last. When a favorite made such a poor showing, the standard blood and urine testing was required. Mike knew he was too late to make it to the paddock, but the Match itself wasn't scheduled till six o'clock, later than usual for the feature race, in order to attract the optimum television audience nationwide. He hoped that the preliminaries would run late; that way, he figured, he would be able to run down to the clockers' stand and catch the race from there.

Always before, Mike had dreaded Ruffian's races. They were stunning exhibitions, they sent chills up his spine, but he worried so much he made himself sick. He could hardly bear to look. He endured each contest only in fits and starts, glancing briefly at the filly, then glancing away. Now, faced with the prospect of having to miss one of her races—perhaps her most important race—he discovered to his surprise how desperately he wanted to be there. Watching her run was agonizing; not watching her would be even worse.

2

Three mornings after winning the Filly Triple Crown with Ruffian, Jacinto climbed aboard Foolish Pleasure and followed LeRoy Jolley out to the main track. This started a buzz among the rumor-hungry. After all, Braulio Baeza had been officially named by Jolley as his rider for the Match, and Baeza had ridden the colt for his last workout, on the morning of the eighteenth.

Foolish Pleasure breezed an easy seven furlongs. After his first eighth, he had been held to a very steady twelve-second clip, finishing out in 1:25. It was what the clockers called a "useful trial."

When they returned to the barn, they were faced by a circle of reporters who demanded to know if Jolley was having second thoughts about Baeza. The trainer shook his head and assured them he had not changed his mind. Why then, they wanted to know, was Jacinto once again working Foolish Pleasure in the morning?

"Because he's a good exercise rider," the trainer answered.

"But aren't you afraid he'll learn some of your secrets, if he keeps handling the colt?"

"Look." Jolley tried not to show his irritation. "If Jacinto doesn't know all about this colt by now, he's not going to learn anything new in these workouts." After all—as he had tried to explain several times already—there were no strategic secrets to ferret out. This was a match race. Neither the filly nor the colt had any choice: They would each try to take the lead and hold it for a mile and a quarter.

"I'll put Braulio on him, too," Jolley added. "Probably for his next work, on Sunday." That workout would be the more important one, for that was when he planned to ask the colt for some real speed. During the remaining twelve days before the Match, his primary goal was sharpening the colt's speed.

Jolley knew his colt could run. He'd racked up some excellent fractions as a two-year-old. This year, however, both Jolley and Jacinto had concentrated on teaching the colt to rate in preparation for the grueling Triple Crown campaign, where sheer speed could take you only so far. Foolish Pleasure was a versatile athlete, though; Jolley was convinced that with a few fast works he could regain that early turn of foot. And he wasn't at all concerned about Jacinto being involved during these final stages of preparation; on the contrary. Jacinto's familiarity with the colt could only help their cause.

Frank Whiteley agreed. That's why he was furious when he heard that Jacinto had worked the colt on the twenty-fourth. Why should his jock be lending his expertise to the other side? For the time being, Whiteley held his tongue, for he had heard that Jolley would use Baeza from now on. If Jacinto was through riding the colt, it was spilt milk and there was no need to complain.

For the next few days, both Ruffian and Foolish Pleasure drew more than the usual number of onlookers as they circled the track in their regular morning gallops. Their upcoming contest meant a lot to everyone associated with Belmont. There had not been a match race in New York since 1947, when Armed and Assault confronted each other in a special, nonwagering event. That had been a popular contest, but nothing like the current match. For one thing, both Foolish Pleasure and Ruffian were hometown horses, regularly stabled on the grounds. One had captured the Kentucky Derby; the other was undefeated, ten for ten.

Plus, to top it all off, one was a colt and one a filly. This immediately became the focus of discussion. Wherever the debate started, it almost always ended on that note. Not content to see which horse was faster—which, ostensibly, was what a race measured—people rushed in from all sides to imbue this contest with symbolic meaning. Not who was faster, but who was *better*, males or females?

Part of its appeal was that it was so simple. In a head-to-head race, only two outcomes were possible: The colt would beat the filly, or the filly would beat the colt.

For five consecutive days prior to the Match, the *Daily Racing Form* ran an informal nationwide poll under the heading "Who D'Ya Like?" In it, they surveyed trainers, jockeys, owners, and officials, the vast majority of whom were men, and published their comments about how they thought the race would shape up. The world of thoroughbred racing had never been a caldron of progressive attitudes—with few exceptions, women had not been permitted to work on the backstretch in any capacity until the late 1960s—yet when it came to choosing sides for the Match, racing people set aside their prejudices and went with the evidence. The prevailing opinion, by a wide margin, was that Ruffian was the better of the two horses, and in a match race, where speed from the start almost always determined the outcome, the filly had a decided edge. The race, they predicted, was Ruffian's to lose.

"Don't kill the bitch out there. You understand me, Por-ta Rican?" Whiteley pulled Sled Dog to a halt.

Jacinto nodded. He was taking Ruffian out for an easy half-mile. He jogged her the wrong way up the track, turned, and eased her into a gallop to warm up. Then he chirped once and off they went. Along the outside rail other riders slowed their mounts so they could watch the black filly breeze.

Ruffian covered the four furlongs quickly and with no fuss. She had probably gone faster than Whiteley wanted, but Jacinto couldn't help that. He'd done his best to hold her to a reasonable pace.

Suddenly, there was a commotion nearby. A horse had thrown its rider and was coming up fast on the outside. As soon as Ruffian heard it, she took off again.

Jacinto screamed at her to stop. He hauled back on the reins and stood straight up in the irons, using his whole body as leverage against the bit, but the filly was determined to outrun the other horse.

"Get that sonofabitch out of here!" Jacinto shouted at the outrider, who had swerved expertly on his pony at the first sign of trouble.

Jacinto felt the sting of leather against his palms as Ruffian continued to fight for her head. She was racing the riderless horse. It didn't matter that she had just breezed four furlongs in 47 seconds. It didn't matter that a piece of metal was tearing at her mouth. Ruffian was normally a well-behaved, responsive horse, but she had one inviolable rule: When she was running on the racetrack, no other horse was allowed to pass.

By the time the outrider had grabbed the bridle of the loose horse, Ruffian was under control. Jacinto's throat was hoarse and his shoulders ached, but he was not worried about himself; he was scared the extra work had drained his filly. With only nine days remaining till the Match, anything that threw her off schedule might prove disastrous.

Then he almost laughed. Whiteley would tear into him, that went without saying, but after two seasons with this filly, Jacinto realized that he was the only one who'd be worn out by the morning's excitement. It didn't matter if Ruffian had given herself a double workout—like he used to give those horses at Remon, when he was desperate to ride races—because she never got tired. Ruffian could run all day.

On Sunday morning Braulio Baeza and his agent Lenny Goodman drove over to LeRoy Jolley's barn. Jolley outlined his basic plan for the final week of preparation: six furlongs today, then three days of galloping, and a final three-furlong blowout on Thursday. The time for these final workouts was crucial, since everything depended on the colt's being sharp. Baeza was to take the colt out and work him in 1:10 or thereabouts. Speed was of the utmost importance, Jolley emphasized, since he had only these two workouts left before the Match. Baeza listened impassively. If he was getting on a man's horse, he was going to do his best. No one had to impress him with the significance of his job.

When they stepped out onto the track, around seven-thirty, the air was hot and sticky and the sky was overcast. The clockers took particular note of Jolley's colt. This was an important work, and they were curious to see how much would be asked of him.

As Baeza warmed the colt up, he could feel that the track was a little deep. It changed every day, sometimes from hour to hour, or race to race, depending on the wind, the sun, the amount of moisture in the soil. There was nothing Baeza could do about that. He brought Foolish Pleasure around, galloped him over to the three-quarter pole, and asked him to run. As much as anyone else, Baeza wanted this colt ready for the Match.

Foolish Pleasure took off smoothly and felt fine, but even with steady urging, he lacked the explosive response Baeza had been looking for. Still, the rider wasn't too worried. He could see that everyone else out there was also bogging down in the dull track. He had no reason to be displeased until ten minutes later, when he caught up to Jolley, who was waiting for him on the pony.

"That wasn't what I wanted at all!" Jolley fumed. All the color had drained from the trainer's face. "He ran in 1:14! Goddamn it, you might have just cost me the race out there!" He was so outraged that his hands were shaking.

Baeza didn't respond. Later, away from the ears and eyes of reporters, he might explain to Jolley about the track and tell him not to worry. He would never allow himself to get into a public argument with a trainer under such circumstances. Jolley was a knowledgeable, experienced horseman; he would understand those things. But when Baeza dismounted, back at the barn, Jolley was still too angry to talk.

He was, in fact, devastated. He had come so far, and now a rider had ruined everything! Why couldn't Baeza have followed orders? Foolish Pleasure had always been a good work horse; he was willing and he always finished strong. A time like 1:14 was totally uncharacteristic. And if it wasn't the jock's fault, the alternatives were worse: Maybe the colt had hurt himself. Or maybe he was ill.

Jolley held himself together long enough to examine the colt and reassure himself there was no physical problem. But what if Foolish Pleasure was just worn out? It happened. The Triple Crown had been a rough grind. Maybe the colt's tank was finally empty, in which case he would be eaten alive by the filly when they met.

The thought literally made Jolley so sick that he bent over and vomited. At that moment, if there were any possible way he could have done so, he would have called off the Match.

3

As July sixth neared, the demand on both camps for media appearances and interviews escalated to such a degree that many offers had to be turned down. Baeza and Vasquez had been invited to appear on the *Tonight* show. The Association would have loved the publicity, but both riders were busy racing and working horses every day, and both were vying for the New York riding title. They had no time—and little inclination—to take the red-eye to the West Coast and back for publicity that neither felt they needed. Money might have lured them, but they were offered only the standard appearance fee. They declined.

There were other requests that they couldn't refuse. Local newspapers did photo spreads on the jockeys and their families, and Jacinto in particular made good copy because of the popular "Women's Liberation" angle—not only had Jacinto chosen the filly, but he also lived surrounded by females: his wife, two daughters, and his mother-in-law.

It was the normally reticent Baeza rather than the outspoken Vasquez who created the only shock in the otherwise predictable wave of coverage. In an appearance on *Sports Extra*, a local television show on Sunday evening, one week before the Match, he made a comment that stunned the audience. "Frank Whiteley is a creep," Baeza said simply. "I hate his guts and he hates mine. I really want to win this race."

Until that moment the Great Match Race had been a more or less impersonal contest. There was no vendetta between Vasquez and Baeza, who were friends, or Whiteley and Jolley, who, while not friends, were certainly not personal enemies, either,

or between the Janneys and the Greers. Even to the public, for
whom the race summoned up emotions that had nothing to do
with racing, it was a general rather than a specific rivalry. Now
a new layer of tension had been revealed, between a jockey who
believed he had been slandered and a trainer who believed he'd
been betrayed.

Their anger went back seven years. Racing insiders had
known about it, but most thought it was water under the bridge.
Unfortunately, it was precisely the kind of disagreement that
would never be resolved. It all stemmed from two outings Baeza
had aboard Damascus. Whiteley had trained Damascus to a
Horse of the Year title in 1967, and when the colt returned as a
four-year-old in January of 1968, in California, Willie Shoemaker was still his regular rider. But before the month was over,
Shoemaker was sidelined as the result of a bad spill, and Whiteley was forced to find substitutes the entire year.

He turned primarily to Manny Ycaza, but he had also used
Baeza, in the DuPont and the Aqueduct, and both times Baeza
had brought Damascus home in front. When the Michigan Mile
and One-Eighth, popularly referred to as "the Michigan Mile,"
rolled around, Whiteley again secured the services of Braulio
Baeza, who had been the top money-winning jockey in the country for the past three years.

Damascus had been assigned high weight of 133 out of a
field of twelve. Baeza was instructed to rate the colt and then
make one move in the latter part of the race, but with less than
half a mile remaining, Damascus was still fifteen lengths back.
When Baeza finally let him go, he made up a ton of ground but
was too late to catch the leader, Nodouble, who was carrying
only 111. Whiteley was disgusted. He thought Baeza had waited
too long on purpose; Baeza felt he was simply the victim of some
bad racing luck.

Whiteley would have preferred not to use Baeza again, but
the owner of the horse, Edith Bancroft, who had been a knowledgeable horsewoman, was extremely ill and no longer able to
communicate. When the trainer explained to her husband what
he felt had happened, Mr. Bancroft appeared shocked. "Frank,
I don't really think the boy would have held him back. I can't
believe that. Let's give him the benefit of the doubt and try him

again." So Baeza rode the horse another time, in the 1968 Woodward Stakes.

This time Damascus went right to the front and, for most of the mile and a quarter race, he held a narrow lead over a horse named Mr. Right. However, in the final strides, Mr. Right swept by to win. Once again, Whiteley was suspicious of the ride. Damascus had to bull his way past horses; if you let him go head to head with someone for awhile, you could not force him away. Baeza, Whiteley thought, had not gotten after the horse when he should have. From the quarter pole to the finish, Beaza had not hit the horse once.

When the horses returned to be unsaddled, Whiteley stormed down from the Bancrofts' box and met them out on the track. "Get the hell off my horse, you goddamn Chinaman, or I'll pull you off!" he shouted, loud enough for several reporters to hear. Baeza refused to look at him, weighed in, and headed for the jockeys' room. He had a very different perspective on the race: he felt there had been something wrong with Damascus, that the big horse was not himself that afternoon. As a rider, Baeza had not wanted to risk putting pressure on a horse that might be hurting, even a little bit.

As long as there had been racetracks, trainers and jockeys had blamed each other for defeats. On the whole, Whiteley was not the type of trainer to cry over a lost race, but this time his fury was unmistakable and on public view. He carried it one step further by filing a complaint with the stewards, charging Baeza with deliberately holding his horse in order to let another horse win. The stewards examined the films of the race and determined they could not substantiate the claim.

Whiteley remained convinced he had a case, right down to the motive. The two biggest rivals on the track that year were Damascus and Dr. Fager, both contenders for Horse of the Year honors. They had hooked up four times over the last two years, and each had come away with two victories. Baeza was the regular rider for Dr. Fager. Since the two horses were not scheduled to meet head on again, the best way to help the Doctor's cause was for Damascus to win fewer races the remainder of the season.

Baeza continued to be bitterly resentful of Whiteley for assaulting his character and dragging his name in the mud. He felt vindicated by the stewards' decision, but he never forgave the trainer for leveling the charge. The anger that had simmered between them for years had now boiled over into the public.

The morning after *Sports Extra* aired, Barney Nagler showed up at Whiteley's barn. "Well," Nagler began, "how does it feel to be called a 'crumb'?"

"Didn't call me a crumb," Whiteley corrected. "Called me a creep."

"Oh," Nagler said with admiration in his voice, "that moves you up a length or two. On my scale, a crumb is less than a creep."

That brought a grin to Whiteley's face, which he quickly erased. "Don't go making too much of that Baeza thing," he said. "I don't like fights at that level."

4

Even earlier that morning, before the first set went over to the track, Fats and Jacinto had met with Whiteley at his barn. After Foolish Pleasure's disastrous six furlongs the day before, Jolley had asked Jacinto to work the colt one more time, for his final sharpener before the race. Naturally, word had filtered back to Whiteley.

"Listen here, Fats." The trainer lit a cigarette and ignored the coffee Fats had offered. "I don't give a damn if Baeza screwed up that work or not. Jacinto is not working that colt, or I'll get another rider for the Match. I mean it." He glanced at Jacinto, but continued to address Fats. "Way I see it, anything Jacinto does to help Foolish Pleasure hurts our chances. He had a choice and he chose the filly. Until the Match is over, he belongs to me. Like part of my own training equipment. He owes it to me and the horse and the public to do everything possible to win this race."

"Well, all right, Frank." Fats was momentarily at a loss for words. "It's just that Jolley asked, and I've been riding his horse all year."

"I know it," Whiteley interrupted. "Jacinto rode a lotta races for LeRoy, and I believe he owes a degree of allegiance to the man. But not now. Until this match is over, he's working for me lock, stock, and barrel or he ain't working for me at all. That's the way it's gotta be."

Jacinto poked at the dirt with his boot. "Okay," he shrugged. "If you say so."

This was going to create tension between him and Jolley, but there was nothing he could do about it. For two years, the web of his career had been woven from the interlocking threads of these two barns and these two horses. Now, with a sinking feeling, Jacinto realized that regardless of the outcome of the Match, these threads were going to unravel.

It didn't take Jolley long to recover from the apparent fiasco of the day before. The first thing he did when the reporters approached—including those who had heard his outburst twenty-four hours earlier—was to reassure them that Baeza was still his rider for the Match.

"I studied all the works at six furlongs for yesterday," Jolley began, "and I've got to conclude that maybe the colt's wasn't that bad after all. The track was very dull; there wasn't a work all day you could really call fast. Everything was in the 1:14 range. Also, we didn't run till after seven-thirty, and you know the earlier you run here, the faster the track. When the sun sucks out the moisture it gets a little slower because of all the sand. It honestly wasn't that bad."

"You gonna work the colt again before the Match?"

"We'll probably hang him over the fence later this week. Don't know for sure, maybe five furlongs. I should think he'll go a lot faster in that one."

"How's the colt feeling?"

"He's fine. Relaxed." Jolley smiled. "He has come this far and beaten just about everything they've thrown at him no matter what I do, so I guess he's smarter than I am. Who knows?"

"Who'll ride him for the next work?"

"Baeza."

"Hey, did you hear him on TV last night? What do think about his feud with Whiteley?"

Jolley shook his head. "I don't know anything about that. You'll have to speak to Braulio about that."

"What will you do tomorrow?"

"Probably just gallop him his regular two miles."

"We'll need to get some pictures, LeRoy. What time are you going to bring him out?"

"Oh, probably around six."

"Six! How come so early?"

"So I can finish early and get out to the golf course!"

A small army of photographers arrived the next day to shoot the colt and the filly as they continued their preparations for the Match. After his bath, Foolish Pleasure was grazed for an hour, and Jolley had instructed his assistant to allow the photographers and cameramen to do their job—as long as they didn't get too close and didn't interrupt the colt's routine activities.

Whiteley wasn't so cooperative. The sawhorses were still up on the path leading to his barn, and he had allowed them to be removed for television cameras only once: He had to let CBS take some footage of the filly. They did a quick shoot of her inside her stall, nibbling on her hay ball, and he let them follow her over to the grassy area nearby where she grazed. But instead of grazing or walking around, Ruffian, who knew just what the cameras were for, simply lifted her head and posed. Frank had to jiggle the shank and lead her around in a circle so they could get some action in the shot.

And one morning after Squeaky finished galloping her, Frank had agreed to let someone from the press office bring around a cameraman for the New York Racing Association. They filmed Dan giving the filly her bath while Mike held her and answered a few questions.

A bunch of still photographers wasn't so lucky. They showed up in the early afternoon while Ruffian and the other horses were resting. Frank was tempted to send them all packing; then he got a funny look on his face. He pointed to the last stall at the far end of the barn.

"That's her down there," he told them. "Mike, go over there with them. Don't let 'em bother her none, though. Can't let her out of the stall."

Red-faced, Mike dutifully led the photographers down to Loud's stall. He hoped no one would ask him questions, because he hated to lie. The gelding was big, like Ruffian; he was dark, life Ruffian; and he had a little irregular star on his forehead, like Ruffian. Otherwise he looked completely different. His head was much broader and coarser, and his muzzle was a much lighter shade of brown; his body was thicker and not so long; and he was not nearly so composed as the filly. Like all the horses in the barn, he wore a halter with a nameplate on it. But Frank had long since discovered that a lot of reporters and photographers—especially those who did not regularly cover racing—were scared of horses; they never got close enough to read the fine print. Their cameras whirred and clicked, Loud snorted a few times but didn't lunge at anyone—he'd smashed Mike's brother in the head once, when he'd come to visit—and finally the photo session came to an end.

Frank had tilted his chair back against the wall, pulled his hat down till it rested just above his eyeglasses, and pretended not to notice what was going on at the other end of the barn. Directly behind him, in her stall, Ruffian was lying down in the straw, taking a nap.

5

On the Tuesday afternoon before the race, Vasquez and Baeza were being honored by the city of New York in a special ceremony on the steps of the public library on Fifth Avenue and Forty-second Street. In spite of the hot weather, they both donned suits and ties, polished their dress boots, and drove in with their wives. For the first time in years they were free on a weekday: On June 8, the day following the Belmont Stakes, the New York Racing Association had instituted Sunday racing, and now Tuesday was the single dark day at the track.

Standing in for Mayor Abe Beame was Neil Walsh, the chairman of the city's Athletic and Community Task Force, who presented each jockey with a specially engraved silver coin commemorating the Great Match Race. Off-duty stewardesses had been hired to hand out NYRA's promotional buttons to the large lunch-hour crowds. The buttons had a picture of either the filly or the colt on them with their name written in green letters underneath and the words THE GREAT MATCH above.

The whole city was excited about this race. For the average taxpayer as well as the politicians, it was a welcome diversion from their growing urban woes, notably the worst fiscal crisis that had ever hit New York. Anything local that generated positive headlines was seized upon with feverish delight.

On Wednesday, Off-Track Betting officially began taking wagers on the Match. They were permitting special use of the letters R for Ruffian and F for Foolish Pleasure rather than the standard A, B, C designations that had come to replace both names and numbers in the off-track operation. Every day through Saturday,

226

from seven-thirty in the morning until eight at night, New York City OTB was accepting bets for the Match. On Sunday their windows would stay open until four-thirty in the afternoon. The race was scheduled for six o'clock.

This was an unusually long period in which to accept wagering on a single race, and OTB made sure it got in on the promotional act as well. They distributed 200,000 buttons, simpler and even more direct than those put out by NYRA. Each button had a single word on it, and you could take your choice: HIM or HER.

If ever there was a race that captured and exploited the emotion of the moment, this was it.

The odds set by the linemaker on that first morning showed Foolish Pleasure listed at better than even money, 4-to-5. However, for the first time in his entire career, he was not the favorite. Ruffian had been listed at 1-to-2.

By six-thirty Ruffian was already untacked. Having watched the filly's workout from the rail, Teddy Cox wandered over to the barn for his morning report.

"She was the first horse out there," Whiteley volunteered as Cox took out his pad. "Soon's the harrows had churned the soil and they opened the gate, in we went."

Whiteley tapped out a cigarette. Both he and Cox settled in under the shedrow to watch the filly get her bath.

"What did you think, Frank?"

"She didn't go too fast. Frenchy got her in :58 and one. Other guy got her a fifth quicker. Don't want her going too fast."

"What's left now? Anything else you can do?"

"That's about it. I've done everything I know to get her ready. She may blow out a little later in the week." For a while the two men were silent, studying the filly. Frank tossed out his cigarette, which he had hardly touched. He immediately lit up another one.

"I wish the race were tomorrow," he said.

6

"**Y**ates, do me a favor." Whiteley pulled the stopwatch out of his pocket and tapped on it a few times with his thumb.

"What do you want, Frank?"

It was quiet time on the backstretch. The horses had finished lunch and were resting in their stalls. The grooms had wiped out the feed tubs and swept the shedrow, bandages had been washed and hung out to dry, and the activity in all the barns had just about ground to a halt.

"Take a walk over to the paddock, will you, like you're bringing over a horse for a race?"

Yates looked puzzled, but he nodded. "All right."

Frank handed him the stopwatch. "And let me know exactly how long it takes to get over there, will you?"

Yates tugged at his ever-present cowboy hat. "Now I gotcha." He pressed the button on the watch and headed off.

There was always a method to Frank's madness. He wasn't going to arrive at the paddock for the match race and then have Ruffian stuck in the middle of a mob scene while Foolish Pleasure took his own sweet time.

Although Ruffian had always been calm before her races, Frank didn't know what to expect on the afternoon of the sixth. The filly was aware that something big was coming up. Maybe it was a projection of their own tensions, but everyone at the barn agreed. Under the shedrow she was her usual businesslike self, but once she hit the track in the mornings, whether she was galloping or going out to breeze, she crackled with energy and threatened to flare up any moment. They were being more cautious than ever with her.

It was worth every penny to Frank to have kept Squeaky in New York. Not to take anything away from Yates, who was as good an exercise rider as they came, but in terms of temperament, Squeaky was the one best suited to the filly, especially now, when she was getting tough. He was really the only one who could relax her on the track. Yates was quick and intense, like Frank, and the filly on occasion could provoke him; Squeaky remained quiet and deliberate, always protective of Ruffian. He respected her as a racehorse, but underneath he still thought of her as the "little schoolgirl" he took care of. No matter how stubborn she became, he never tried to push her around. When he was on the filly's back, he saw his job as that of older brother: the equivalent of holding her hand, getting her across the busy streets, and guiding her safely home.

Not only was Frank determined not to enter the paddock ahead of Jolley, he had even considered getting there late. What could the stewards do? They could fine him, that was all. He'd been fined for similar tactics plenty of times. Under the circumstances, they couldn't scratch his horse. The race was being broadcast on national television, and without his horse there was no race.

He had already made it clear to the press office that no TV crews could interview him or any of his people once they left the barn. Just in case CBS didn't respect his wishes, he would have Sled Dog along to help enforce them. Sled Dog, strategically placed, could discourage anyone from getting too close.

He had the timing question down to an art. Yates would let him know how long the walk over would take. Then, on Sunday, just before the seventh race, he would send someone to the spitbox to get the precise post time for the feature. The official times were set from there, and he would adjust his watch to be in sync with them.

Frank didn't want any surprises. He had to know exactly when to expect the burst of static over the loudspeakers: "Horsemen, get your horses ready . . ."

Ting! Ting! Ting!

Frank leaned against the fence and listened to the sound of hammer against metal. The aluminum plates had a light, musical tone. Jarboe worked quickly, making a few slight adjustments so that the shoes would conform more perfectly to each of the filly's hooves.

"So." Jarboe didn't look up as he worked. "Those New York officials didn't know I'd been shoeing your horses all this time, hey, Frank?"

"That's right. If you believe it. Hell, they don't know nothing around here till somebody complains. Or it gets into the papers." Frank watched as Jarboe finished up. Not surprisingly, NYRA had granted a special thirty-day license permitting the blacksmith to work at the track.

Jarboe was doing nothing different for the Match. The filly was getting her standard size fives with caulks in the rear. The caulk gave the heel a slight lift that enabled the toe, the front part of the shoe, to grab the dirt a little more firmly, giving the horse a better footing. After each shoe was nailed into place, Jarboe carefully filed each hoof with his rasp. When he was finished, he folded up his leather apron and packed away his tools.

"Whyn't you stay up here a few days," Frank said, "watch the race with us?"

"Nah, got to get back. My grandson's coming over Sunday, we're gonna watch her on the television."

"All right, then, you old son of a gun. Safe trip home, you hear?"

Jarboe started for his truck. "I'll come up and watch her in the fall, when she takes on the big boys. That'll be something, won't it? All of 'em at once?"

Frank nodded. He was staring at Ruffian, who was busy chewing on some hay. "Looks good, don't she, Jarboe?" Frank said over his shoulder. "What do you think?"

"Hell, yes!" Jarboe answered. "Goddamn soundest good horse I ever worked on!"

7

The draw for post positions was held on Thursday morning. Frank chose to remain at the barn with his horses, but plenty of photographers, reporters, officials, and other trainers had gathered for the event. Tom FitzGerald, president of NYRA, was going to pick the numbers. The positions were labeled "One" and "Two," but it had been agreed that the horses would actually break from the third and fourth stalls of the starting gate so that neither horse would be stuck too near the rail.

Without a full field, a draw such as this lacked the usual element of suspense. Neither horse was going to lose a lot of ground because of its position in the gate, and neither was going to encounter traffic jams. But if post positions didn't make much difference, a question was raised about something else that might. Trainer Allen Jerkens, the "Giant Killer" who had beaten Secretariat twice, pointed out to a reporter that there could be problems when races started from the chute. The chute was a long straightaway that crossed the training track and blended into the main track along the backstretch, past the clubhouse turn. Horses starting from the chute had to travel over three different surfaces, which was not a desirable situation. No matter how it was harrowed, the training track could never be made absolutely level with the chute.

"I think the key could be that start," Jerkens said. "There is always a slight dip, either right before the crossing on the training track or right after it. It could be a big factor."

The jockeys would want to move towards the outside, where the difference in levels was less noticeable. In this respect, whoever drew the outside position would hold a very minor advantage. However, the basic risk—guiding their horses over a changing surface—was something both riders would share.

The press hardly reacted when Foolish Pleasure drew the number 2 post and Ruffian the number 1, but there was much excitement in the room over something else: Word had spread about Foolish Pleasure's latest work.

Earlier that morning he had zipped five furlongs in :56⅖. That wasn't just good or even excellent time, that was phenomenal. That was the kind of work Ruffian had been known to knock off on occasion. Even Jolley was surprised, and briefly worried it would prove too much. Horses who used themselves that hard in the mornings sometimes came up empty in the afternoons. But the colt returned to the barn in good spirits and ate up all his oats. True, the track that morning had been lightning fast. Jolley had noticed that one of Mack Miller's sprinters, a colt named Queen City Lad who worked just before Foolish Pleasure, was clocked in :57⅗. It was a hard, fast track, one of the fastest anyone at Belmont had seen in quite a while. In fact, several trainers had complained about the surface, insisting that their horses were coming back sore.

Regardless of the track condition, Foolish Pleasure had turned in an outstanding work. Even observers who strongly favored Ruffian began to think the Match would be a real contest and not the walkover they had initially envisioned. Five furlongs in :56⅖ meant only one thing: Foolish Pleasure was ready. This was going to be a horserace.

Early that afternoon, when Ruffian had finished her midday nap, Mike held her near the webbing in her stall for about thirty minutes while her front legs soaked in two buckets filled with ice cubes and cold water. Afterwards, Dan would rebandage her. Whiteley was seated nearby, chatting with Teddy Cox.

Cox had one thing on his mind. "You heard about the colt's work this morning, didn't you, Frank? He went in :56 and two."

Whiteley nodded. "That's a real fast work. Should put him on his toes."

"Fifty-six and two is more than fast, Frank! That's a sensational time!"

"It sure is," Frank agreed. "Do you think we should scratch

Ruffian?" He paused a moment, letting the sarcasm sink in, then he relented. "Look, he's a fine colt who is as honest as they come. He's got all kinds of speed. LeRoy's done an excellent job of keeping him in good form." What did everyone expect? If the colt hadn't been good, there wouldn't have been any interest in a match. There was no point running Ruffian against a dog. That's what competition was about—testing yourself. No matter how much you were favored, they never paid you the money for staying in the barn.

Behind them, in the growing silence, the stall fans whirred.

8

Jacinto sat up in bed. Beside him, his wife Patty slept peacefully. It was the morning of the Match, and a single sentence had flashed into his mind: *Something's not gonna go my way.*

He tried to account for it. Ruffian was as sound as she had ever been. Security had been double- and triple-checked the last few weeks; no one could have gotten to her. He himself was in excellent shape. The feeling was irrational—it had to be—and yet it had disturbed him.

Maybe it was a reaction to the stresses of the past few weeks. That would make sense. He had been forced to choose between the two biggest horses of his life. The fact that he might have some doubts—subconscious doubts—was not at all surprising. Especially since he knew, no matter how the race turned out, that there would be a price to pay.

Of course, he couldn't tell anyone. If he expressed these vague misgivings, Whiteley would not want him on the filly, and Jacinto was determined not to lose the mount. Not just for today, but in the future. That's what made the feeling so unsettling: He genuinely believed Ruffian was the better horse. He didn't see how she could lose this race.

It was earlier than he usually woke up, but he knew instantly he would not get back to sleep. He dressed and drove himself over to the barn.

Jacinto was not the only one to show up early, but Frank found extra work for everyone to do. He refused to let the stablehands just hang around Ruffian. No matter what they said, Frank knew

they all were tense and nervous, and horses picked up on people's moods. He wanted business to go on as usual. Dan walked
the filly under the shedrow. She grazed and had her ankles iced.
Dan bandaged her. She took her midday nap.

Jacinto stepped over the cables that lay stretched out across the
floor of the jockeys' room. Earlier, CBS had taped a segment
there with Eddie Arcaro. Chic Anderson, who was calling the
race on TV, had asked him about the 1955 match race between
Nashua and Swaps, in Washington Park, Illinois, in which Arcaro had ridden Nashua to an upset victory, and the cameras
had been left in place so they could catch both Jacinto and Braulio for live, postrace interviews.

Because the feature would not go off until after six, Jacinto
had more time than usual between races. He stripped off the
red polka dot silks of the Bancrofts' Pen-Y-Bryn Farm. He had
no idea why Honorable Miss had done so poorly in the Nassau
County Handicap. She had broken well, she had stayed clear of
traffic, but she had not responded when he asked her to run.
He shrugged his undershirt off over his head and ducked in for
a quick shower.

Her performance had not been the strangest thing about
that race. The strangest thing had been the weather. All day, the
temperature had stayed around 80 degrees, and for the first
three races there was bright sun. During the next three races a
soft cloud cover drifted in, muting the light. But just before
Honorable Miss's race, there were violent thunderclaps and staggering bolts of lightning to the west, in Manhattan, where the
skies had darkened like a bruise into an angry purplish-red. It
was such a sudden, overwhelming change that the announcers
for CBS commented on it, wondering how soon the storm would
cross the river and hit Belmont. Would the eighth race—the
Match—be run in a thunderstorm? Could the day get any more
dramatic than this?

By the time Jacinto emerged from the shower a few minutes
later, he had put the Nassau County Handicap, the weather, and
the media out of his mind. His focus now was on the Match. He
peered into the mirror nailed inside his locker. There were
hollows under his eyes, though he was not aware of feeling

tired. He ran a comb through his hair, changed into clean whites, and looked up to see Timmy holding out the Janneys' silks.

He slid them on, twisted a rubber band over each wrist, then tucked in his shirttail. He glanced back at his reflection and once again slid the comb through his hair.

Across the aisle from him, Braulio Baeza went through virtually the same routine. They had each done this tens of thousands of times, and thousands of times they had each come home winners. In fact, they were tied for the lead in the jockey standings for the Belmont summer meet, with 23 wins apiece.

Jack O'Hara stood up from behind his desk and straightened his sport jacket. "First call for the eighth race," he intoned into the microphone. "First call for the Great Match Race." He went through the formalities as if they were part of an everyday occurrence. Cradling his clipboard in his arm, he stared intently at the needle on the scale as Braulio and Jacinto took turns stepping up with their tack. A cluster of jockeys stood around watching, and as the pair strode out through the crowd of reporters, several other riders called after them, "Good luck!"

On another occasion Jacinto and Braulio might have climbed the stairs and headed for the paddock together, but not today. Without having exchanged a word, they understood that each preferred to go up on his own.

The paddock was always crowded for a major stakes, but for the match race it was mobbed. Jockey Club members mingled with politicians and NYRA officials; the huge press corps had descended, along with scores of photographers and the television crew. The Janneys and the Greers and their immediate families were joined by Phippses and Whitneys and Mellons and Vanderbilts. They pressed together inside the iron rails that had been decorated all weekend with red, white, and blue bunting in the spirit of the Fourth of July.

Outside the rails, thousands of onlookers surrounded the paddock, trying to catch sight of the filly and the colt. Frank had positioned Sled Dog in front of the saddling enclosure, so even the television cameras could not catch Ruffian being tacked up. When both horses were ready and the riders lifted aboard, the grooms led them once around the walking ring. Then they exited the paddock and disappeared into the tunnel to the track.

9

Ruffian emerged first. The cheers that followed her rolled out like a wave, crashing along the length of the stands.

No lead pony accompanied her, but Dan stayed with her right up to the gap. She didn't miss a beat as he reached over and unsnapped the shank. With a nod to Jacinto, he let the filly go.

Jacinto steered Ruffian the wrong way up the track. She flicked her ears back and forth, tracing the sounds. She was calm, regal, poised. Jacinto allowed her to proceed at her own pace. When she lowered her head, he gave her more rein. At one point Ruffian stopped dead still. She turned her head to the right, drawn by some unknown distraction. Jacinto let her have a look. After a moment, with no prompting from her rider, she resumed her stately procession.

Behind her, Foolish Pleasure drew his share of cheers as well. He was accompanied as usual by his lead pony, but he, too, appeared calm and well under control. Earlier, in the paddock, Jolley had joked to the TV crew that the colt could afford to be relaxed: He didn't know what was at stake. He didn't know he was facing a superstar. He didn't know he was going after the biggest payday of his career. He didn't know that, to large segments of the population, he represented the entire male sex in his quest for victory. He was just putting in another day at the office. He would, of course, give it his best shot, because he always did.

Foolish Pleasure and Ruffian were models of comportment as they paraded in front of the huge crowd. The noise didn't upset them, nor did the darkened skies and the distant flash of lightning. It was a few minutes before six.

The horses broke into a trot. They continued clockwise towards the top of the stretch, paused, turned left, and passed once more in front of the stands, this time traveling in the right direction. Behind them, dominating the infield, the tote board proclaimed the odds: Foolish Pleasure was listed at 4-to-5; Ruffian was 2-to-5.

The screams of the crowd faded as the two horses galloped along the clubhouse turn and onto the backstretch. As they headed back along the straightaway, towards the gate, they were so far from the stands that they looked like small, carved toys, separated from the spectators by the vastness of the largest track in North America.

The crowd jamming the grandstand was laughing and light-hearted. They polished off the last of their beers, flaunted their T-shirts and long hair, kissed and hugged and pounded the air with clenched fists. In the clubhouse people were more formal and subdued, but they, too, were smiling and eager for the contest to begin, tense with a happy tension, for in those final minutes before the starting bell rang, everyone believed that they would win.

The Janneys had graciously endured an interview with Phyllis George for CBS, but even as they answered the same question over and over—"How are you feeling? How are your spirits?"—their eyes remained riveted on the track where their filly was warming up. Mr. Janney expressed some concern about the impending thunderstorms, and, in his understated manner, refused to predict the outcome of the race.

"I have confidence our filly's gonna do well, but whether she's equal to the task, I don't know," Mr. Janney explained. "That's what we're here to find out."

As soon as they were released from camera and microphone, Mr. and Mrs. Janney were on their feet and heading back to the Phippses' box. Within a few minutes Whiteley was able to join them.

From that point on, they didn't say much to one another. Everything was out of their hands. All they could do was watch.

George Cassidy climbed the stairs to the starter's platform. He straightened his beige sport coat and knocked the sand off his immaculate white bucks. Ruffian and Foolish Pleasure were still a quarter-mile up the track. They had finished warming up and were walking towards the starting gate. Both horses appeared calm. Cassidy didn't anticipate any trouble, but he was prepared.

The colt had never been a problem in the gate, but a few times that spring, Ruffian had seemed a bit anxious. It was nothing Jacinto couldn't cope with, but Cassidy wasn't about to take any chances. His job was to get both horses off fairly and cleanly. This was always his job, regardless of the size or quality of the field, but in a match race the importance of a good start was magnified: first, because the early lead was considered crucial; and second, because if one horse was even slightly disadvantaged at the break, the benefit was not spread out among a whole field of contenders, but went directly to the other horse.

Cassidy called instructions to his assistants. "Harry, you handle Foolish Pleasure. Frank, you handle Ruffian. And both boys be careful."

The jockeys perched above their mounts like fine-boned birds. The filly and the colt were beautifully behaved as they were guided around to the back of the gate. Ruffian turned to enter first. A few feet from the opening she paused. Jacinto tapped her lightly with the stick three times and she walked calmly into the enclosure. Foolish Pleasure entered with equal aplomb.

There was a split second while Cassidy looked down at them; when the assistant starters felt their hearts spinning as they kept a steadying hand on the bridle of their respective horses. The jockeys each grabbed a fistful of mane. Suddenly, Ruffian twisted her head down and to the left—too late! Cassidy had already pressed the starter's gun! The gates had flown open, the race had begun.

A roar went up from the crowd.

From the stands it looked as if both horses had broken cleanly. Foolish Pleasure was a step in front, which surprised no one who had followed Ruffian's career. She had only to relax and find her stride, that long, flowing, trademark stride that had borne her aloft so effortlessly in the past. Jacinto encouraged her, he could not afford to let her lag behind, and if he was a little more tense, more anxious to get going, it was because he knew what no one else would know until they replayed the head-on tapes from the start: Ruffian had been caught off guard and had broken so sharply to her left that she had crashed into the side of the gate, banging her shoulder, and for a fraction of a second was almost perpendicular to Foolish Pleasure, facing the inner rail. She straightened herself immediately by plunging back to the right and began driving hard after her rival.

Within seconds she was rolling. Jacinto felt her settle into her stride as she drew even with the colt. The two horses raced as one down the backstretch. This was the battle everyone had dreamed of, the colt and the filly neck and neck right from the start, both of them burning up the track.

For everyone watching from ground level, much of the first part of the race was obscured by the shrubbery lining the infield, with the horses flashing in and out between the bushes. They were so small, they hardly seemed real.

There was one thing Jacinto had to do for his filly. He figured that Baeza would try to squeeze them over towards the rail, and he did not want to get stuck on that inner strip of track. He steered her out—there was some brushing, they bumped a few times, but nothing serious—this was raceriding; as long as no one was thrown off stride, there was no harm. Crossing from the chute to the main track there was that slight bump in the dirt, banked higher on the inside, and Jacinto did not want Ruffian running over the high part. It would be all right as soon as she made her move and pulled away. Then she could have whatever part of the track she wanted.

Ruffian stuck her nose in front and was timed at the quarter in :22⅕. Dave Johnson noted it at the track, Chic Anderson commented on TV—but for the filly that meant nothing. She had run the first quarter of both her maiden race and the Spinaway in identical time. And those had not even been her fastest starts. In the Astoria she'd gone in :21⅘, and against Hot n Nasty, her toughest competitor prior to the colt, she had blazed an unbelievable first quarter in :21⅗. The filly could move. Oh, this filly could move!

The colt had glued himself to her, but now the glue began to come unstuck. Ruffian was drawing away, slowly, inch by inch; the horses were no longer eye to eye, the filly was stretching out her lead. She stuck her head in front, her neck—you could distinguish two distinct silhouettes—she was picking it up, running smoothly—both riders were encouraging their mounts, pushing, pumping with their hands—it was much too early to even think of going to their sticks, they knew their horses were giving everything they had—this was everybody's wildest dream, a speed duel right from the start—an all-out battle for the lead—three furlongs down the backstretch, three and a half—the filly changed leads, she was running smoothly—now she was half a length in front!

Ruffian was half a length in front and everyone was on their feet, screaming. The noise in the stands was deafening, but it reached the riders only as a distant hum. What they heard was the thundering of hooves, the sharp and steady intake of breath, the ancient and unchanging rhythms of the running horse.

Then both riders heard something else. A quick, bright sound, like the snapping of a twig. Suddenly Foolish Pleasure was a length in front, then two—three—*four!*—and Dave Johnson was crying out into the microphone, his own voice tinged with disbelief: *"Ruffian has broken down! Ruffian has broken down!"*

Fifty thousand people stopped screaming. On the television broadcast, Chic Anderson had called out the same words, in the same stricken voice, to eighteen million more people sitting in homes all across the country. Stunned, they watched the nightmare unfolding on their screens.

Ruffian kept on running.

Jacinto knew instantly what had happened, he had heard the crack of bone, he tried to pull the filly up as quickly as possible but the filly was having none of it. She wanted to run. She was in the race of her life; she was pulling away from the colt and she couldn't understand the sudden pain, the way her balance shifted as she went from four working legs to three. She did not want the other horse in front, she would not let this happen, she was determined to regain the lead. *Let me run!* she shrieked at Jacinto, as silent, as unmistakable as ever, her only demand, fighting the bit, clearer than words, *Let me run!* And Jacinto pulled with all his might, tears stinging the back of his eyes, desperate to hold her up because, at least, oh God, there was a chance if she did not go down! But she was so strong and so determined that she kept on running, and Jacinto had to beg her, beg her to stop, stop! Because if she kept running on three legs she would go down on the track, and then he knew that she would never get back up.

But the filly wouldn't stop. She ignored Vasquez, ignored the bit tearing at her mouth, ignored the pain. She went on running, pulverizing her sesamoids, ripping the skin of her fetlock as the bones burst through, driving the open wound into the stinging sand of the Belmont track, tearing her ligaments, until her hoof was flopping uselessly, bent up like the tip of a ski, as she pounded down the track on the exposed bone, running on and on—it seemed to Jacinto like forever—until finally he managed to pull the valiant, mutilated filly to a halt.

Frank had rushed from the box without a word as soon as the filly stumbled. David met him at the edge of the track, ready to run across, when the Pinkerton stretched out his arm and stopped them both. "I'm sorry," he said. "You can't go out there till the colt crosses. I'm sorry."

There was no time to fight and no argument to make. People couldn't just dart out in front of a horse that was still running on the racetrack. Frank knew that; he understood. He looked up and down the track for some other solution. He had to get to the filly.

Jacinto jumped down, keeping the reins in his left hand, and immediately tried to support the wild-eyed Ruffian by pushing with his right hand against her shoulder. He leaned into her, a human brace, as she tried to circle to her left, to her good side, the only support she had left. Vasquez glanced once at her right foreleg. The foot was hanging by some shreds of skin. It was a useless tangle of blood and filth and protruding bone. He would not look at it again. His goal was just to keep her upright. The vets would have to deal with the rest.

The first person to reach them was Frank Calvarese, the assistant starter who had loaded Ruffian into the gate. As soon as the filly bobbled, he had jumped into the patrol car with Cassidy and Dr. Gilman, the track vet. A grateful Jacinto let Calvarese take the reins while he reached under the filly. He was barely conscious of his own movements; these were acts he had done thousands of times, unbuckling a girth and sliding off a saddle. Up close, he saw the sweat-soaked hair of her back—Ruffian had not broken a sweat going a mile and a half in the Oaks! She had run six furlongs in 1:08⅗ without even getting damp!—and was aware of the dank smell of fear that rose up from the filly's flanks. Jacinto gathered the saddle and blanket and girth under his arm and walked off, slowly, head down. He had had a feeling something would not go his way today. But not this! Not this!

The army-green horse ambulance slowly made its way along the backside. While Calvarese held the filly, Dr. Gilman tried to apply an inflatable plastic cast. Ruffian was not making it easy. She was jumping around and rearing up in desperation. Calvarese, his heart aching to help her, could do nothing to relieve her panic and her pain. He gave her lots of rein and kept talking to her, trying to calm her down while Gilman affixed the cast which would temporarily immobilize the flopping ankle. By the time Gilman was finished, his hands were covered with blood.

Calvarese felt sick to his stomach. He had loaded the filly in the gate for each of her eleven starts. He had seen up close what a proud, intelligent animal she was. Now the stricken look in her eyes told him that she knew how bad it was—*she knew*—and there was nothing he could do to help.

Jimmy Dailey, the outrider, had arrived and remained nearby in case they should need his help. But it was an unnecessary gesture: Ruffian could not run away. She could no longer run at all.

Foolish Pleasure circled the track on his own. If he wanted to collect the $225,000 purse, he had to cross the finish line with his rider on board. Baeza didn't enjoy the trip, but he had no choice. He had wanted to beat the filly because he had wanted to beat Frank Whiteley, but not like this.

He had heard the snap and knew immediately what it meant. One glance over his shoulder as the colt pulled away confirmed it—the filly had broken down; the Great Match Race was over. Foolish Pleasure was running at a terrific clip and the track was lightning fast. His time for the first three-quarters was 1:08⅗. To run that fast on his own steam was fantastic, a tribute in part to what both he and the filly had been honed to do. But there was no point to it now. It wasn't a horserace anymore. Baeza began to ease him up.

Dan and Squeaky eluded the Pinkertons and ran across the infield together. Dan was not young, nor was he used to running, and he was gasping for air as they crossed the huge expanse of green. Squeaky wished he could have carried his friend. More than any single person, Dan had taken care of the filly in the day-to-day sense: fed her, cleaned up after her, bathed her, brushed her, bandaged her, walked her. He had wiped the sleep from her eyes and the snot from her nose. Several times a day he had picked out her feet. He was the one who rode with her every time she stepped inside the van, the one who led her to the track before each race and to the spit-box after she had won. Now, whatever happened, he wanted to be with her. He was no doctor, but he knew Ruffian as well as anyone. He knew that in her terror and her pain, she would be difficult to deal with. If anyone could help to keep her calm, if anyone could ease her, it would be Dan. Because the filly needed him, Dan's sixty-year-old legs found a way to race across the infield grass.

As soon as he saw her falter, Mike, too, sprinted over the track. He ran diagonally across the field from the clockers' stand, as fast as he could, until his breath was cutting at his lungs and throat. He had lived this moment over and over in his mind; every time the filly ran he had been afraid to watch. Now that the very thing he feared the most had happened, all he could think was that it seemed unreal.

The horse ambulance was specially equipped with a hydraulic floor panel that could be lowered to ground level so an injured horse would not have to step up to enter the van. Horace "Blue" Rapelyea, the van operator, slowly lowered the platform. He could see figures converging from across the track, photographers had already started to show up, and several other cars were now approaching. He was relieved to see Dan and Squeaky arrive in time to help the filly into the van. They were familiar with her, and their presence would ensure that the least possible harm was done. Inside the ambulance Dan was able to slip the filly's halter on and ease the bridle off over her head. For the last time, he lifted the bit from her mouth.

On the other side of the track, Foolish Pleasure crossed the finish line, galloping, in 2:02⅘. For LeRoy Jolley it was the longest race of his career. It felt like it had taken the colt over an hour to complete the mile and a quarter, and then there was no sense of victory, no joy, no vindication, not even a shred of satisfaction. No matter what anyone said—and he himself would say, later that evening, that he thought Foolish Pleasure would have won anyway—the better horse was once again only a matter of belief, just as it had been before the race. The Match had proved nothing. It had all been for nothing.

Jim Prendergast had been watching the race on television on the backstretch. Now he rushed to his truck, which was loaded with his vet supplies, and drove over to the track. He spotted Frank and David waiting at the gap and slowed down to let them in. He drove as fast as he dared around the clubhouse turn, but when they reached the far side of the track, the ambulance had already started to roll.

Frank rushed over to it. "I want to get in with her!" he called. Dr. Gilman started back to open the door, but Frank realized he'd only be causing further delay. "Never mind! I'll ride up here." He jumped onto the space between the cab and the van, where Squeaky and Mike were standing, and Blue took off again.

Yates had been watching from the tunnel when the filly broke down. As Dan and Squeaky took off across the infield, Yates rushed back to the paddock and unhitched Sled Dog. He could do nothing for Ruffian on the track, but he could help out over at the barn. If they were going to bring the injured filly back to her stall, he knew he'd better clean it out.

He kicked the pony over to the backside in record time, jumped off and grabbed a pitchfork. He emptied out the stall and swept the dirt away out front. When he stopped to catch his breath, he noticed a crowd of reporters, photographers, and on-lookers converging on the barn.

The jockeys' room was silent as Jacinto entered. Many of the riders remained in front of the television, watching the coverage of the accident. They shook their heads or looked away as Jacinto headed towards his locker. Everyone felt awful. They would have said something, if they thought that it would help, but the accepted wisdom among them was that talking would only make things worse. Jacinto understood their silence.

He would have preferred not to say anything himself, but Chic Anderson was waiting for him with a microphone, looking for once as if he wished he didn't have to do his job. But there was a huge television audience that had been saddened and con-fused by the unexpected turn of events.

"Jacinto, I know this is a bad time, but could we get you on the air just briefly? To give the people at home some idea what happened? It would mean a lot to them."

"I don't know." Jacinto's voice was flat. All he wanted was to dress and go see Frank Whiteley and Ruffian. Yet he understood that millions of people out there loved his filly—were watching just because of her—and they would be desperate for any scrap of news. What he had to report would not be optimistic, but at least it would be honest. "Just give me a minute, okay, let me wash my face?"

Off camera he unsnapped the red and white silks and handed them to Timmy. He tossed the rubber bands into his locker. When he returned from the bathroom, he headed for the desk of the Clerk of Scales. He had one more piece of busi-ness to attend to.

Jack O'Hara watched him approach. Even O'Hara, with his formidable command of the English language, could not find words to tell Jacinto how sorry he was.

Jacinto tapped his fingers on the desk. "Can you get me off that horse in the ninth race?" he said.

"It's already taken care of. I would never ask you to ride again today." O'Hara nodded towards the television cameras. "Go on, finish up. I know you want to get over to the barn."

Baeza guided Foolish Pleasure into the winner's circle. The jockey looked grim. He tossed his stick to his valet, the photos were taken, and he dismounted. There was a flurry of weak cheers, then a chorus of boos and hisses as the officials carried out what was, without question, the least popular ceremony that had ever taken place in the Belmont winner's circle.

There was no dispute that Foolish Pleasure had won the race, but it was a hollow victory, for he had not beaten anyone. Certainly he had not beaten the filly. And, through no fault of his own, he had failed to answer any of the questions that had prompted the Match in the first place.

Yet John Greer and his wife were beaming, accepting the trophy even as Ruffian was being loaded into the ambulance. Congratulations were offered, and a handful of press and publicity people crowded around the colt's connections. LeRoy Jolley remained low-key. He was in a difficult position. His owners were openly pleased, they had just won $225,000—of which LeRoy was due ten percent—but to the trainer, in spite of his big payday, the Match had proved nothing. And it had cost the racing world a great champion. All the spirit was drained from the day.

His father, however, was exultant. Two years ago Moody Jolley had picked out this son of What a Pleasure for $20,000 up at Saratoga, and now he could not refrain from gloating. When asked what he thought of the turn of events, the senior Jolley grinned. Away from the television microphones, but loud enough for those around him to hear, he exclaimed, "First time they threw some speed at her, and the bitch comes unbuckled!"

Reporters who thought they had heard everything were shocked. A great racehorse had just broken down. They didn't expect Moody to be gracious, but they didn't expect such ugliness, either.

Dan never stopped talking to the filly. He spoke gently, quietly, as they rode inside the van, but everything he said now was a lie, and he knew it. Nothing was all right anymore, and from the looks of it, things were only going to get worse.

Blue was as careful as any driver could possibly be, but every bump over the dirt track seemed like a mountain to Dan. He was determined to prevent any further harm to his distraught filly. In the past, Ruffian had always been so placid when she traveled, but now she was tossing her head, kicking out, trying to back away. Dan kept a firm hold on the shank and a steady hand on her shoulder. He kept talking, talking, soothing her with his voice. He tried to reassure her. It was the only thing he could do.

Outside, in the space between the cab and the van, Squeaky, Mike, and Frank rode without saying a word. They didn't even look at one another. Each man was alone with his own thoughts, his own unspoken fears. Then suddenly, without any warning, Mike burst into tears. He couldn't help it, he hadn't meant to, he just started to sob.

"Stop it!" Whiteley's voice had a clipped, military edge to it. "Goddamn it, stop it right now and get ahold of yourself!"

In that instant Mike realized one thing about Frank White-ley: No matter what happened—today, tomorrow, the rest of his life—the trainer would never be allowed the luxury of tears, of any outward sign of grief. Too many people, too many horses, were counting on him. Even if he had been granted it, after a lifetime of learning to do without, Whiteley would have refused. Only by plowing straight ahead could he survive. If he stopped in the middle of his pain, he would be lost.

Mike put none of this into words at the time, but he also faced something about himself. Breakdowns—and worse—were a part of the racetrack. If he wanted a life in this world, he would have to learn to deal with that unalterable fact.

He rubbed a hand across his face and composed himself. Whiteley was right. This was not the time for tears.

Louis Otero had been struggling to keep the strangers out of the way, and was relieved when his colleague, Buck Jones, who had been watching the race from the grandstand, managed to work his way through the crowd to help out. Even though Buck was off duty and in street clothes, he was big and imposing and no one questioned his authority as a Pinkerton. The two guards set up the sawhorses and tried to keep the people back. Finally the ambulance arrived.

If Ruffian's stall had not been where it was—across from the opening in the shedrow fence—they would have moved whoever was there out, because this was the only stall that a truck could get near. But even this short distance between the van and the stall loomed like a desert once Dan coaxed the uncomprehending filly out of the ambulance. Her injured leg could not support any weight and had already bled so extensively it had ruptured the air cast. With Mike at the filly's head, Dan and Frank locked hands under Ruffian's belly, Yates and Squeaky gripped arms to support her from the rear, and in this awkward manner they managed to help her to the stall. Off to the side, watching with her husband, Barbara Janney wept.

Jim Prendergast went into action. He knew that before they could make any major decisions about the filly's leg, they had to calm her down and attend to the immediate issues of infection, hemorrhage, and shock. They would also have to take X rays. Everything was complicated because she had broken down in the middle of a race, running as hard as she could; since there was no chance to cool her out, she had arrived back at the barn a very "hot" horse, her respiration and circulation way up, her veins bulging. Under those circumstances, the vets had to be exceptionally careful. Drugs had to be administered more slowly and in smaller doses than usual, because they tended to have a greater and more cumulative effect.

Inside the stall, Prendergast moved to the near side of her neck and gave her the first injection. It was a half cc of aceprom-azine, a tranquilizer. The normal dose for a horse you were going to work on was between two and three cc's, but he knew the importance of proceeding cautiously. Dan and Mike stayed near the filly's head; David Whiteley, Squeaky, Yates, and Frank were all nearby. Dr. Harthill, who was in New York just to see the race, had hurried over from the clubhouse to help out. A little ways beyond, on the embankment nearby, the Janneys waited with their family and friends, while an ever-growing circle of reporters, NYRA personnel, officials, guards, concerned colleagues, and curiosity seekers pressed closer and closer.

Prendergast tried to shut out the noise and confusion as he made a mental checklist of all the shots the filly needed: Premarin, to help stop the hemorrhaging by aiding in the coagulation of the blood; penicillin, as an all-purpose antibiotic; tetanus, because of the contamination of the wound; Butazolidin, an anti-inflammatory; and Talwin, a narcotic antagonist, which had the effects of a painkiller such as Demerol.

The cast was useless now and had been removed. Someone was sent to get another one. Dan had wrapped a thin cold-water bandage around the ankle, and it was decided to immerse the foot in a bucket of icy water while the filly calmed down and they figured out what to do next. Harthill and Prendergast conferred along the way. Although other vets were offering opinions in the confusion and near panic that ensued, Whiteley assumed that these two men, the vets who had actually cared for Ruffian in the past, were in charge.

They knew as well as anyone that submerging the foot in water would further contaminate it, but they wanted to stop the bleeding and it was already such a mess—that was obvious to anyone—that it was really a matter of choosing the lesser of two evils. After soaking the leg, they needed to get X rays. Dr. Gilman had already said that the sesamoids had shattered, which everyone agreed with, but they needed to get pictures of the ensuing destruction as well—then they needed to make one crucial decision: Should they operate on her immediately or should they immobilize the leg as best they could and wait until tomorrow?

Each choice had disadvantages. If they operated now, they would be forced to put Ruffian under anesthesia before she had been stabilized. She was in shock and had lost tremendous quantities of fluid. Her heart and respiration were still accelerated. These factors would increase the risks of surgery and anesthesia. If, however, they waited for her to cool down, they would have to make sure she was compliant enough to accept some form of temporary casting on the leg and enough restraint to prevent further injury.

Neither choice was going to be a picnic. Still, Ruffian was beginning to calm down. Almost twenty minutes had passed since Dr. Prendergast had administered the drugs, and everyone around her noticed the change. She was no longer rearing in the stall, and she was allowing her leg to rest in the bucket of ice and water. Most important, it looked as if she had stopped sweating. This was a positive sign.

In this interlude of relative calm, Prendergast decided to run out to his truck to get the portable X-ray machine and some plates. Frank had stepped out of the stall and was a few yards away, conferring with Harthill and the Janneys. Dr. Gilman remained nearby, and by then several other vets had stopped off in case they could be of help. As Prendergast headed for his truck he passed one of them, William O. Reed, who was walking towards the barn. Reed owned the equine hospital right across the street on Plainfield Avenue.

Dr. Edward Keefer, an orthopedic doctor at New York Hospital—not a veterinarian—had also stopped by. He was friends with Cynthia Phipps, Mrs. Janney's niece, and in 1973 he had helped devise the first successful artificial foot for a horse. He, too, offered his services.

A stall was normally a roomy place, but, filled with people and an unpredictable horse, it shrank quickly. The men who had always been close to Ruffian remained with her now. They tried to keep everything under control, but it was a chaotic scene, with people wandering back and forth, ducking into and out of the stall, asking questions, trying to take notes, offering suggestions. Horses broke down during races, but rarely horses of such prominence, and never in the middle of a major nationwide television broadcast. Most of the horsemen who had seen Ruffian right after the break agreed that it was so bad any other horse would have been destroyed right there in the van. Instead, heroic attempts were going to be made to save the filly. There was no script for a drama such as this, and Whiteley, who had always before been the director, had no choice but to turn the decision-making authority over to the vets. All the players had to improvise, and there were no easy parts.

Prendergast returned in a few minutes and set up the X-ray machine. Dan and David and Mike were ready. Ruffian's leg was lifted from the now-murky water and, at first, she was allowing them to proceed.

Then, unexpectedly, she went berserk. She rose up on her

hind legs again and again, lashing out with the good foot. Whiteley and Harthill immediately rushed back to her side.

"We've got to settle her down!" cried Prendergast. "We've got to get these X rays!" Prendergast tried one more time to position the machine close enough to the leg to get accurate pictures. They would need them if there was to be surgery. "The other leg's bleeding, too. Look at it. We really should get pictures of that one, too." The back of the left fetlock had been rubbed raw from the sand grinding against it; the filly's full weight had shifted after she broke down, forcing the good front foot deeper into the track.

"You can try," Whiteley said, "but watch her, will you? She's gonna hurt herself even more in a minute." He wanted them to get her out of there while they still could. There had been a sudden change in the filly. She was lashing out at everyone and throwing herself against the walls. The people in the stall scurried to avoid her three still-powerful hooves.

Mike and David remained at her head, along with Dan and Frank, and there were no better horsemen in the world, but Ruffian had become irrational and they were losing control. She tried more than once to fling herself onto the ground. She had started to sweat again, profusely; within minutes her skin was soaked through.

The men who worked with her were usually quiet and steady; now they were shouting orders, pushing, stepping on each other's toes as they rushed to protect the filly from herself. And though they tried to keep their own panic from breaking through the surface, fear curdled their voices as they spoke. They all knew that the filly had a very slim chance; if they couldn't keep her calm enough to undergo treatment, she wouldn't have any chance at all.

It had become total bedlam in the stall. Prendergast dodged her hooves as he examined her. In the midst of all this confusion, he noticed what several other people had seen, too: there was blood dripping from the right side of the filly's neck, from an intramuscular injection. All of Prendergast's injections had been given on the left.

"Who gave her a shot?" Prendergast cried.

No one answered.

"Goddamn it! Who gave her a shot?" Jim Prendergast was the youngest and the most self-effacing of all the vets in attendance, a normally soft-spoken and undemanding man. But this time there was something in his voice that commanded an answer.

"Doc Reed give it to her."

Prendergast was furious. He had no way of knowing whether the extra shot was having an adverse effect on the filly or not, since Reed had walked away without letting anyone know what he had given, but the idea that anybody would administer drugs to another man's horse without consulting the attending vet or getting permission from the owners or trainer was an outrage. But it was an outrage he had to ignore for the moment. To him and to the others who had actually seen Reed give the shot, the questions that it raised were overwhelmed by the immediate problem at hand: Ruffian was going berserk. If she kept throwing herself against the walls, she was going to destroy herself in front of everyone. The injured foot had no fixation on it; it was dangling uselessly as Ruffian banged herself around.

There was no longer any choice about the course of action. To leave the filly in the stall now meant a violent and ugly death. She was going to tear herself apart. It became imperative to get her under anesthesia and attempt to operate right away, or there would be no chance to save her. They attached another inflatable cast to her leg.

Mr. and Mrs. Janney had been pacing back and forth, talking quietly, then lapsing into silence. After a moment Stuart Janney motioned to Dr. Harthill. "It's not good, Doc, I can see that. What are her chances, do you think?"

Harthill shook his head. "I'd say something less than ten percent."

Mr. Janney looked away from the filly, over in the direction of the track. "Well, then, go ahead and try," he said. "Do whatever you can."

Frank left Ruffian's side and crossed over to where his wife, Louise, was waiting by the car. He spoke to her briefly, then returned to the shedrow. For a moment he cradled his face

against the wall. Everyone had a breaking point. No one watching in the crowd would have blamed him if Frank Whiteley had
reached his.

What he thought or felt for that instant no one else would
ever know, but he did not break down. When he pushed himself
away from the wall, he was pale and drawn, but his jaw was set
as he rejoined the men inside the stall. The decision had been
made and there was work to do. The filly had to be moved across
the street to Dr. Reed's hospital. They were going to operate.

10

There were only two places where the surgery could be done immediately. NYRA had a little-known facility on the grounds, but it was not as modern or as well-equipped as Dr. Reed's nearby hospital. After a brief conference, Ruffian's vets agreed that Reed's place was by far the better choice. Reed was informed of their decision and went on ahead to get things ready. The hospital had been closed up all afternoon while he was at the races, and the first thing he did was to turn on the air-conditioning, knowing it would be a long, hot night.

The filly was still agitated when the ambulance reached the hospital, but sheer exhaustion was beginning to take its toll, and Dan and Mike were able to lead her without incident onto the operating table. This specially padded platform was at floor level, so a horse could be walked onto it. Once the horse was sedated and in a prone position, the table could be raised hydraulically to the desired height.

Ruffian had been injected with Seratal, a short-acting barbiturate that enabled the vets to lay her down and intubate her. Dr. Tom Gorman, another vet who had offered his assistance, was in charge of the anesthesia; he slid the thin tube down her throat into her trachea. Through this tube would flow the mixture of fluothane gas and oxygen. Dr. Prendergast supervised the IV fluids. Ruffian needed a continual flow of electrolytes to replace the salts that shock had drained from her bloodstream. A catheter was inserted into her bladder. In addition, throughout the entire procedure she remained hooked up to a heart monitor.

When they put Ruffian under, her pulse was racing but her

breathing was very slow. Because she had not been able to cool out after the race, there was a much greater risk in administering gas. She was already suffering from the vicious cycle of her own reactions: shock and pain and—possibly—a drug interaction had caused her to respond violently, and these exertions had further upset her system, which in turn intensified the shock and pain. The vets would have to be alert every second.

Reed and Harthill were to perform the surgery. They scrubbed and pulled on sterile gowns and gloves, then they prepped Ruffian: the injured leg had to be clipped, shaved, and scrubbed. Surgical drapes were applied to prevent any further contamination of the area as they worked, and a green surgical gown was arranged over the filly's glistening bulk.

Getting Ruffian stabilized became a heroic task. She would go so far under the anesthesia that they had to apply stimulants. The stimulants got her so high that they had to increase the anesthesia. For almost an hour the doctors rode up and down with the filly on the roller coaster of these reactions. Twice, the line on the monitor completely flattened out. Gorman had to administer straight oxygen while the others pounded on Ruffian's chest to revive her. The atmosphere was tense but not panicky; under the circumstances, these reactions were not entirely unexpected. Gorman deftly adjusted the flow of the anesthesia and oxygen and they began to get a relatively normal pulse. Finally, the filly's vital signs were under control. The operation could begin.

Although the bones had ripped through the skin, leaving a two-inch gash, the doctors extended the incision slightly, cleaning up the ragged, torn edges of the wound. First they flushed the area with sterile saline solution and antibiotics. They attached half a dozen Penrose drains, from the point of injury up past her knee. They would remain sutured to the filly throughout the surgery, continuously trying to eliminate the dirt and grit that had been driven up into the leg. If the filly had stopped running after the initial fracture, the prognosis would not have been so grim. But that was the nature of great horses: Their hearts drove them forward when their bodies could no longer carry them.

Harthill and Reed then began the laborious process of debriding the area, picking out all the contamination and the particles of bone, cutting away the dead tissue. They stopped and flushed the area again. They worked in this painstaking fashion for almost an hour, alternately cleaning and flushing out the wound. The shattered sesamoids were too small to pin together, and the vets would not be sure for days whether they had salvaged enough bone to allow the leg to heal, or whether, if it healed, it would be able to support Ruffian's weight so she could function. Whole and sound, a thoroughbred's leg was a fragile affair; broken, it was a risky proposition at best. Ruffian's leg had been smashed to bits; the vets who worked on it were charting unknown waters. If they had been guided by the odds, the filly never would have left the track alive.

It had taken almost an hour to stabilize Ruffian, and another hour had passed during the operation itself. In the middle of everything the air conditioner went on the blink, and the men finished their task in the heat of the July night. Opening the door helped only a little, for the air outside was thick and damp. The rains that had been threatening since the seventh race still had not fallen. The men were sweating right through their shirts and the green hospital gowns.

Normally, surgery was performed in a subdued and placid atmosphere, but there had been nothing normal about this night. The operating room became a circus, with people traipsing in and out—trainers with no connection to the filly, members of the press who slipped inside. There was no one to keep order; no clear-cut chain of command, because so many people were working together for the first time, under pressured and difficult circumstances. Some vets thought Reed should order the intruders out, since it was his hospital. Reed felt all his attention needed to be focused on the filly, since he and Harthill were performing the surgery on the leg. There were no guidelines for a crisis like this, and despite the fact that conditions were disturbing, they did not actually affect the filly's care. What affected the filly's care was a combination of her condition, the state of medical knowledge at the time, the public's need for action, some genuinely selfless efforts, men's egos, and luck.

Everything was being carried out in a fishbowl. The press was camped outside the hospital door, NYRA's media people were trying to obtain information and updates which they could relay back to their offices at the track, and a scattering of ad-mirers—from both the backstretch and the public—simply re-fused to leave. They settled themselves in the waiting room and on the steps. They wandered in and out of the building. They hiked back and forth to Esposito's, bringing back coffee for the men inside.

While the veterinarians labored over the filly's leg, Edward Keefer—the NYU doctor, who lived out on Long Island—had driven home to get an orthopedic brace he had devised for another horse, whose shoe size was the same as Ruffian's. The brace consisted of padded steel supports that ran up both sides of the horse's leg, from the shoe to the knee, and it was to be fitted to the leg with cushioned metal clamps. The idea was to have it support the leg, relieve pressure from the break, and therefore buy time for the ankle to heal.

There were many difficulties in affixing this brace and at-taching the shoe. It took Keefer and a local blacksmith, who had been called out of bed to help, over an hour, during which time the filly had to continue under anesthesia. The vets were appre-hensive about this unusually long period of sedation. Horses sometimes became violent as they emerged from the gas, and they could not be strapped down like human beings.

After the brace was attached, Keefer engineered a plaster of paris cast to go over it. The entire apparatus weighed between forty and fifty pounds. Nine months earlier Ruffian had refused to tolerate a much lighter, smaller cast for a minor hairline frac-ture. What would she do when she woke up and found this bulky contraption on her leg? There was no way to explain to her that, however frightening this cost might be, she had to tolerate it or she would die. Mr. Janney thought it looked "difficult," to say the least; Harthill thought it "cumbersome." The men who knew the filly best—Frank and Dan and Mike and Squeaky and Yates—watched with growing dread. They could not, however, think of an alternative.

It was, as Harthill would later say, a "destruction case" from the very beginning. That's what would have been called for un-der any standard medical protocol. But the public wouldn't al-low Ruffian to be destroyed until all avenues for saving her, however unlikely, had been explored. Mr. Janney had under-stood that. If the chance was one in one hundred, or one in one thousand, or even one in one million, they had to try.

Ruffian had been under the anesthesia for a very long time: an hour while she was being stabilized, an hour for the surgery, an hour for the casting procedure. Finally, she was slid into the padded recovery room. It was twelve-thirty in the morning, and it was now the seventh of July.

All night, reporters had shuttled back and forth up Plainfield Avenue between the hospital and Esposito's, where the two phone booths in the back remained their pipeline to the outside world. John Esposito had done everything he could to accommodate not only the press, but everyone who had gathered in the area, hoping for word of the filly's progress. He did not usually serve food, but that night he went out and bought cold cuts and bread and laid them out along the bar for anyone who wanted a sandwich. He made pot after pot of strong black coffee.

Back in the press office, the staff was getting ready to end the longest and most depressing day they had ever spent at the track. Phone calls were still coming in, but they had finally stopped answering them. For six hours they had replied to the same questions, listened to the same criticisms, and fielded the same offers of help. They repeated the little information they had over and over again: Ruffian had broken down in her right front leg, she was undergoing surgery, everything was being done to save her, they would know more in the morning. The outpour-ing of sympathy and support was unlike anything they had heard before: I'll send my vet, people volunteered. I'll send my private plane. I'll pay the hospital fees. What do you need? How can I help? What can I do?

Hundreds of calls came in locally, but they also came in from across the United States, from Canada, and from overseas. Save the filly, everyone begged. Please save the filly. Tell me what it costs, tell me what you need. Just, please, please, don't let her die. *Please don't let her die.*

Barbara Janney had not been in the best of health, and, heart-broken by the turn of events, she had returned earlier in the evening to her brother's estate in Old Westbury. Stuart Janney remained at the hospital until the surgery was complete. Not until Ruffian went into the recovery room did he leave the hospital and drive out to join his wife.

They were scheduled to leave early the next day for their summer home in Northeast Harbor, Maine. Mr. Janney assured Frank that they would stop by in the morning and see how the filly was before they headed out. He thanked the doctors and left.

Ruffian lay on the floor of the recovery room. All the surfaces were padded with Ensolite mats, to protect the horses as much as possible as they scrambled about in that hazy state between sedation and consciousness. Her body was being rubbed with alcohol to refresh her muscles and help eliminate the waste products that had built up, creating a toxic condition.

Except for the rising and falling of her chest, the big filly was still. She had lost so much fluid that her body seemed shrunken and caved in; each rib was outlined with a painful, delicate precision. Even her face had grown gaunt in the last few hours. She had been through so much, and her trials were not yet over. She had to regain consciousness and get back on her feet. Horses couldn't remain on their side for extended periods of time or the radial nerve in their shoulder could become paralyzed. It was this transitional period, the emergence from the anesthesia, that was so often dangerous for horses.

Reed had retreated to his office, and Harthill had made the trek to Esposito's for his first food since noon, but Jim Prendergast remained in the recovery room. Yates and Dan and Squeaky and Mike and David and Frank were all there. Jacinto had stopped by earlier in the evening, but he could not bring himself to stay. A few other helpers had remained, sometimes inside the room, sometimes in the waiting area outside. A couple of men were always near the filly's head to hold it down should she try to rise before she was fully conscious.

Dr. Keefer had stepped outside on the steps to talk to some of the remaining reporters. He sipped his coffee and appeared relaxed, as if the worst were over. Prendergast suspected otherwise.

Equine instinct says to run from danger. About an hour and fifteen minutes after entering the recovery room, when she began emerging from the anesthesia, Ruffian started to run. At least, that was what it looked like to the men surrounding her.

The filly, still lying on her side, stretched her neck out and began paddling with her legs. It seemed as if she had awakened in the middle of the race she had started almost eight hours earlier, a race she was now desperately trying to finish.

"This is it," Prendergast warned. "Be careful."

A couple of men bent over near her neck. The ones who had been rubbing her with alcohol had to jump out of the way when she started thrashing. As weakened as she was, she was still an enormously powerful horse.

She rested for a while, and the men moved in closer, but soon she was trying to run again, leading with her injured right leg, reaching, reaching, increasingly frantic. Squeaky and Yates exchanged looks. Dan covered his mouth with the palm of his hand in a gesture that expressed the depths of his dismay.

"Hold her down! She's gonna rip the cast off if we don't keep her down!" The men leaned into her with all their weight. She was violent now, angered and confused by her inability to do what she had always done; what she had done so easily, with such authority; what she had been doing that very afternoon when her leg had exploded beneath her.

She had found some reservoir of strength, and she was using it to throw these men around every time they tried to hold her back. She thrashed about so furiously, gaining traction on the rubber mats, that she began spinning herself in circles on the floor. As she flailed about with her legs, she repeatedly knocked the heavy plaster cast against her own elbow until the elbow, too, was smashed to pieces.

And still, she kept on running. The men who witnessed her struggle would later offer different explanations for this desperate paddling motion: It was either an involuntary reaction, or she was trying to shake off the cast, or she was still attempting to open up her lead on Foolish Pleasure, or she was trying to outrun her present horror.

They tried for her own good to restrain her, but she refused to be restrained. Even half-conscious, weak, and battered, she managed to throw off every one of them. The cast was slipping, and as it was being dislodged it was ripping open her leg all over again, undoing whatever good the operation had done.

Reed was called in from his office, and a few minutes later Harthill returned from Esposito's. Ruffian's leg was once more swollen and bleeding and she was still thrashing wildly on the floor. She was given a shot of xylazine to calm her down, a small amount to buy some time while the vets conferred with Whiteley. They couldn't sedate her again because she had taken so much anesthesia into her system. Any tranquilizing agent they gave now could prove fatal.

When the possibility of further surgery was raised, Prendergast emphatically spoke out against it. All night he had watched the filly suffer, struggling with pain and shock and terror. Who would the surgery be for? Surgery was futile now. To insist on it would only be for show, a chance for grown men to play hero at Ruffian's expense. The outcome would not be changed. Ruffian would never have a leg, and if by some miracle she withstood more anesthesia and a second operation, necrosis and gangrene were almost certain to set in, given the initial state of the wound and the way it had been reopened. If she was not tolerating this cast and these restrictions, why would she tolerate new ones in three or four hours?

They had tried to save her, not because they really thought she had a chance, but because they were buying time for a miracle. The Janneys felt they owed that much to the millions of people who had grown to love their filly. The demands of that love had, ironically, caused Ruffian nothing but more agony. And the miracle had not happened.

They had run out of alternatives. The vets spoke briefly with Frank, then Frank went into Reed's office and dialed the Phipps estate.

"It doesn't look good, Mr. Janney," he began. He briefly recounted what had happened.

Mr. Janney didn't hesitate. "Please," he told Frank. "Don't let her suffer anymore."

All night long Frank had functioned. When there was something to do, he did it. When they wanted his opinion, he gave it. In

the interim he smoked an endless chain of cigarettes as he
slumped in the armchair outside Reed's office. Everyone who
passed him averted their eyes. They all had the same eerie
impression: They thought Frank Whiteley looked like a dead
man.

In the next few minutes the men who had been helping all night
spoke quietly, passing the word, offering what little comfort they
could to one another. Everyone who had been close to Ruffian,
except for Yates, chose to leave the hospital before she was put
down.

Mike and Squeaky and Dan took their turns saying good-
bye. As long as the filly was alive, they would do anything
they could to help her. But they would not stay and watch her
die.

When almost everyone else had left, Whiteley stood up. He,
too, knew his limits. Yates came up behind him but remained
silent. In the recovery room, the xylazine had taken effect and
the filly was temporarily at rest.

The door to the outside was open, had been left open ever
since the air conditioning went off. It was twenty minutes past
two, and sometime in the last hour the rains that had been men-
acing for so long had finally begun to fall.

Frank took a step forward, then paused, his hands resting
on either side of the doorframe. He stood there for a moment,
staring into the darkness. Finally he cleared his throat. "Yates,"
he said. He had to clear his throat a second time. "Get her halter
for me, will you?"

Then Frank Whiteley stepped out into the night.

Yates knelt beside the filly's head while Reed prepared the shot
of phenobarbital. Ruffian was starting to run again, leading with
her right leg, as she had been doing in the race, reaching with
her head, slowly at first, not fully conscious, then faster and
faster, running down the backstretch once again, she was rolling
now, picking up steam, everything was all right, that's all she
had been asking—*Let me run!*—half a length in front of the colt,
smoothly now, pulling steadily away, she had found her stride
at last, she was opening up daylight, it was so simple, all she ever

wanted was to run, morning or afternoon, that was all she ever asked—*Let me run!*—faster now and faster, finally released, no more bit in her mouth, no rider on her back, no cast, no pain, no terror anymore, she had pulled away from everything, she was flying, the sun blazed all around her, she was running easily now, easily, straight into the light, *free*

11

Updates on Ruffian's condition were broadcast over radio and television until late into the night, when she went into recovery. As a result, millions of people fell asleep believing she would live. They woke to the news that she had been destroyed. Morning papers had gone to press while Ruffian was still alive, prompting more vain hopes. The later editions announced her death on their front pages.

"Please." Dan looked up from inside the stall where he was brushing Honorable Miss. His eyes were red. "Don't ask me no more questions 'bout what happened. I just don't want to talk to nobody. I done lost my best friend. I feel too bad to talk."

Mike had tried to fend off the reporters, but they kept circling back. Once again he asked them politely to leave. "Really, you guys, nobody around here feels like talking today, all right?" He returned to his work.

The rain had been so heavy during the night that huge puddles had collected at the end of the shedrow. Mike was sweeping out the water and unclogging the gutters. It was morning on the backside; they had horses to get ready. Life couldn't stop because there was an empty stall.

Around five-thirty, Frank had shown up. He looked as if he hadn't slept. There was no color in his cheeks, and he was moving a half step slower than usual. Still, he was there; he was functioning. If he could do it, everyone else thought, so could they.

He almost hadn't made it. Only an hour earlier he had

turned to his wife and announced, "I'm not going to the barn this morning."

She had stared at him for a moment. He had never missed a day of work. "But, Frank, you have to go," she said.

"No," he had answered. "I've got nothing to go there for."

"Squeaky, you gonna get on them horses today?"

"Yessuh." Squeaky's face was streaked with tears. "I can ride, Mr. Whiteley."

"That's good. I want you on them, just like always."

"Yessuh."

Mike passed them on his way to the tackroom. "There's an awful damn lot of reporters, Mr. Whiteley. Some of them are getting kinda pushy."

"Well, just try to get rid of 'em. I got Buck Jones over here again to help out. Try to keep everything as close to normal as possible, hear?"

Mike nodded. As close to normal as possible. What did those words mean anymore?

Ruffian was buried a little after nine o'clock that night, when the long summer evening had started to fade. Two hours earlier a clamshell shovel had pulled up to a spot under the NYRA flagpole and started biting off huge mouthfuls of dirt. It spit them out into a mound nearby until a hole approximately twelve feet square had been carved out. That was roughly the size of the stall Ruffian had lived in all her life.

The Janneys had left for Maine early in the day, as planned, because of Mrs. Janney's health. Stuart Janney had consulted with Frank before making the practical arrangements with the Association. Whiteley insisted that the funeral be private. The last thing he wanted was a circus, another show. Except for his friends Bill Rudy and Teddy Cox, he had asked that no reporters be allowed.

He didn't quite get his way on that one. Too many writers protested to the press office that they had covered Ruffian's entire career and did not deserve to be shut out at this point. A few exceptions were made.

Frank had come straight over from the barn. His hat was low

on his forehead and he was carrying something under his arm. He was joined by Louise and his son David. Jacinto stood nearby, as did Dan and Squeaky and Mike. A Pinkerton, not recognizing Yates, had tried to bar him from crossing to the infield, but to no one's surprise Yates had prevailed.

Across the track, standing at the fence along the clubhouse turn, near the clockers' shed, Vince Bracciale looked on at the proceedings. Frank would have allowed him to attend, but in the confusion and exhaustion of the last twenty-four hours he had not thought of it, and Bracciale was too proud to ask. But he was intent on paying his respects, so he stood at a distance and watched. He was grateful for his two trips on the filly, storybook rides he would never forget. He doubted he would ever ride a horse like her again. When he glanced around, he was astonished to see that hundreds of backstretch workers had spread out all along the rail, waiting, as he was, for the chance to say good-bye.

By the time the hole was dug, lights had been turned on in the stands across from the track. Photographers, barred from the gravesite, had set up their equipment in the clubhouse seats.

The clamshell rumbled off across the grass, and in the growing darkness the beams of two approaching headlights caught everyone's attention. It was the horse ambulance, carrying Ruffian's body, with Blue Rapelyea once again at the wheel. Blue drove slowly, carefully, across the grass, turned, and backed up to the edge of the grave. The rear door was lowered to form a ramp that inclined directly into the pit at the base of the flagpole. Several members of the grounds crew jumped onto the back of the van and tugged the filly to the edge of the ramp.

Many of the onlookers were shocked by what they saw: The filly had been wrapped from head to hoof in white canvas, like a gigantic mummy. In a way, there was something dignified about it; the shroud preserved her privacy and kept the mangled leg from being exposed. Yet there was something missing also: a chance to see the filly herself one last time—the small identifiable star high on her forehead, the white band circling her left hind foot.

The men grunted with the effort of maneuvering the huge form along the ramp. They guided it as gently as they could, but it was not easy to control the progress of 1100 pounds down an incline into the pit. No one took their eyes off the filly. No one moved.

Ruffian's eulogy was silence.

Frank turned abruptly to Mike Bell. "Here," he said. "Go put these on her." He had been carrying the filly's two red blankets, the good ones, with the initials of Locust Hill Farm embroidered in bright white letters in the corner.

Mike hesitated, then climbed down the ladder into the pit. He could put a cooler on a live horse blindfolded, but Whiteley had said nothing to him about this in advance, and he had no idea how he was supposed to cover the lifeless body of the filly that he loved. He knelt beside the white-wrapped form. He didn't want to draw attention to himself, and he didn't want to dramatize the moment. But he wanted everything connected with Ruffian to be exactly right. He owed her that, because of her perfection. Everyone was watching him. He unfolded the first blanket and laid it carefully over her side and hindquarters. With the second cooler he overlapped the first, covering her head and neck. Then he smoothed out the creases.

When Mike climbed out of the hole, people stirred and glanced around, waiting for some signal. Was there more? Was it over? In her arms, Louise Whiteley held a box of long-stemmed red roses. They had been handed to her by a man named John Allen, who stood off to the side. He was one of the backstretch regulars known to everyone, a sometime night watchman who had been around the track forever.

"I think we'll save these for tomorrow, when they've covered over the grave, don't you think?" Mrs. Whiteley said. The people around her nodded.

But John Allen, who seemed to stand in for all the nameless people paying tribute to the filly, thought otherwise. He politely reached into the box and lifted out a single flower. He stepped to the edge of the grave and dropped it in. It landed soundlessly by the filly's head.

"Well, time we're getting along." Frank gestured for Louise and David, and everyone else slowly followed.

Blue drove the ambulance off. In its place came the power shovel. The first spray of dirt hit the white-wrapped body with a thud, then gradually the hole filled up with dirt. In the morning the grounds crew would clean up and replace the turf. Once again there would be a seamless blanket of green under the flagpole.

12

Frank Whiteley stayed busy, but for a long time he wasn't the same. He didn't come in as early in the morning and he didn't spend every waking moment at the barn. The quiet hours in the early afternoon were sometimes just too hard, with no Ruffian there to graze.

Other horses occupied his thoughts, and he seldom spoke about the filly. Gradually, though, over the years, he began to let the memories come back. Sometimes, sitting with a visitor under his shedrow at the end of the day, he might even tip his chair back, push his hat up on his forehead, and talk. Then, as he gazed into the distance, recalling one particular day, he would almost be transported back in time.

It was an autumn afternoon in 1973, and Frank had driven out to Claiborne, unsuspecting, to preview the babies that would ship to him for training. That's when he'd seen Ruffian for the first time.

She was just a nameless yearling to him then, but she caught his eye right away. She was big and beautiful, and she stood out over everything. With her long easy stride, her breeding and her conformation, she looked like she might be a good one.

Of course, there was no way of knowing till she ran. That was a long way off, and Frank tried not to look too far into the future. In this game, with all its ups and downs, you lasted longer if you took one day at a time.

Still, when the filly charged across the paddock, mane and tail streaming, it was hard not to picture her tearing up the track. Reviewer had been full of speed; Shenanigans, too. Minor injuries had ended both of their careers. Someday, with a little luck, their daughter might be winning races and breaking other horses' hearts.

But Frank was getting ahead of himself. One day at a time. He took a last look at the big filly and smiled. He couldn't wait for her to join him out in Camden. With a horse like that, anything was possible.

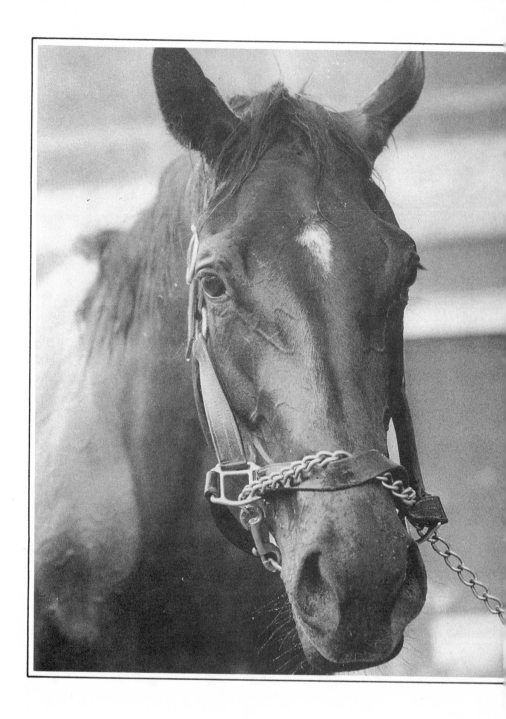